What's New in This Edition

This book has been completely revised so that readers are learning the best techniques available under Java 2, including each of the following:

- Five chapters dealing with Swing, Java's method of developing graphical programs you can control with a mouse
- A chapter on the enhanced sound features introduced in Java 2 for the playback of audio files in numerous formats
- The latest enhancements to Java's style of object-oriented programming, including inner classes
- Tutorials that make it easy to learn multithreaded programming, animation, and graphical user interface design
- Coverage of advanced features such as JavaBeans and Java2D

Comments from Readers and Reviewers

"I've read dozens of Java books and this one by far outclasses them all. For a simplified discussion of the language and how to work with it, this can't be beat."

—A reader's review on Amazon.com

"[W]hen all is said and done, there's just no substitute for the cold hard act of coding for facing the evil that Rogers Cadenhead calls "compiler angst." Read more about it in his (intentionally) hilarious, yet sharp and thorough beginner's book, *[Sams] Teach Yourself Java 1.1 Programming in 24 Hours*—my current favorite Java companion."

—Michelle Murdock, *NC World*

"I just wanted to drop you a line to say thanks. Your book just got me a promotion at work and I have several other possible job opportunities now."

—Reader Terry Bockover

This Book's Web Site

The solutions to each of the hour-ending activities are just one of the offerings on the book's World Wide Web site. Author Rogers Cadenhead offers the answers to reader questions, supplemental material, and the book's source code at the following address:

http://www.prefect.com/java24

You can contact the author at any time by visiting the Web site. Feel free to drop Rogers a line with any questions, comments, criticisms, or error reports, and be sure to let him know if you share his opinion that the Dallas Stars need one more front-line scoring forward who is in his 20s.

How to Use This Book

This book offers 24 separate hours that are devoted to specific topics. You should read them in order, picking the timeframe you prefer best—one hour a day, a few hours a week, or one continuous 24-hour frenzy that sets your carpal tunnel nerves on fire and leaves you mumbling "Java...Java...Java" over and over like someone in a meditative trance.

Special Highlighted Elements

If something needs a little extra attention, the 24-hour clock stops for a bit and it's described in a Note like this one.

Tips will help you save time but are not necessarily essential to the lesson at hand.

These warn you of what to pay close attention to as you follow the book's exercises.

Q&A, Quiz, and Activities

Each hour ends with a brief Q&A section covering some questions you might want to ask. After that, there's a three-question quiz you can take, and a few suggested activities for you to expand your knowledge of the material that was covered.

The *Sams Teach Yourself in 24 Hours* Series

Sams Teach Yourself in 24 Hours books provide quick and easy answers in a proven step-by-step approach that works for you. In just 24 sessions of one hour or less, you will tackle every task you need to get the results you want. Let our experienced authors present the most accurate information to get you reliable answers—fast!

Integer Types

There are four data types that can be used to store integers. The one to use depends on the size of the integer, as indicated:

TYPE	SIZE	VALUES THAT CAN BE STORED
byte	8 bits	-128 to 127
short	16 bits	-32,768 to 32,767
int	32 bits	-2,147,483,648 to 2,147,483,647
long	64 bits	-9,223,372,036,854,775,808 to 9,223,372,036,854,775,807

Special Characters

You can insert several special characters into strings. The following list shows these special characters; note that each is preceded by a backslash (\).

SPECIAL CHARACTERS	DISPLAY
\'	Single quotation mark
\"	Double quotation mark
\\	Backslash
\t	Tab
\b	Backspace
\r	Carriage return
\f	Formfeed
\n	Newline

Arithmetic Operators

There are five operators used to accomplish basic arithmetic in Java.

OPERATOR	MEANING	EXAMPLE
+	Addition	3 + 4
-	Subtraction	5 - 7
*	Multiplication	5 * 5
/	Division	14 / 7
%	Modulus	20 % 7

Comparison Operators

These operators are used in expressions that return Boolean values of `true` or `false`, depending on whether the comparison being made is true.

OPERATOR	MEANING	EXAMPLE
==	Equal	x == 3
!=	Not equal	x != 3
<	Less than	x < 3
>	Greater than	x > 3
<=	Less than or equal to	x <= 3
>=	Greater than or equal to	x >= 3

Operator Precedence

If two operations have the same precedence, the one on the left in the actual expression is handled before the one on the right. Operators farther up the table are evaluated first.

OPERATOR	NOTES
. [] ()	Parentheses (()) are used to group expressions; a period (.) is used for access to methods and variables within objects and classes (discussed tomorrow); square brackets ([]) are used for arrays. (This operator is discussed later in the week.)
++ -- ! ~ instanceof	The `instanceof` operator returns `true` or `false` based on whether the object is an instance of the named class or any of that class's subclasses (discussed tomorrow).
new (type)expression	The `new` operator is used for creating new instances of classes; () in this case is for casting a value to another type. (You learn about both of these tomorrow.)
* / %	Multiplication, division, modulus
+ -	Addition, subtraction
<< >> >>>	Bitwise left and right shift
< > <= >=	Relational comparison tests
== !=	Equality
&	AND
^	XOR
¦	OR
&&	Logical AND
¦¦	Logical OR
? :	Shorthand for `if...then...else` (discussed on Day 5)
= += -= *= /= %= ^=	Various assignments
&= ¦= <<= >>= >>>=	More assignments

Rogers Cadenhead

SAMS
Teach Yourself

Java™ 2

in 24 Hours

SAMS

A Division of Macmillan Computer Publishing
201 West 103rd St., Indianapolis, Indiana, 46290 USA

Sams Teach Yourself Java 2 in 24 Hours
Copyright © 1999 by Sams Publishing

International Standard Book Number: 0-672-31630-7

Library of Congress Catalog Card Number: 97-80858

Printed in the United States of America

First Printing: January 1999

01   00   99   4   3

Trademarks

All terms mentioned in this book that are known to be trademarks or service marks have been appropriately capitalized. Sams cannot attest to the accuracy of this information. Use of a term in this book should not be regarded as affecting the validity of any trademark or service mark. Java is a trademark of Sun Microsystems, Inc.

Warning and Disclaimer

Every effort has been made to make this book as complete and as accurate as possible, but no warranty or fitness is implied. The information provided is on an "as is" basis. The authors and the publisher shall have neither liability or responsibility to any person or entity with respect to any loss or damages arising from the information contained in this book or from the use of the Web site or programs accompanying it.

EXECUTIVE EDITOR
Mark Taber

DEVELOPMENT EDITOR
Scott D. Meyers

MANAGING EDITOR
Patrick Kanouse

PROJECT EDITOR
Andrew Cupp

COPY EDITOR
Patricia Kinyon

INDEXER
Erika Millen

TECHNICAL EDITOR
Eric A. Wolf

PRODUCTION
Carol Bowers
Mona Brown
Ayanna Lacey
Gene Redding

Overview

Contents

About the Author

Rogers Cadenhead is a writer, journalist, and Web developer whose inner child is a stay-at-home goalie with a weak glove hand and poor stick-handling skills. He is the co-author of *Sams Teach Yourself Java 2 in 21 Days*, and author of *Sams Teach Yourself to Create a Home Page in 24 Hours* and *Sams Teach Yourself Java 1.1 Programming in 24 Hours*. He also writes a question-and-answer trivia column for the *Fort Worth Star-Telegram*, *Knight-Ridder News Service*, and *New York Times News Syndicate*. He lives in northern Florida, where he waits patiently for one of his former high school classmates to become famous so he can sell stories about the person to the tabloid newspapers. You can visit his Web site at `http://www.prefect.com/java24`.

Dedication

To Wade DuChene, Jonathan Bourne, Mark Winner, Phil Weinstock, Eric Manuel, and Andrew Borokove. No person has closer intergender friendships outside of a women's prison movie, and I dedicate 16.66 percent of the book to each of you in alphabetical order. The remaining 0.04 percent is dedicated to world peace.

Acknowledgments

To the folks at Sams—especially Mark Taber, Scott Meyers, Eric Wolf, and Drew Cupp. No author can produce a book like this on his own, regardless of what my agent told Sams during contract negotiations. Their excellent visions and revisions will give me plenty to take credit for later on.

To my he-agent and she-agent team, David and Sherry Rogelberg, who helped me hide from all the people in the preceding paragraph during a critical two-day period in which I needed to catch up on my soaps.

To my wife, M.C., and my son, Max. Although our family has not fulfilled my dream of becoming a high-wire trapeze team like the Flying Wallendas, I'm the world's proudest husband in a non-acrobatic family.

Tell Us What You Think!

As the reader of this book, *you* are our most important critic and commentator. We value your opinion and want to know what we're doing right, what we could do better, what areas you'd like to see us publish in, and any other words of wisdom you're willing to pass our way.

As the Executive Editor for the Web Development team at Macmillan Computer Publishing, I welcome your comments. You can fax, email, or write me directly to let me know what you did or didn't like about this book—as well as what we can do to make our books stronger.

Please note that I cannot help you with technical problems related to the topic of this book, and that due to the high volume of mail I receive, I might not be able to reply to every message.

When you write, please be sure to include this book's title and author as well as your name and phone or fax number. I will carefully review your comments and share them with the author and editors who worked on the book.

Fax: 317-817-7070

Email: webdev@mcp.com

Mail: Mark Taber
         Executive Editor, Web Development
         Macmillan Computer Publishing
         201 West 103rd Street
         Indianapolis, IN 46290 USA

Introduction

You might not feel this way if you're currently wandering through a bookstore's computer section, but this stuff is a lot easier than it looks.

Anyone who has persistence and a little free time can learn how to create computer software using the hottest computer language of the decade: Java. By working your way through the tutorial projects in *Sams Teach Yourself Java 2 in 24 Hours*, you'll be able to learn Java programming quickly.

Anyone can learn how to write computer programs—even if they can't program a VCR. Java is one of the best programming languages to learn, because it's a useful, powerful, modern technology that's being used by thousands of programmers around the world.

This book is aimed at non-programmers, new programmers who hated learning the subject, and experienced programmers who want to quickly get up to speed with Java. It uses Java 2, the greatly enhanced new version of the language.

Java is the decade's most exciting programming language because of the things it makes possible. You can add animation and sound to a World Wide Web page, write games and useful utilities, create programs that feature a graphical user interface, and design software that makes the most of the Internet.

This book teaches Java programming from the ground up. It introduces the concepts in English instead of jargon, with plenty of step-by-step examples of working programs you will create. Spend 24 hours with this book and you'll be writing your own Java programs, confident in your ability to use the language and learn more about it. You also will have skills that are becoming increasingly important—such as network computing, graphical user interface design, and object-oriented programming.

These terms might not mean much to you now. In fact, they're probably the kind of things that make programming seem like a secret ritual known only to a small group of humans who have a language of their own and a unique approach to wellness. However, if you can use a computer to create an attractive resume, balance your checkbook, or create a home page, you can write computer programs by reading *Sams Teach Yourself Java 2 in 24 Hours*.

If you're at a store and you make the decision not to purchase this book, please reshelve it with the front cover facing outward on an endcap with access to a lot of the store's foot traffic. In the event that an employee raises any questions about your effort to rearrange products, you didn't get this idea from the author of this book. He will disavow any knowledge of your activities faster than you can say "plausible deniability."

Part I
Getting Started

Hour

Hour 1

Becoming a Programmer

Computer programming is insanely difficult. It requires a four-year degree in computer science, thousands of dollars in computer hardware and software, a keen analytical intellect, the patience of Job, and a strong liking for caffeinated drinks. If you're a programming novice, this is probably what you've heard about computer programming. Aside from the part about caffeine, all of the rumors are greatly exaggerated.

Programming is a lot easier than most people think. However, there are several reasons why you might believe otherwise:

- Computer programmers have been telling people for years that programming is hard. This belief makes it easier for us to find high-paying jobs (or so I've heard) and gives us more leeway to goof off during business hours.

- Computer programming manuals are often written in a language that only a Scrabble player could appreciate. Strange acronyms like OOP, RAD, COM, and MUMPS are used frequently along with newly invented jargon like instantiation, bytecode, and makefile.

- Many computer programming languages have been available only with software packages costing $200 or more, which is a lot of cabbage.

Because of the growth of the Internet and other factors, this is a great time to learn programming. Useful programming tools are being made available at low cost (or no cost), often as downloads from World Wide Web sites. The goal of this book is to teach programming to the person who has never tried to program before and the person who tried programming but hated it with an intense passion. The English language will be used as much as possible instead of jargon and obscure acronyms, and all new programming terms will be thoroughly explained as they are introduced.

If I've succeeded, you will finish *Sams Teach Yourself Java 2 in 24 Hours* with enough programming skill to be a danger to yourself and others. You'll be able to write programs, dive into other programming books with more confidence, and learn programming languages more easily. You also will have developed skills with Java, the most exciting programming language to be introduced in a decade.

The first hour of this book provides some introductory material about programming and gives you instructions on how to set up your computer so you can write Java programs. The following topics will be covered:

- Choosing which programming language to learn first
- What Java is
- Using programs to boss your computer around
- How programs work
- How program errors (called *bugs*) are fixed
- Acquiring the free Java Development Kit
- Installing the Kit
- Getting ready to write programs

Choosing a Language

As you might have surmised at this point, computer programming is not as hard as it's cracked up to be. If you're comfortable enough with a computer to create a nice-looking resume, balance a checkbook with software such as Intuit Quicken, or create your own home page on the Web, you can write programs.

The key to learning how to program is to start with the right language. The programming language you choose to use often depends on the tasks you want the computer to accomplish. Each language has things it is well-suited for and things that are difficult, or perhaps impossible, to do with the language. For example, many people use some form of the BASIC language when they are learning how to program because BASIC is good for learning how to write programs.

The BASIC language was invented in the 1960s to be easy for students and beginners to learn (the B in BASIC stands for *Beginner's*). The downside to using some form of BASIC is that it's easy to fall into some sloppy programming habits with the language. Those habits can make it much more difficult to write complex programs and improve them later.

Microsoft Visual Basic combines the ease of BASIC with some powerful features to aid in the design of Windows software. (VBScript, which is short for Visual Basic Script, offers the simplicity of BASIC for small programs that run in conjunction with World Wide Web pages.) Visual Basic has been used to write thousands of sophisticated programs for commercial, business, and personal use. However, Visual Basic programs can be slower than Windows programs written in other languages, such as Borland C++. This difference is especially noticeable in programs that use a lot of graphics—games, screen savers, and the like. Because of that, game programmers and other multimedia developers don't use Visual Basic to create graphical programs such as Age of Empires and Quake.

This book uses the Java programming language, which was developed by Sun Microsystems. Though Java is more difficult to learn than a language such as Visual Basic, it is a good starting place for several reasons. One of the biggest advantages of learning Java is that you can use it on the World Wide Web. If you're an experienced Web surfer, you have seen numerous Java programs in action. They can be used to create animated graphics, present text in new ways, play games, and help in other interactive efforts.

Another important advantage is that Java requires an organized approach for programs to work. The language is very particular about the way programs must be written, and it balks if programmers do not follow all of its rules. When you start writing Java programs, you might not see the language's choosy behavior as an advantage. You'll write a program and will have several errors to fix before the program is finished. Some of your fixes might not be correct, and they will have to be redone. If you don't structure a program correctly as you are writing it, errors will result. In the coming hours, you'll learn about these rules and the pitfalls to avoid. The positive side of this extra effort is that your programs will be more reliable, useful, and error-free.

Java was invented by Sun Microsystems developer James Gosling as a better way to create computer programs. Gosling was unhappy with the way that the C++ programming language was working on a project he was doing, so he created a new language that did the job better. It's a matter of contentious debate whether Java is superior to other programming languages, of course, but the amount of attention paid to the language today shows that it has a large number of adherents. Book publishers obviously dig it—more than 1,000 books have been published about the language since its introduction. (This is my fourth, and I will write more of them until prohibited by municipal, state, or federal law.) Regardless of whether Java is the best language, it definitely is a great language to learn today. There are numerous resources for Java programmers on the Web, Java job openings are increasing, and the language has become a major part of the Internet's past, present, and future. You'll get a chance to try out Java during Hour 2, "Writing Your First Program."

Learning Java or any other programming language makes it much easier to learn subsequent languages. Many languages are similar to each other, so you won't be starting from scratch when you dive into a new one. For instance, many C++ programmers find it fairly easy to learn Java because Java borrows a lot of its structure and ideas from C++. Many programmers are comfortable using several different languages and will learn new ones as needed.

C++ has been mentioned several times in this hour, and you might be tripping over the term wondering what it means and, more importantly, how it's pronounced. C++ is pronounced *C-Plus-Plus*, and it's a programming language that was developed by Bjarne Stroustrop and others at Bell Laboratories. C++ is an enhancement of the C programming language, hence the *Plus-Plus* part of the name. Why not just C+, then? The *Plus-Plus* part is a computer programming joke you'll understand later on.

Telling the Computer What to Do

A computer program, also called *software*, is a way to tell a computer what to do. Everything the computer does, from booting up to shutting down, is done by a program. Windows 95 is a program. Ms. Pac-Man is a program. The `dir` command used in MS-DOS to display file names is also a program. Even the Michaelangelo virus is a program.

Computer programs are made up of a list of commands the computer handles in a specific order when the program is run. Each of these commands is called a *statement*.

If you're a science fiction fan, you're probably familiar with the concept of household robots. If not, you might be familiar with the concept of henpecked spouses. In either case, someone gives very specific instructions telling the robot or spouse what to do, something like the following:

Dear Theobald,

Please take care of these errands for me while I'm out lobbying members of Congress:

Item 1: Vacuum the living room.

Item 2: Go to the store.

Item 3: Pick up butter, lozenges, and as many *SnackWells Devil's Food Cakes* as you can carry.

Item 4: Return home.

Love,

Snookie Lumps

If you tell a loved one or artificially intelligent robot what to do, there's a certain amount of leeway in how your requests are fulfilled. If lozenges aren't available, cough medicine might be brought to you instead. Also, the trip to the store can be accomplished through a variety of routes. Computers don't do leeway. They follow instructions literally. The programs that you write will be followed precisely, one statement at a time.

The following is one of the simplest examples of a computer program, written in BASIC. Take a look at it, but don't worry yet about what each line is supposed to mean.

```
1 PRINT "Shall we play a game?"
2 INPUT A$
```

Translated into English, this program is equivalent to giving a computer the following to-do list:

Dear personal computer,

Item 1: Display the question, "Shall we play a game?"

Item 2: Give the user a chance to answer the question.

Love,

Snookie Lumps

Each of the lines in the computer program is a statement. A computer handles each statement in a program in a specific order, in the same way that a cook follows a recipe or Theobald the robot followed the orders of Snookie Lumps when he vacuumed and shopped at the market. In BASIC, the line numbers are used to put the statements in the correct order. Other languages, such as Java, do not use line numbers, favoring different ways to tell the computer how to run a program.

Figure 1.1 shows the sample BASIC program running on the Bywater BASIC interpreter, which is available for free in several shareware file repositories on the World Wide Web and can run on any DOS or UNIX platform. Bywater BASIC is among many free BASIC interpreters that can be found on the Internet for Microsoft Windows, Apple Macintosh, UNIX, and Linux systems.

FIGURE 1.1

An example of a BASIC program running on the Bywater BASIC shell and interpreter developed by Ted A. Campbell.

The quote "Shall we play a game?" is from the 1983 movie *WarGames*, in which a young computer programmer (played by Matthew Broderick) saves mankind after nearly causing global thermonuclear war and the near-extinction of humankind. You'll learn how to do that in the next book of this series, *Sams Teach Yourself to Create International Incidents with Java in 24 Hours*.

Because of the way programs operate, it's hard to blame the computer when something goes wrong while your program runs. After all, the computer was just doing exactly what you told it to do. Unless your hardware is on the fritz, a pesky virus is attacking your system, or your operating system is having a bad day, the blame for program errors lies with the programmer. That's the bad news. The good news is that you can't do any permanent harm to your computer with the programming errors you make. No one was harmed during the making of this book, and no computers will be injured as you learn how to program with Java.

How Programs Work

Most computer programs are written in the same way that you write a letter—by typing each statement into a word processor. Some programming tools come with their own word processor, and others can be used with any text-editing software. You can use the Java Development Kit, which you will learn about later in this hour, with any of your favorite editors.

When you have finished writing a computer program, you save the file just like saving any other document to disk. Computer programs often have their own filename extension to indicate what type of file they are. Java programs have the extension `.java`; an example of a Java program file name is `Calculator.java`.

If you use a fancy word processing program that has features such as bold-faced text, different font sizes, and other stylistic touches, do not use those features while writing a computer program. Programs should be prepared as text files with no special formatting. For example, when using Microsoft Word to write a program, save the file in Text Only mode instead of saving it as a Word document. Notepad, a word processor that comes with Windows, saves all files as unformatted text.

For this program to run, you need some help. The kind of help that's needed depends on the programming language you're using. Some languages require an interpreter to run their programs. The *interpreter* is a program that interprets each line of a computer program and tells the computer what to do. Most versions of BASIC are interpreted languages. The advantage of interpreted languages is that they are faster to test. When you are writing a BASIC program, you can try it out immediately, spot any errors, fix them, and try again. The primary disadvantage is that interpreted languages run more slowly than other programs.

Other programming languages require a compiler. The *compiler* takes a computer program and translates it into a form that the computer can understand. It also does what it can to make the program run as efficiently as possible. The compiled program can be run directly, without the need for an interpreter. Compiled programs run more quickly than interpreted programs, but they take more time to test. You have to write your program and compile it before trying it out. If you find an error and fix it, you must compile the program again to verify that the error is gone.

Java is unusual because it requires a compiler and an interpreter. You'll learn more about this later as you write Java programs.

How Programs Don't Work

Many new programmers become discouraged when they start to test their programs. Errors appear everywhere. Some of these are *syntax errors*, which are identified by the computer as it looks at the program and becomes confused by what you wrote. Other errors are *logic errors*, which are only noticed by the programmer as the program is being tested, if they are noticed at all. Logic errors sneak by the computer unnoticed, but they will cause it to do something unintended.

As you start to write your own programs, expect to encounter errors. They're a natural part of the process. Programming errors are called *bugs*, a term that dates back a century or more to describe errors in technical devices. The process of fixing errors has its own term also: *debugging*. Whether you want to or not, you'll get a lot of debugging experience as you learn how to write computer programs.

While you're learning Java by reading this book, it's likely that many thousands of your programming colleagues will be hard at work on the biggest debugging project in history: the "Year 2000 problem." This crisis is caused by computer programs that will experience logic errors on January 1, 2000, because of the way the programs incorrectly handle year values beyond 1999.

The biggest contributor to this problem is that many programmers decided to store year dates as two-digit values: 1967 became 67, 1998 became 98, and so on. Memory was at a premium for most programmers in the past decades when most of the affected programs were written, so the two digits saved came in handy elsewhere.

The Year 2000 problem rears its head when a computer compares two of these two-digit dates and one of them is higher than 99. A person who is 32 years old in 1999 (99–67=32) becomes –67 years old in 2000 (00–67=–67). Try buying the right number of candles for that person's birthday cake.

If you're wondering how programmers could have let this happen, most didn't think their work would still be running in 2000. This lack of foresight has turned into the Godzilla of all logic bugs.

Next Stop: Java

Before you can start writing Java programs, you need to acquire and set up some kind of Java programming software. Although several different products are available for the development of Java programs, including many terrific ones that make programming much easier, the starting place for most new Java programmers is the Java Development Kit. All of the examples in this book use the Kit, and you are encouraged to forsake all

other Java programming tools as you go through the remaining 23 hours of tutelage. The material will make more sense to programmers using the Kit, and it builds experience that will be beneficial no matter which development software you use later on.

The Java Development Kit (also referred to as the JDK) is in version 1.2 as of this writing. It is a set of tools that enable you to write and test Java programs, and the version number of the Kit usually corresponds with a version number of the language itself—though not, presently, in the case of Java 2.

This book teaches the techniques of Java 2, the edition of the language introduced in 1998. The first programming tool to offer full support for Java 2 is version 1.2 of the Java Development Kit.

To create all of the programs in this book, you must either use Java Development Kit 1.2 or another Java programming tool that fully supports Java 2. There are many different software packages that offer the ability to create Java programs, but all of these are not created equal when language support is concerned.

Some of these programming tools only support Java 1.0.2, the initial version of the language, which was released by Sun Microsystems in late 1995. Other tools support Java 1.1, which was released in mid-1997.

Users of Microsoft Windows systems may be dismayed to learn that the Java Development Kit is not graphical. You run programs from a command line (the `C:\>` prompt that will be familiar to MS-DOS users) instead of using a mouse and a point-and-click environment. Figure 1.2 shows the Kit in use in an MS-DOS window on a Windows 95 system. The Java program `WarGames.java` is compiled, and then it is run.

The examples of this book were prepared on a Microsoft Windows 95 system, and some references in the text are specific to Windows users. However, all of the material is intended for users of the Java Development Kit on any of the platforms it is currently available for. All of the code in this book's tutorial programs will work regardless of the system you're using.

At the time of this writing, the Java Development Kit version 1.2 is available directly from Sun Microsystems for the following systems:

- Microsoft Windows NT or Windows 95 systems
- Solaris SPARC and Solaris x86 systems

FIGURE 1.2

A program being compiled and run with the Java Development Kit.

The Windows 95/NT version of the Kit is provided in two versions. One version is listed as an EXE file, which means that you can install it by clicking the file's icon when you download it. This version is the easiest to set up. The other version can be downloaded as a .Zip archive file.

The World Wide Web page from which to download versions of the Kit is found at http://java.sun.com/products/JDK/.

Although Sun Microsystems has not announced plans to make the Kit available for other systems, other companies have created implementations of the Java language for non-Windows and non-Solaris systems. Details about these implementations are provided in the "Products and APIs" section of Sun's official Java site, which is available at http://java.sun.com.

If your system can handle the Java Development Kit, download it from the Web and save it on your system in a temporary folder. The file is several megabytes in size, so you'll have time during the download to make coffee, knit a cardigan, or gnaw your foot off to escape any bear traps it might be caught in.

Workshop: Installing the JDK

After the Java Development Kit has been downloaded to a temporary folder, you're ready to install it. Sun's own installation documentation supplements the information provided during this hour, so be sure to consult it if you have any questions about how the installation should be handled.

Windows Installation

Windows 95 and Windows NT versions of the Kit can be installed by double-clicking the name of the downloaded file. After you confirm that you're ready to install the Kit, a dialog box will open enabling you to determine how it will be installed on your system (see Figure 1.3).

FIGURE 1.3

Selecting how Java Development Kit will be installed.

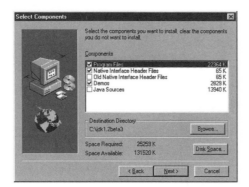

The default settings for this wizard should be fine for the work you'll be during in this book, with the possible exception of the Destination Directory setting. The JDK will be installed in a folder with a name based on the version you're downloading, such as \jdk1.2). You can select a different folder by using the Browse button.

As a hedge against any configuration problems that may occur, you should install the Kit into the folder \jdk1.2 either by accepting it as the default choice or by using Browse, if necessary, to select it. All troubleshooting sections will refer to \jdk1.2 as the place where the Kit has been installed.

Solaris Installation

Other versions of the Kit are packed as an archive file that has been compressed to reduce its size. These versions will have a filename extension such as .zip, .z, .gz, or .tar in the name. To use these, you must use decompressing software such as WinZip, untar, gzip, or PKZip.

If you don't own any software that can handle archive files, you can find programs for all common archive types on the Web. The file search engine at http://www. share-ware.com offers a way to find archive utilities for all popular operating systems. Searching for text such as unzip or untar will turn up several programs that can handle these archive formats.

The Kit's installation archive should be decompressed into a directory that does not already have a subdirectory called jdk1.2. Otherwise, you might overwrite some existing files.

Next, you should make sure you can access the file correctly by using the chmod a+x shell command on the filename.

For example, SPARC users would use the following command:

```
% chmod a+x jdk12-solaris2-sparc.bin
```

To install the JDK after making the chmod change, use a shell window to enter the command ./ followed by the archive filename. The following is an example:

```
% ./jdk12 -solaris2-sparc.bin
```

If you already have ./ in your $PATH environment variable, you won't have to include it in the command. However, you should consider removing ./ from your $PATH, because it makes it easier for your personal files to be deleted either by accident or as a result of someone's intentionally damaging script.

Testing the Installation

The Java Development Kit includes a Readme file in the main folder where the Kit was installed. This file gets its name for a good reason: You should read it right away to find out about any last-minute notes from the developers of the Kit. Any bugs, warnings, and major announcements about the Kit will be included in Readme.

Once you have installed the Kit and followed the instructions from Sun's Web site, it should work right away. Along the same lines, rush hour should really rush, nothing should ever be described as "completely unfinished," and ATMs should be described as AT machines, not ATM machines.

The most commonplace errors to watch for during the first several hours of this book are a result of a misconfigured Kit.

Windows users can test their Kit installation by using the MS-DOS Prompt command (Start, Programs, MS-DOS Prompt on most systems). This brings up an MS-DOS window where you can enter commands with your keyboard. You'll explore this feature fully during the next hour.

For now, you need to enter a command that tests whether your system can find the Java Development Kit you just installed. Enter the following in the MS-DOS window:

```
java -version
```

If you're using version 1.2 of the Kit, you should see the following message in response:

```
java version "1.2"
```

The version number might be more specific than 1.2 if you have downloaded a newer release of Java Development Kit 1.2. The more specific number should be displayed in response to the java -version command.

If you see the wrong version number or get a Bad command or file name error, your system can't find the right version of java.exe, the program that runs Java programs. This must be corrected before you can start writing Java programs. Read Appendix C, "Configuring the Java Development Kit," to learn how to take care of this problem.

Sun Microsystems also offers help on the installation process at http://java.sun.com/products/JDK/1.2/.

Official Documentation

In addition to the Java Development Kit, Sun Microsystems offers comprehensive documentation for the Java language in Web page format. You don't need this information to use this book because each topic is discussed fully as it is introduced, but these pages will come in handy when you write your own programs.

You can download the entire documentation, but it might be more convenient to browse it as needed from Sun's Web site. The most up-to-date Java documentation is available at http://java.sun.com/products/JDK/1.2/docs/index.html.

Summary

During this hour, you were introduced to the concept of programming a computer—giving it a set of instructions that tell it what to do. You also downloaded and installed the Java Development Kit that will be used as you write sample programs throughout the book.

If you are still confused about programs, programming languages, or Java in general, that's understandable at this point. Everything will make more sense to you in the next hour, "Writing Your First Program," which takes a slow trip through the process of creating a Java program.

Q&A

Q **What does the Internet have to do with making it easier to learn programming?**

A Because of the dramatic growth of the World Wide Web, companies such as Microsoft, Netscape, and Sun Microsystems are trying to attract as many programmers as possible to their languages and related technology. To do this, they are offering many programming tools for free over the Web, such as the Java Development Kit and the Microsoft Visual Basic 5 Control Creation Edition, and are offering others for free 30- or 90-day trial periods, such as SunSoft Java

WorkShop. There also are numerous free products distributed over the Internet for programmers. To find out where these products are, visit a Web directory such as Yahoo! at `http://www.yahoo.com` and search for a language that interests you. It's much cheaper today to learn programming than it was five years ago.

Q What is it about BASIC that makes it easier to fall into bad habits while writing programs?

A One thing you'll learn as you start writing Java programs is that you have to be organized. If you don't structure your program in the correct way, it won't work. BASIC doesn't have this kind of requirement. You can write in a disorganized manner and still get the program to work successfully. Later on, however, you'll have a much harder time figuring out the program if you try to fix a bug or add an improvement.

Q BASIC? C++? Java? What are the names of these languages supposed to mean?

A Like many programming languages, BASIC gets its name from an acronym that describes what it is: Beginner's All Symbolic Instruction Code. C++ is a programming language that was created to be an improvement on the C language, which itself was an improvement of the B programming language. Java goes against the tradition of naming a language with an acronym or other meaningful term. It's just the name that Java's developers liked the best when brainstorming for possible monikers—beating out WebRunner, Silk, Ruby, and others.

Q There are more than 1,000 books about Java programming?

A According to the official *JavaWorld* count, there are at least that many. The online Java magazine, which is available at `http://www.javaworld.com`, maintains a guide to all upcoming and in-print books related to Java and other Internet technology. This guide is available at `http://www.javaworld.com/javaworld/books/jw-books-index.html`.

Q Why are interpreted languages slower than compiled ones?

A For the same reason that a person interpreting a live speech is a lot slower than a translator interpreting the printed speech later on. The live interpreter has to think about each statement that's being made as it happens, while the other interpreter can work on the speech as a whole and take some shortcuts to speed up the process. Compiled languages can be much faster than interpreted languages because they can do things to make the program more efficient.

Q Is C++ harder to learn than Java?

A It's a matter of personal opinion, but Java does seem more approachable for beginners than C++. The previous language and its predecessor, C, are widely regarded as "programmer's languages," meaning that they were designed for the needs of experienced programmers. There are a lot of features in C and C++ that make them faster—and more powerful—during program creation, but these features often come at the expense of understandability. Java takes a more simplified approach to programming than C++ and is probably a better place to start.

Quiz

Test your knowledge of the material covered in this chapter by answering the following questions.

Questions

1. Which of the following is *not* a reason that people think computer programming is painfully difficult?

    (a) Programmers spread that rumor to improve their employment prospects.

    (b) Jargon and acronyms are all over the place.

    (c) Mind-control waves are sent out by the CIA promoting this belief.

2. What kind of tool runs a computer program by figuring out one line at a time?

    (a) A slow tool

    (b) An interpreter

    (c) A compiler

3. Why did James Gosling hole up in his office and create Java?

    (a) He was unhappy with the language he was using on a project.

    (b) His rock band wasn't getting any gigs.

    (c) When you can't download any image files at work, the World Wide Web is pretty dull.

Answers

1. c. Of course, the CIA could have forced me to say this.

2. b. Compilers figure out the instructions beforehand so the program can run faster.

3. a. The Web was still a little-known idea when Gosling wrote Java.

Activities

If you'd like to better introduce yourself to the subjects of Java and computer programming, do the following activities:

- Visit Sun's official Java site at `http://java.sun.com` and read some of the introductory articles that are presented in the "Read About Java" section.

- Using English sentences instead of a programming language, write a set of instructions to add 10 to a number selected by a user and then multiply the result by 5. Break the instructions into as many short one-sentence lines as you can.

To see solutions to the activities at the end of each hour, visit the book's Web site at `http://www.prefect.com/java24`.

Hour 2

Writing Your First Program

As you learned during Hour 1, "Becoming a Programmer," a computer program is a set of instructions that tell a computer what to do. These instructions are prepared in the same way instructions could be given to a person: You type them into a word processor. However, that's where the similarity ends. Instructions given to a computer must be written using a programming language. Dozens of computer programming languages have been created; you might have heard of some of them, such as BASIC or Pascal.

During this hour, you will create your first Java program by entering it using any word processor you like. When that's done, you will save the program, compile it, and test it out. The following topics will be covered during this hour:

- Entering a program into a word processor
- Naming a Java program with the `class` statement
- Organizing a program with bracket marks

- Storing information in a variable
- Changing the value of a variable
- Displaying the information stored in a variable
- Saving a program
- Compiling a program
- Running a program
- Fixing errors
- Modifying a program

What You Need to Write Programs

As explained in Hour 1, you must have the current version of the Java Development Kit installed on your system. The kit contains tools that enable you to compile and test Java programs. You also need a word processor to write programs.

With most programming languages, computer programs are written by entering text into a word processor (also called a *text editor*). Some programming languages, such as Visual C++ from Microsoft, come with their own word processor. SunSoft Java WorkShop, an advanced programming tool from Java's developers, also comes with its own editor.

Java programs are simple text files without any special features such as centered text, boldface text, or other enhancements. They can be written with any word processing program that can create text files. Microsoft Windows systems have several word processors you can use, including Notepad, WordPad, and the DOS program Edit. Apple Macintosh users can create programs with Simple Text or other editors such as BBEdit Lite. Any of these will work fine.

You also can use more sophisticated word processors, such as Microsoft Word, if you remember to save the programs as text. This option has different names depending on the program you are using. In Word, the file should be saved as a file of type Text Only. Other programs call these files DOS text, ASCII text, or something similar.

If you're in doubt about whether a word processor can save files as text files, you can always use one of the simple programs that comes with your operating system. For instance, Windows 95 users can rely on Notepad to create Java programs because text files created with Notepad are always saved as text-only files.

Windows 95 users have some special issues to deal with when selecting a word processing program and configuring it to create Java source files, so these issues will be described next. Everyone else should immediately skip to the "Creating the BigDebt Program" section later this hour to begin writing a Java program right away.

If you're still here, are you feeling special yet? You'll be up to speed with a text editor in a few minutes.

Choosing a Windows 95 Word Processing Program

If you're using Windows 95, there are several word processors included with the operating system, so you might wonder which one is best to select.

Notepad, available by selecting Start, Programs, Accessories, Notepad, is a no-frills text editor that only works with plain-text files. It can only handle one document at a time.

WordPad (Start, Programs, Accessories, WordPad) is a step above Notepad. It can handle more than one document at a time and can deal with both normal text and Microsoft Word formats. It also remembers the last several documents it has worked on, making it possible for you to load them easily from the File pull-down menu.

DOS Edit, which can be run from an MS-DOS prompt by typing the command edit, is another simple editor that handles normal text documents. It will appear crude to a Windows 95 user who isn't familiar with MS-DOS, but it does have one feature that Notepad and WordPad both lack: Edit displays your cursor's line number.

DOS Edit, like many editors other than Notepad and WordPad, shows the number of the line you're currently editing. The topmost line of the document takes the number 1, and numbers increase as you move downward.

You'll see why line numbering is a nice feature during this hour when you start working on your first Java program. Before you get too excited about DOS Edit, though, you should realize that it doesn't do Windows. Features like cut-and-paste and sophisticated mouse control, which are part of all current Windows software, either don't work in DOS Edit or don't work the way you might expect them to. The program is a throwback to the days when a mouse was an optional component on your computer.

Setting Up a Java File Extension

After a word processor has been selected, Windows 95 users should associate that editor with the .java file extension. This accomplishes two things:

- A .java source file can be opened by double-clicking its name in a folder.
- Editors such as Windows Notepad will be prevented from incorrectly adding a .txt file extension to the name of .java source files.

To create a file association, you first must have a file on which to work. Open a folder in Windows 95 and create a new text document by selecting File, New, Text Document from the folder menu bar. This is shown in Figure 2.1.

A new text document is created with the fitting name of New Text Document.txt. You can immediately rename the file by clicking its name and then selecting File, Rename from the folder's menu bar. Change the name to Anything.java and confirm the new name when Windows 95 asks if you really want to change the file extension.

Once you have created Anything.java, double-click the file. If your system has never encountered the .java file extension before, you will see an Open With window. You can use this window to associate the .java file extension with your chosen word processor. Skip directly to the "Creating a New Association" section later this hour.

If anything else happens, you must delete the existing .java association before you can create a new one.

Delete an Existing File Association

If your system already has something associated with the .java file extension, you can remove this association while inside any Windows 95 folder. Select View, Options from a folder menu bar and an Options window with three tabbed dialog boxes will open. Select the File Types tab to see its dialog box, which is shown in Figure 2.2.

The Registered File Types list box in this window shows all file extensions that are associated with programs on your system. Highlight a file type in the list box and two other fields will provide information about that file type:

- The Extension field displays all file extensions that work with this file type.
- The Opens With field displays the program that is used to open this file type.

FIGURE 2.2

The File Types tabbed dialog box.

The file type 1-2-3 Worksheets in Figure 2.2 has four file extensions: WK4, WT4, WK1, and WK3. Any file with these extensions can be opened with the program 123W (which is the Lotus 1-2-3 spreadsheet application).

Scroll through the Registered File Types list until you find one that includes JAVA in its Extension field. The most likely place to find it is under a heading such as Java files or Java programs, but that might not be the case on your computer.

When you find the right file type, you need to delete the existing association so you can replace it with a new one. Select Remove to delete the existing association and click Yes to confirm that you want to remove it.

Once you do this, you can create a new association for the .java file extension.

Creating a New Association

Windows 95 makes it easy to associate an unused file extension like .java with a program. After you create an association, you'll be able to click files that have the .java extension and load them immediately with the right word processor.

In a file folder, if you double-click a file that has no known association for its extension, an Open With window appears. This is shown in Figure 2.3.

Use the following steps to create a .java file association:

1. In the Description of '.java' Files text box, enter Java source files.

FIGURE 2.3

Associating a file extension with a program.

2. In the Choose the Program You Want to Use list box, scroll until you find the word processor you want to use when creating and editing Java source files. If you don't find it, select the Other button and find the program manually. If you're looking for DOS Edit, it can be found in the \Windows\Command folder on most systems under the filename edit or edit.exe.

3. Make sure that the Always Use This Program to Open This File option is selected (checked).

When you click OK to confirm these settings, your chosen word processor opens the Anything.java file. From this point on, it gives you double-click access to any file on your system with the .java file extension.

Associating an Icon with a File Type

At this point, you can create and edit Java source files with your desired word processor. You're ready to get to work on a program, but there's one last thing you might want to tinker with: the icon that represents Java source files.

An icon is assigned by default to all .java files on your system. This icon probably will incorporate a Microsoft Windows logo of some kind, though your system might be configured to use something else as the default icon. Unless your mind immediately thinks of Java when you see the Windows logo, you might want to pick a different icon.

When I see the Windows logo, my mind immediately thinks of all the Microsoft stock that could have been purchased in January 1988 for under $5 per share if I hadn't invested all of my money in parachute pant manufacturing.

If you want to change the icon for Java source files, select View, Options, File Types from a folder menu bar to see the File Types dialog box. Scroll through the Registered File Types to find the one associated with the .java file extension.

When this file type is highlighted, select Edit to open an Edit File Type window, which is shown in Figure 2.4.

FIGURE 2.4

The Edit File Type window.

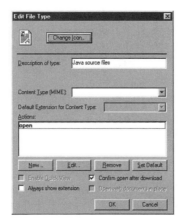

Select Change Icon from the Edit File Type window, and you can choose a different icon to display for all .java files. If you see an error message indicating that no icons are available, click OK to choose from the default set of icons.

If you like one of the icons displayed in the Current Icon window, highlight that icon and click OK to make the change.

To do some window shopping for other icons on your system, select Browse and you can look inside many files to see the icons that they contain. You can open any icon file, Windows 95 program, or .DLL file, and many of these will include one or more icons. After you select a file, any icons it contains are displayed in the Current Icon window.

Once you find an icon you like, highlight it and click OK to select it. This icon will be displayed for all Java source files on your system.

Creating the BigDebt Program

One of the things that computers are best at is math, a task that most humans are happy to pass off to someone else (or something else, in this case). For your first Java program, you will use the computer to determine a depressing fact about the financial condition of the United States. Your program will be called BigDebt. The program figures out how much the National Debt increases in an average minute. In order to determine this amount, the computer will be told how much the debt increases in an average day.

> The National Debt is the amount the United States government has borrowed to compensate for budget deficits over the years. It was approaching $5.48 trillion at last count, which equals $20,300 in indebtedness for each resident of the United States.
>
> The following list shows the debt since 1960:
>
> 1960: $290.2 billion
>
> 1965: $320.9 billion
>
> 1970: $389.2 billion
>
> 1975: $576.6 billion
>
> 1980: $930.2 billion
>
> 1985: $1.946 trillion
>
> 1990: $3.365 trillion
>
> 1995: $4.989 trillion
>
> Ed Hall maintains a Web page with the current National Debt, updated continuously. It's available at `http://www.brillig.com/debt_clock/`.

Beginning the Program

Using your word processor, begin your Java programming career by entering each line from Listing 2.1. Don't enter the line number and colon at the beginning of each line—these are used in this book so that specific line numbers can be referred to.

LISTING 2.1 THE BigDebt PROGRAM

```
1: class BigDebt {
2:     public static void main (String[] arguments) {
3:         // My first Java program goes here
4:     }
5: }
```

Make sure to capitalize everything exactly as shown, and use your space bar or Tab key to insert the blank spaces in front of some lines. When you're done, save the file with the file name BigDebt.java.

> If you're using Notepad or WordPad as your word processor, put quotation marks around the filename when saving it, as in "BigDebt.java". This will ensure that the file extension .txt is not added to the filename automatically. Setting up the .java file extension should have prevented this problem, making the quote marks unnecessary, but go ahead and use them here as a safeguard.

At this point, `BigDebt.java` contains the bare-bones form of a Java program. You will create several programs that start off exactly like this one, except for the word `BigDebt` on Line 1. This word represents the name of your program and changes with each program you write. Line 3 also should make sense—it's a sentence in actual English. The rest is completely new, however, and each part is introduced in the following sections.

The `class` Statement

The first line of the program is the following:

```
class BigDebt {
```

Translated into English, this line means, "Computer, give my Java program the name `BigDebt`."

As you might recall from Hour 1, each instruction you give a computer is called a *statement*. The `class` statement is the way you give your computer program a name. It also is used to determine other things about the program, as you will see later. The significance of the term `class` is that Java programs are also called *classes*.

In this example, the program name `BigDebt` matches the file name you gave your document, `BigDebt.java`. As a rule, a Java program should have a name that matches the first part of its filename, and they should be capitalized in the same way.

If the program name doesn't match the filename, you will get an error when you try to compile some Java programs, depending on how the `class` statement is being used to configure the program. Although some programs can have a filename that doesn't match its program name, this makes it more difficult to work with the file later on.

What the `main` Statement Does

The next line of the program is the following:

```
public static void main(String[] arguments) {
```

This line tells the computer, "The main part of the program begins here." Java programs are organized into different sections, so there needs to be a way to identify the part of a program that will be handled first. All of the programs you will write during the next several hours use main as the starting point.

Those Squiggly Bracket Marks

In the BigDebt program, every line except Line 3 contains a squiggly bracket of some kind—either an { or an }. These brackets are a way to group parts of your program (in the same way that parentheses are used in this sentence to group words). Everything between the opening bracket, {, and the closing bracket, }, is part of the same group.

These groupings are called *blocks*. In Listing 2.1, the opening bracket on Line 1 is associated with the closing bracket on Line 5, which makes your entire program a block. You always will use brackets in this way to show the beginning and end of your programs.

Blocks can be located inside other blocks (just as parentheses are used here (and a second set is used here)). The BigDebt program has brackets on Line 2 and Line 4 that establish another block. This block begins with the main statement. Everything that is inside the main statement's block is a command for the computer to handle when the program is run.

The following statement is the only thing located inside the block:

```
// My first Java program goes here
```

This line is a placeholder. The // at the beginning of the line tells the computer to ignore this line—it is put in the program solely for the benefit of humans who are looking at the program's text. Lines that serve this purpose are called *comments*.

Right now, you have written a complete Java program. It can be compiled, but if you run it, nothing will happen. The reason is that you have not told the computer to do anything yet. The main statement block contains only a line of comments, which is ignored. If the BigDebt program is going to provide sobering details about the United States Treasury, you will have to add some commands inside the opening and closing brackets of the main statement block.

Storing Information in the debt Variable

The National Debt is increasing at a present rate of $446 million per day. To put this number into perspective, overpaid sports athletes could donate their salaries to the United States Treasury and barely make a dent in it. Minnesota Timberwolves forward Kevin Garnett's six-year, $126 million deal stops the debt from increasing for around seven hours.

Aside from the publishers of computer books, most of us don't make the same kind of money as pro athletes. If we want to slow down the growing debt ourselves, a place to start is by breaking it down into minutes. Your Java program will figure this out for you.

The first step is to tell the computer what you were just told: The National Debt goes up $446 million per day. Load the BigDebt.java file into your word processor if it's not still loaded, and replace Line 3 with the following:

```
int debt = 446000000;
```

This statement tells the computer to store the value 446,000,000 into a variable called debt. *Variables* are special storage places where a computer program can store information. The value of variables can be changed.

Variables can be used to hold several different types of information, such as integers, floating-point numbers, lines of text, and characters of text. In a Java program, you must tell the computer what type of information a variable will hold. In this program, debt is an integer. Putting int in the statement int debt = 446000000; sets up the variable to hold integer values.

The int variable type can store values from -2.1 billion to 2.1 billion in Java programs. There are other variable types for different types of numbers and other types of information.

When you enter this statement into the computer program, a semi-colon must be included at the end of the line. Semi-colons are used at the end of each command in your Java programs. They're like periods at the end of a sentence; the computer uses them to determine when one command ends and the next command begins.

Changing the Information Stored in debt

As it stands, the program you have written does one thing: It uses the debt variable to hold the value 446,000,000—a day's worth of growing debt. However, you want to determine the amount of debt per minute, not per day. To determine this amount, you need to tell the computer to change the value that has been stored in the debt variable. There are 1,440 minutes in each day, so tell the computer to divide the value in debt by 1,440.

Insert a blank line after the int debt = 446000000; statement. In the blank line, enter the following:

```
debt = debt / 1440;
```

If you haven't been able to suppress all memories of new math, this statement probably looks like an algebra problem to you. It gives the computer the following assignment: Set the debt variable equal to its current value divided by 1,440.

You now have a program that does what you wanted it to do. It determines the amount the National Debt grows in a minute. However, if you ran the program at this point, it wouldn't display anything. The two commands you have given the computer in the BigDebt program occur behind the scenes. To show the computer's result, you have to display the contents of the debt variable.

Displaying the Contents of debt

Insert another blank line in the BigDebt program after the debt = debt / 1440; statement. Use that space to enter the following statement:

```
System.out.println("A minute's worth of debt is $" + debt);
```

This statement tells the computer to display the text A minute's worth of debt is $ followed by the value stored in the debt variable. The System.out.println command tells the computer to display a line on the system output device. In this case, the system output device is your computer monitor. Everything within the parentheses is displayed.

> If you learned to type on a typewriter rather than a computer, watch out for hitting the "1" key as an alternative to the "l" key (lowercase "L"). Although your cerebra1 cortex is perfectly happy to treat the numera1 as the 1etter when it appears, the computer isn't as adaptab1e as your brain. Your program won't compile if you use print1n instead of println, for example.

Saving the Finished Product

Your program should now resemble Listing 2.2, although you might have used slightly different spacing in Lines 3–5. Make any corrections that are needed and save the file as BigDebt.java. Keep in mind that all Java programs are created as text files and are saved with the .java file extension.

LISTING 2.2 THE FINISHED VERSION OF THE BigDebt PROGRAM

```
1: class BigDebt {
2:     public static void main(String[] arguments) {
3:         int debt = 446000000;
4:         debt = debt / 1440;
```

```
5:          System.out.println("A minute's worth of debt is $" + debt);
6:      }
7: }
```

When the computer runs this program, it will run each of the statements in the main statement block on lines 3–5. Listing 2.3 shows what the program would look like if it were written in the English language instead of Java.

LISTING 2.3 A LINE-BY-LINE BREAKDOWN OF THE BigDebt PROGRAM

```
1: The BigDebt program begins here:
2:      The main part of the program begins here:
3:          Store the value 446000000 in an integer variable called debt
4:          Set debt equal to its current value divided by 1440
5:          Display "A minute's worth of debt is $" and the new value of
               debt
6:      The main part of the program ends here.
7: The BigDebt program ends here.
```

Compiling the Program into a `Class` File

Before you can try out the program, it must be compiled. The term *compile* might be unfamiliar to you now, but you will become quite familiar with it in the coming hours. When you compile a program, you take the instructions you have given the computer and convert them into a form the computer can better understand. You also make the program run as efficiently as possible. Java programs must be compiled before you can run them. With the Java Development Kit, programs are compiled using the `javac` program.

The `javac` program, like all programs included with the Java Development Kit, is a command-line utility. You run the program by using your keyboard to type a command at a place that can accept the input. This place is what the term *command-line* refers to.

Because most UNIX usage is handled at the command-line, readers with a UNIX operating system will be familiar with how the Java Development Kit programs are used.

Many Windows 95 users might not be aware that their operating system includes a command-line feature of its own: the MS-DOS window.

The Command Line in Windows 95

Windows 95 users can get to a command line by using their system's MS-DOS Prompt feature (Start, Programs, MS-DOS Prompt). This opens up a window where MS-DOS commands can be entered, as shown in the following output:

OUTPUT
```
Microsoft(R) Windows 95
    (C)Copyright Microsoft Corp. 1981-1996.

C:\WINDOWS>
```

In this output, the text C:\WINDOWS> is the command line. A blinking cursor on this line indicates that commands can be entered here. MS-DOS is the operating system that preceded Microsoft Windows, and you'll need to use some MS-DOS commands to work with the Java Development Kit.

The main MS-DOS command you'll be using is CD, which moves from one folder to another. CD is short for "change directory," because a file folder is called a *directory* in MS-DOS.

The CD command is followed by a space and the name of the folder to which to move. If you're changing to the C:\JAVA folder on your system, the following command would be entered:

```
CD C:\JAVA
```

After a command is completed, you'll be brought back to a command line. Under most configurations, the command line will include the full name of the current folder. For example, if you switched to a C:\JAVA folder on your system, the command line is likely to be the following:

```
C:\JAVA>
```

To close the MS-DOS window and return to Windows 95, use the EXIT command. You also can press ALT-TAB to return to Windows 95 while leaving the MS-DOS window open.

Asking someone to learn Java and MS-DOS at the same time constitutes cruel and unusual punishment in some western European countries. To use as little MS-DOS as possible, do the following:

1. While in Windows 95, open the main file folder on your main hard drive, which is (C:) for most people.

2. Create a new folder by selecting File, New, Folder from the folder's menu bar and name this folder J24Work.

3. Save all the programs you write while working through this book in the J24Work folder.

At an MS-DOS command line, you can change to this folder with the following command:

```
CD \J24Work
```

Using `javac` to Compile the Program

To compile the `BigDebt` program, go to the folder on your system where the `BigDebt.java` file is located, and type the following at the command line:

```
javac BigDebt.java
```

When the program compiles successfully, a new file called `BigDebt.class` is created in the same folder as `BigDebt.java`. (If you have any error messages, refer to the following section, "Fixing Errors.") The `.class` extension was chosen because all Java programs are called classes. A Java program can be made up of several classes that work together, but in a simple program such as `BigDebt` only one class is needed.

> Did you ever have a relative, spouse, or other loved one who only says something when things go wrong? (Me neither.) The `javac` tool only speaks up when there's an error to complain about. If you compile a program successfully without any errors, nothing happens in response.

Fixing Errors

If errors exist in your program when you compile it, the `javac` tool displays a message explaining each error and the lines on which they occurred. The following output illustrates an attempt to compile a program that has errors, and the error messages that are displayed as a result:

OUTPUT

```
C:\J24Work>javac BigDebt.java
BigDebt.java:4: Invalid type expression.
          debt = debt / 1400
                      ^

BigDebt.java:5: Invalid declaration.
          System.out.println("A minute's worth of debt is $" + debt);
                          ^

2 errors

C:\J24Work>
```

Error messages displayed by the `javac` tool include the following information:

- The name of the Java program
- The number of the line where the error was found
- The type of error
- The line where the error was found

As you learned during the past hour, errors in programs are called bugs. Finding those errors and squashing them is called *debugging*. The following is an example of an error message from the preceding output:

```
BigDebt.java:4: Invalid type expression.
              debt = debt / 1440
```

In this example, the 4 that follows the file name BigDebt.java indicates that the error is on Line 4. This is where having a line-numbering word processor comes in handy—you can jump more easily to the Java statement that's associated with the error.

The actual error message, Invalid type expression in this case, often can be confusing to new programmers. In some cases, the message can be confusing to any programmer. When the error message doesn't make sense to you, take a look at the line where the error occurred.

For instance, can you determine what's wrong with the following statement?

```
debt = debt / 1440
```

The problem is that there's no semi-colon at the end of the statement, which is required in Java programs.

If you get error messages when compiling the BigDebt program, double-check that your program matches Listing 2.2 and correct any differences you find. Make sure that everything is capitalized correctly and that all punctuation marks (such as {, }, and ;) are included.

Often, a close look at the statement included with the error message is enough to reveal the error, or errors, that need to be fixed. If the Java compiler responds with error messages such as Bad command or filename or error: Can't read, the most likely culprit is a Java Development Kit that needs to be reconfigured. For help fixing this, read Appendix C, "Configuring the Java Development Kit."

Running the Program

The Java Development Kit provides a Java interpreter so you can try the program you have created. The interpreter, which is a command-line program called java, makes the computer follow the instructions you gave it when you wrote the program.

To run a Java program, the command java is followed by a space and the name of the class file that contains the program. Although the class file's name includes the .class extension, this part of the name must be left off when running the program with the Java interpreter.

To see whether the BigDebt program does what you want, go to the folder that contains the BigDebt.class file, and type the following at a command line:

```
java BigDebt
```

When the program runs, it should state the following:

```
A minute's worth of debt is $309722
```

The computer has provided the answer you wanted! With this information, you now know that if you want to donate your salary to slow one minute's growth of the National Debt, you need to make more than $300,000 per year. You also have to avoid paying any taxes.

> Neither the author nor Macmillan Computer Publishing makes any guarantees expressed or implied that the Internal Revenue Service will accept the excuse that you spent all your money on the National Debt.

Workshop: Modifying the Program

The BigDebt program calculated the amount the National Debt increases in a minute. If you'd like to make a dent in the debt but can't spare $309,702, you might want to see how much a second's worth of debt would cost you.

Load the file BigDebt.java into your word processor again. You need to change the following statement:

```
debt = debt / 1440;
```

This line divided the value in the debt variable by 1,440 because there are 1,440 minutes in a day. Change the line in the BigDebt program so that it divides the debt variable by 86,400, the number of seconds in a day.

> When you change the line of code, don't include a comma in the number (as in 86,400). If you do, you will get an error message when you compile the program. Commas may make it easier for people to read the numbers in your code, but the compiler doesn't appreciate the gesture.

You also need to change the following line:

```
System.out.println("A minute's worth of debt is $" + debt);
```

Now that you're calculating a second's worth of debt, you need to replace the word minute with second. Make the change and save the file BigDebt.java. Your version of BigDebt.java should match Listing 2.4.

LISTING 2.4   THE MODIFIED VERSION OF THE BigDebt PROGRAM

```
1: class BigDebt {
2:     public static void main(String arguments[]) {
3:         int debt = 446000000;
4:         debt = debt / 86400;
5:         System.out.println("A second's worth of debt is $" + debt);
6:     }
7: }
```

Compile the file with the same command you used previously:

```
javac BigDebt.java
```

When you run the program, you should get the following output:

OUTPUT   A second's worth of debt is $5162

Summary

During this hour, you got your first chance to create a Java program. You learned that to develop a Java program you need to complete these three basic steps:

1. Write the program with a word processor.

2. Compile the program.

3. Tell the interpreter to run the program.

Along the way, you were introduced to some basic computer programming concepts such as compilers, interpreters, blocks, statements, and variables. These things will become clearer to you in successive hours. As long as you got the two versions of the BigDebt program to work during this hour, you're ready to proceed.

Q&A

Q **Is SunSoft Java WorkShop another programming language like Java, or is it something else?**

A Java WorkShop is a way to write Java programs in a graphical, point-and-click environment. It was produced by a division of Sun Microsystems, the developer of Java, as an improvement on the Java Development Kit. Other products in the market offer similar features, such as Symantec Visual Café and Borland JBuilder.

Q **I have several word processing programs on my system. Which should I use to write Java programs?**

A Any of them will suffice, as long as it can save files as text without any special formatting. A word processor that shows the line number your cursor is located on is especially useful. (Microsoft Word, for example, shows the line number at the bottom edge of the window along with the column number.) Because the javac compiler lists line numbers with its error messages, the line-numbering feature helps you debug a program more quickly.

Q **How important is it to put the right number of blank spaces on a line in a Java program?**

A Spacing is strictly for the benefit of people looking at a computer program. You could have written the BigDebt program without using blank spaces or the Tab key to indent lines, and it would compile successfully. Although the number of spaces in front of the lines isn't important, you should use spacing in your Java programs. Spacing indicates how a program is organized and to which programming block a statement belongs. When you start writing more sophisticated programs, you'll find it much more difficult to do without spacing.

Q **A Java program has been described as a class, and it also has been described as a group of classes. Which is it?**

A Both. The simple Java programs you create during the next few hours will create a single file with the extension .class. You can run these with the java interpreter. Java programs also can be made up of a set of classes that work together. In fact, even simple programs like BigDebt use other Java classes behind the scenes. This topic will be fully explored during Hour 10, "Creating Your First Object."

Q **If semi-colons are needed at the end of each statement, why does the comment line // My first Java program goes here not end with a semi-colon?**

A Comments are completely ignored by the compiler. If you put // on a line in your program, this tells the Java compiler to ignore everything to the right of the // on that line. The following example shows a comment on the same line as a statement:

```
debt = debt / 86400; // divide debt by the number of seconds
```

In this example, the compiler will handle the statement debt = debt / 86400; and ignore the comments afterward.

Q What is a character?

A A *character* is a single letter, number, punctuation mark, or other symbol. Examples are *T*, *5*, and %. Characters are stored in variables as text.

Q I get an Invalid argument error message when I use the javac tool to compile the BigDebt program. What can I do to correct this?

A You are probably leaving off the .java extension and typing the following command:

```
javac BigDebt
```

Make sure you are in the same folder as the file BigDebt.java and type the following command to compile the program:

```
javac BigDebt.java
```

Q I couldn't find any errors in the line where the compiler noted an error. What can I do?

A The line number displayed with the error message isn't always the place where an error needs to be fixed in your program. Examine the statements that are directly above the error message to see whether you can spot any typos or other bugs. The error usually is within the same programming block.

Quiz

Test your knowledge of the material covered in this chapter by answering the following questions.

Questions

1. When you compile a Java program, what are you doing?
    (a) Saving it to disk
    (b) Converting it into a form the computer can better understand
    (c) Adding it to your program collection

2. What is a variable?

    (a) Something that wobbles but doesn't fall down

    (b) Text in a program that the compiler ignores

    (c) A place to store information in a program

3. What is the process of fixing errors called?

    (a) Defrosting

    (b) Debugging

    (c) Decomposing

Answers

1. b. Compiling converts a `.java` file into a `.class` file or set of `.class` files.

2. c. Variables are one place to store information; later you'll learn about others such as arrays and constants. Weebles wobble but they don't fall down, and comments are text in a program that the compiler ignores.

3. b. Because errors in a computer program are called bugs, fixing those errors is called debugging. Some programming tools come with a tool called a debugger that helps you fix errors.

Activities

If you'd like to explore the topics covered in this hour a little more fully, try the following activities:

- Multiplication is handled in Java using the `*` character. An example of its use is the statement `int answer = x * 5;`. Write a program for megamillionaires who have a yen to help fight the National Debt: Calculate the amount the debt increases in three days.

- Go back to the `BigDebt` program and add one or two errors. For example, take a semi-colon off the end of a line or change the text `println` on one line to `print1n`. Save the program and try to compile it. Compare the error messages you get to the errors you caused.

To see solutions to these activities, visit the book's Web site at
`http://www.prefect.com/java24`.

HOUR 3

Vacationing in Java

Java is a huge opportunity for all of us.

—Marc Andreesen of Netscape at the JavaOne Conference,
May 31, 1996

Before you venture further into Java programming, it's worthwhile to learn more about the language and see what Java programmers are doing today. One of the reasons that Java has become popular quickly is that it can be used to offer programs on the World Wide Web. Because of this capability, the best examples of how to use Java are also on the Web. During this hour, we'll take a look at some sites that feature Java programs and talk about the history and development of the language.

To go on this vacation, you need a Web browser that can handle Java programs. The current versions of Netscape Navigator and Microsoft Internet Explorer can run Java programs that are found on Web pages.

> If you're using a current version of Netscape Navigator and it isn't working with Java programs, check your setup configuration from one of the program's pull-down menus (select Edit, Preferences, Advanced in Navigator). Make sure your browser software has Java enabled in its settings.

Load your browser software of choice, put on your best Hawaiian shirt, and get ready to vacate. Because you won't be leaving your house, you won't get a chance to experience the simpler pleasures of tourism: odd driving rituals, exotic food, exotic members of the opposite sex, exotic members of the opposite sex with food, and so on. But look on the bright side: no antibacterial shots, traveler's checks, or passports are required either.

The following topics will be covered during this hour:

- A definition of the Java language
- The benefits of using Java
- Some examples of Java at work
- An explanation of object-oriented programming
- Sites of note for Java programmers

> The Web siteseeing examples you visit during today's vacation are just a small sampling of the Java programs in use on the Web. A search of the AltaVista Web search database finds more than a million pages that have included a Java program as of this writing.

First Stop: Sun Microsystems

The Java vacation begins at a place you'll be visiting regularly now that you're a Java programmer: the Web site of Sun Microsystems, the company that developed the Java language. To get there, go to `http://java.sun.com`.

The Java division of Sun Microsystems is responsible for the advancement of the Java language and the development of related software. To see a simple example of Java in action, choose the hyperlink on the Java division's main page that offers a "Java version" of the site. If you can't find one, you can reach the Java front page by visiting `http://java.sun.com:81/index.html`.

A Java program is used on this page to add pull-down menus on top of the main navigation menu of the site. Drag your mouse across the different section titles on the page to see the pull-down menus that appear. Figure 3.1 shows a pull-down menu that appears when the mouse is over the "Read About Java" text.

FIGURE 3.1

Sun's official Java Web site uses a Java program to add pull-down menus on top of a Web page.

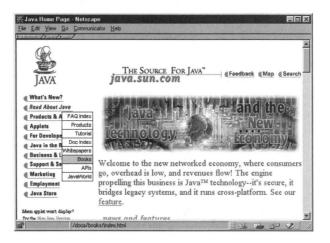

This Web site is the place to find the latest released versions of the Java Development Kit, as well as other programmer's resources. This site also has press releases about Java-related products, full documentation for Java, and sample Java programs that run on the Web. Sun Microsystems first made Java available for free via this Web site in 1995.

A Brief History of Java

Sun cofounder Bill Joy called Java the end result of fifteen years of work to produce a better, more reliable way to write computer programs. Java's creation was a little more complicated than that.

Java was invented six years ago by Sun engineer James Gosling as a language to use as the brains for smart appliances (interactive TVs, omniscient ovens, and the like). Gosling was unhappy with the results he was getting by writing programs with C++, another programming language, so he holed up in his office and wrote a new language to better suit his needs.

Most people who are holed up in their office aren't producing new programming languages or other achievements. They're playing Quake. How many lasting contributions to mankind have been lost because of Id Software?

At the time, Gosling named his language Oak after a tree he could see from his office window. The language was part of Sun's strategy to make millions when interactive TV became a multimillion-dollar industry. That still hasn't happened today (six years down the road), but something completely different took place. Just as Sun was ready to scrap Oak development and scatter its workers to other parts of the company, the World Wide Web became popular.

In a fortuitous circumstance, many of the qualities that made Gosling's language good on its appliance project made it suitable for adaptation to the World Wide Web. Sun developers devised a way for programs to be run safely from Web pages and chose a catchy new name to accompany the language's new focus: Java.

You might have heard that Java is an acronym that stands for Just Another Vague Acronym. You also might have heard that it was named for the developers' love of coffee, especially the percolating product from a shop near Sun's offices. Actually, the story behind Java's naming contains no secret messages or declarations of liquid love. Instead, Java was chosen for the same reason that comedian Jerry Seinfeld likes to say the word *salsa*. It sounds cool.

Although Java can be used for many other things, the Web provided the showcase it needed to capture international attention. A programmer who puts a Java program on a Web page makes it instantly accessible to the entire Web-surfing planet. Because Java was the first tool that could offer this capability, it became the first computer language to receive as much press as Dennis Rodman, Madonna's baby, and the alien autopsy. When the language rose to prominence in 1996, you had to be in solitary confinement or a long-term orbital mission to avoid hearing about Java.

There have been three major releases of the Java language:

- Fall 1995: Java 1.0—A version best suited for use on the World Wide Web that showed potential for expansion into other types of programming
- Spring 1997: Java 1.1—An upgrade to the language that included numerous improvements to the way user interfaces are created and handled
- Fall 1998: Java 2—More than three times as large as Java 1.0, with enhancements that make the language a worthy competitor to other general-purpose programming languages

Going to School with Java

As a medium that offers a potential audience of millions, the World Wide Web includes numerous resources for educators and schoolchildren. Because Java programs can offer a more interactive experience than standard Web pages, some programmers have used the language to write learning programs for the Internet.

For one of the strongest examples of this use of Java, visit
`http://www.npac.syr.edu/projects/vishuman/VisibleHuman.html`.

This Web site uses data from the National Library of Medicine's Visible Human Project. The project is a database of thousands of cross-sectional images of human anatomy. A Java program is being used to enable users to search the collection and view images. Instead of making requests by text commands, users make the requests to see different parts of the body by using the mouse, and the results are shown immediately in graphic detail. The Java program is shown in Figure 3.2.

FIGURE 3.2

Images from the National Library of Medicine's Visible Human Project can be viewed interactively on the Web using a Java program.

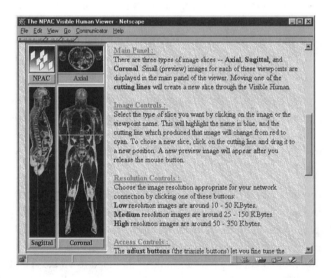

Numerous educational programs are available for many different computer systems, but what makes this program remarkable is its versatility. The Visible Human Project tool is similar in function and performance to CD-ROM software that users might run on their computer systems. However, it is run directly from a Web page. No special installation is needed, and unlike most CD-ROM software, it isn't limited to PC-compatible and Macintosh systems. Just like Web pages, Java programs can be run on any computer system that can handle them.

In order to handle Java programs, a Web browser must have a Java interpreter. The interpreter included with a browser serves a similar function as the interpreter you used to run the BigDebt program during Hour 2, "Writing Your First Program." The difference is that a browser's interpreter can only run Java programs that are set up to run on Web pages and cannot handle programs set up to run from the command line. Currently, Java-enabled browsers are available for most common systems, including PCs running a version of Microsoft Windows, Apple Macintosh systems, SPARC workstations, and computers running the Linux operating system.

The primary Java-capable browsers in use today are Netscape Navigator and Microsoft Internet Explorer. Although versions of these browsers support Java, they might not necessarily support Java 2. Browser developers have not been able to keep up with new versions of the language as quickly as Sun produces them. At the time of this writing, Navigator does not yet support Java 1.1 fully, and Microsoft does not plan to add full 1.1 or 2 support to Internet Explorer at any time.

To make it possible for Java programmers to rely on Java 2 support in browsers, Sun is developing the Java plug-in, a Java interpreter that works as a browser enhancement for Navigator and Internet Explorer. By specifying that this interpreter should be used instead of the one built into the browser, Java programmers can take advantage of all features of the language in their Web-based programs.

A Java program such as the Visible Human Project database does not have to be written for a specific computer system. This advantage is called *platform independence*. Java was created to work on multiple systems. Originally, Java's developers believed it needed to be multiplatform because it would be used on a variety of appliances and other electronic devices.

The programs you write with Java can be run on a variety of computer systems without requiring any extra work from you. This advantage is one of the primary reasons so many people are learning to write Java programs and are using them on software projects. Many professional software companies are using Java for the same reason. Under the right circumstances, Java can remove the need to create specific versions of a program for different computer systems. The potential audience for software grows with a multiplatform solution such as Java.

Lunch in JavaWorld

If you didn't lose your appetite after searching through the innards of a visible human, take a lunch break with *JavaWorld*, an online magazine for Java programmers and other Internet developers. The *JavaWorld* Web site is available at
http://www.javaworld.com.

JavaWorld offers how-to articles, news stories related to Java development, and other features in each monthly edition. One of the advantages of the publication's Web format is that it can display functional Java programs in conjunction with articles. Figure 3.3 shows a Java "poetry magnet board" in a tutorial that describes how it is written.

FIGURE 3.3

A JavaWorld *how-to article on how to create a "poetry magnet board" includes a working example of the program.*

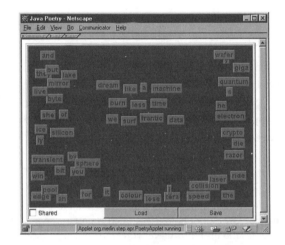

In addition to offering information of benefit to Java programmers, *JavaWorld* publishes articles and commentary about the language and its development. One issue that has been hotly debated since Java's release is whether the language is secure. Security is important because of the way Java programs work when they are placed on a Web page. The Java programs you have tried during this hour were downloaded to your computer first. When each program was finished downloading, it ran on your computer. It was as though someone sat down at your computer, popped in a disk, and ran their own program.

Unless you know a lot of people, most of the Web pages you visit will be published by strangers. In terms of security, running their programs isn't a lot different than letting the general public use your computer on alternate weekends. If the Java language did not have safeguards to prevent abuse, its programs could introduce viruses onto your system, delete files, and do other malicious things. Java includes several different types of security to make sure that its programs are safe when run from Web pages.

The main security is provided by the following general restrictions on Java programs running over the Web:

- No program can open, read, write, or delete files on the user's system.
- No program can run other programs on the user's system.

- All windows created by the program will be identified clearly as Java windows. This identification prevents someone from creating a fake window asking for the user's name and password.
- Programs cannot make connections to Web sites other than the one from which they came.
- All programs will be verified to make sure that nothing was modified after they were compiled.

The general consensus among Java developers is that the language has enough safeguards in place to be usable over the Web. Several security holes have been found, often by programming security experts, and these holes have been dealt with quickly by Sun or the Web browser programmers. Because *JavaWorld* covers the latest news of note in the Java development community, it is a good way to keep track of any security issues that arise.

> None of the safeguards in place are a complete block against malicious programs. Just as loopholes have been found in the past, more will undoubtedly be found in the future. If you are concerned about running Java programs through your Web browser, you might want to run programs only from a source such as developer.com because it tests the programs before including them in the directory. You also should back up anything you can't afford to lose on your computer, which is good practice for anyone who runs programs received from the Internet.

Version 1.2 of the Java language has introduced a more flexible security policy for programs that run in a browser. You can designate some companies and programmers as "trusted developers," which enables their Java programs to run in your browser without the restrictions that normally would be in place.

This system of trust is established through the use of *digital signatures*, files that clearly identify the author of a Java program. These signatures are created in collaboration with independent verification groups like VeriSign, which has a World Wide Web site at http://www.verisign.com.

If you have ever authorized an ActiveX control to run in Internet Explorer, you have worked with a similar system of trust and identity verification.

Taking in a Ball Game at ESPN SportsZone

The first afternoon stop on the Java tour will be a trip to the old ball game. ESPN SportsZone, the leading sports site on the World Wide Web, is using Java to present baseball games as they happen in a visual, pitch-by-pitch fashion. To see how baseball is played in cyberspace, visit http://espn.sportszone.com/.

The Java program called ESPN GameCast presents each pitch in a Major League game. Runners are shown on base, player changes are reflected immediately, and all stats in the game are updated in real time.

The program is a unique way to follow live games. Figure 3.4 shows GameCast after the last pitch in a heartbreaking 7-2 loss that the Texas Rangers received at the hands of the Cleveland Indians. (Heartbreaking to me, at least.)

FIGURE 3.4

The Cleveland Indians defeat the Texas Rangers 7-2 in a game broadcast through ESPN GameCast, a Java program that displays comprehensive information about a game while it is taking place.

One of the things you might notice about ESPN GameCast is that it updates the day's scores from other games as you are using the program. This update is relatively easy to do because the Java language is multithreaded. *Multithreading* is a way for the computer to do more than one thing at a time. One part of a program takes care of one task, another part takes care of a different task, and the two parts can pay no attention to each other. Each part of a program in this example is called a *thread*.

In a program such as ESPN GameCast, the league scoreboard along one edge of the window could run in its own thread. The rest of the program could be another thread. If you use an operating system such as Microsoft Windows 95, you're using a type of this behavior when you run more than one program simultaneously. If you're at work and you surf the Web for European aerobics videos in one window while running a company sales report in another window, congratulate yourself—you're multithreading!

Getting Down to Business

At this point in your travels, you might be getting the impression that Java is primarily of use to baseball fans and those who have body parts to show the world. Although those two subject areas are enough to keep most of us entertained for hours, the next stop on our trip shows an example of Java getting down to business.

Direct your Web browser to `http://www.engine.com/java/engbrowse/Employee.html`.

This example is an employee payroll database managed as a pair of Java programs. Employee information is viewed in one program, and the other program is used to edit items from the payroll record of a specific employee. Figure 3.5 shows Bart Simpson's record as it is being edited.

Unlike other payroll tracking systems that require the installation of software on the computers of each employee who needs access, the use of Java enables Software Engine to make the program available to any employee with a Web browser. With some kind of password security system in place, the program could even be used by employees who are away from the office on business trips. All the employees would have to do is access the company's Web site.

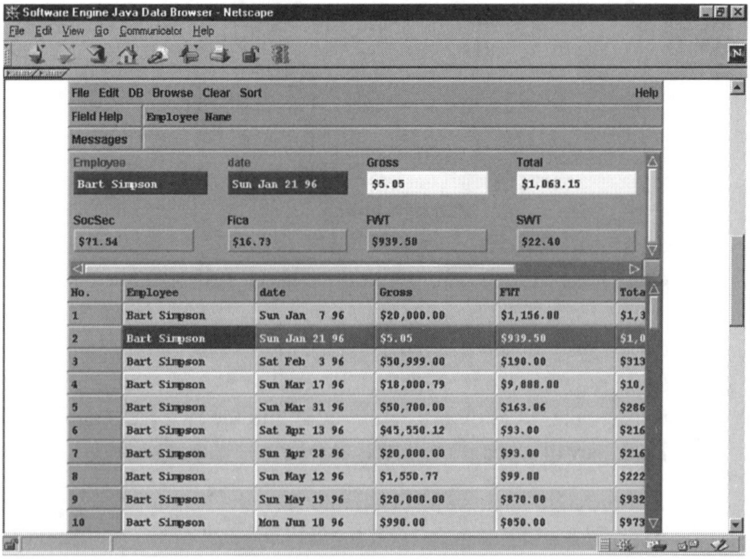

FIGURE 3.5

A Java program from Software Engine that is used to maintain employee payroll records.

A database program such as Software Engine's can be thought of in several different ways. One way is to think of a program as an object—something that exists in the world, takes up space, and has certain things it can do. Java, like the C++ language, uses object-oriented programming, as you will see during Hour 10, "Creating Your First Object." Object-oriented programming (OOP) is a way of thinking about computer programs. A program is thought of as a group of objects. Each object handles a specific task and knows how to speak to other objects. For example, a word processing program could be set up as the following group of objects:

- A document object, which is the area where you type in text
- A spell-checking object, which can look over the document object to find any possible spelling errors
- A printer object, which handles the printing of the document
- A menu object, a mouse object, and many others

Each of these objects is an independent computer program that doesn't need the others to do its job. The word processing software is a collection of all the objects necessary to get work done.

OOP is a powerful way to create programs, and it makes the programs you write more useful. Consider the word processing software. If the programmer wants to use the spell-checking capabilities of that program with some other software, the spell-checking object is ready for use with the new program. No changes need to be made.

Stopping by developer.com to Ask Directions

This world tour of Java programs is being led by a professional who is well-versed in the hazards and highlights of Web-based travel. You'll be venturing out on your own trips soon, so it's worthwhile to stop at the best tour guide currently available for the Java-hungry tourist, the developer.com Web site at `http://www.developer.com/`.

developer.com features the most comprehensive directory of Java programs, programming resources, and other information related to the language. Most of the programs visited during this hour were originally found on a trek through the searchable database maintained by developer.com. Updates are made on a daily basis, so this is another place you'll be visiting often as you develop your Java programming skills.

One of the best uses of developer.com for programmers is to see what programs are available that offer source code. In case you're unfamiliar with the term, *source code* is another name for the text files that are used to create computer programs. The BigDebt.java file you developed during Hour 2 is an example of source code.

developer.com's directory listings indicate when a compiled Java program is accompanied by the source code used to create it. After you have finished your first 24 hours as a Java programmer, you ought to take a look at some of these programs. Figure 3.6 shows developer.com being used to search for "3-D graphics" resources.

FIGURE 3.6

The developer.com Java directory offers more than 13,000 Java resources and links to programs.

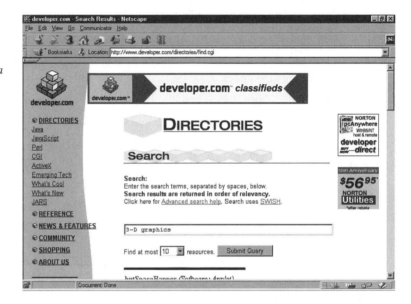

The large number of Java programs listed in developer.com shows that the language has become adopted quickly by thousands of programmers around the world. Part of the reason is that Java's popularity inspires people to learn it, which is the same principle that caused parachute pants and break dancing to be briefly popular in the mid-80s. Another reason for the swiftly growing population of Java programmers is the simplicity of the language.

One of the goals of Java's design was to make it easier to learn than C++, the language James Gosling was having fits with on Sun's smart-appliance project. Much of Java is based on C++, so programmers who have learned to use that language will find it easier to learn Java. However, some of the elements of C++ that are the hardest to learn—and the hardest to use correctly—have been removed from Java.

For people who are learning programming for the first time, Java is easier to learn than C++ would be. Also, Java will not work if its variables and other elements of a program are used incorrectly. This adherence to rules can be painful for experienced programmers, but it forces everyone to develop good habits as they create programs.

Some languages are created to make it easier for experienced programmers to harness the capabilities of the computer in their programs. These languages include shortcuts and other features that programming veterans easily understand. Java does not use these features, preferring to make the language as simple as an object-oriented programming language can be. Java was created to be easy to learn, easy to debug, and easy to use.

A Big Finish with Castanets

The second-to-last stop on your Java vacation has a certain Caribbean flair to it—castanets, marimbas, and bongos are involved. If you packed a ruffly Cuban bandleader shirt just like the one Carmine Ragusa used to wear on episodes of *Laverne and Shirley*, now's the best chance you'll ever have to wear it. Visit `http://www.marimba.com`.

Unlike the other sightseeing locations you have visited, this site can't be viewed with a Web browser alone. Marimba, a startup company formed by several former Java developers at Sun, has used Java to create Castanet, a way to receive and run software over the Internet.

Castanet is a way to send out computer programs that automatically update themselves on the computers of people who request them. It's a service not unlike television, where you turn to a channel and immediately start receiving the broadcast signal of that channel. In fact, the Java programs sent by this method are called *channels*. Figure 3.7 shows a Castanet channel offered by *TV Guide* that presents TV listings. When new listings are added to *TV Guide*'s channel and other features are added, Castanet sends the update automatically over the Internet. No effort is required on the user's end to keep up with new versions of the software.

To provide this automatic-updating feature, Castanet provides special software called the Tuner. The Castanet Tuner is a sophisticated Java program that runs from the command line. To find out more about downloading the Tuner for your system, visit `http://www.marimba.com/products/`.

The Tuner is several megabytes in size, so you might not want to install it on your system immediately. Visit the Marimba Web site to find out more about channels and what services they offer.

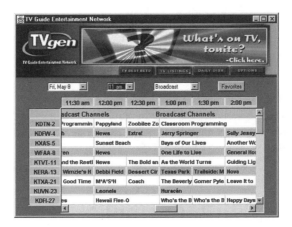

The TV Guide Castanet channel provides constantly updated TV listings via Java.

Castanet illustrates a point about Java that sometimes gets lost: Although Java is most popular as a way to write Web page programs, it is not limited to use on the Internet. You can use it to write any kind of software.

The newest version of the language, Java 2, includes numerous enhancements that make Java a worthy competitor to more established languages such as Microsoft Visual C++ and Borland Delphi.

One of these enhancements is Swing, a feature that makes it possible to create sophisticated user interfaces for Java programs. These interfaces have a special feature called *look-and-feel* that enables a Java program to mimic the appearance of different operating systems. Programs can be written to look like Windows software, Motif software, or even Java's own look-and-feel, which is called Metal.

Early versions of the Java language were best when used on the World Wide Web, so it often is perceived as a Web technology. Sun Microsystems has put its emphasis in recent years on turning Java into a fully capable software development language no matter where the program will run.

Workshop: Putting Java on Your Desktop

The last stop on your whirlwind tour of Java is ABCNEWS.com, the electronic edition of the ABC TV network's news division. So far, your guides have asked nothing of you other than an occasional wardrobe change, but that's going to change. Redirect your Web browser to http://www.abcnews.com.

If you're using a browser such as Netscape Navigator or Microsoft Internet Explorer, your first assignment is to find the Java programs on this page. This ought to be a lot easier than finding Waldo in those *Where's Waldo?* children's books, but if you need a hint, here it is: They're the parts with changing text and graphics.

ABCNEWS.com uses Java programs to provide constant headline updates. In the Your News Summary feature, text is frequently updated along with graphical advertisements.

Your News Summary is offered as part of a Web page, but it has a special feature that adds to its usefulness. It can be detached from the page and placed on your system's desktop as a stand-alone window. Click the `remote control` link and then minimize your Web browser. This might be more information than you're able to handle in a short period of time, but it shows how Java can present it in a way much different from standard Web pages. Figure 3.8 shows Your News Summary on a Windows 95 desktop.

FIGURE 3.8

News headlines and ads are presented in a desktop window with the ABCNEWS.com Your News Summary program.

Once you're completely caught up on the news events that have taken place during your world-in-a-day jaunt, it's time to put away your luggage and get ready for a return to programming. More Web sites and other items of note for Java programmers are described in Appendix A, "Where to Go From Here: Java Resources."

Q&A

Q Can I use the sample Java programs from the Sun Microsystems Web site on my own home page?

A Sun encourages the use of its sample programs on Web sites. In addition to the programs available at `http://java.sun.com`, take a look at the folders that were created when you installed the Java Development Kit on your system. You will find more than two dozen sample programs along with the `.java` files that were used to compile them. These programs can be a valuable resource when you're working on your own Java programs later.

Q What other ways have been devised to offer programs on Web pages?

A Several programming strategies are aimed at making Web pages smarter. The main competitor to Java is ActiveX, an extension of Microsoft technology called the Component Object Model. ActiveX programs are similar in function to Java programs—they are placed on Web pages and are run when browsers are equipped to handle them. The primary differences are that ActiveX uses a way to verify the identity of ActiveX programmers, and ActiveX programs are not downloaded each time they are encountered. Unlike Java programs, an ActiveX program stays on a user's system. Also, an ActiveX program is not restricted in what it can do on a system, whereas Java programs run from Web pages face very strong restrictions in what they can do. In addition to ActiveX, JavaScript and VBScript offer some programming capabilities on Web pages. These programs must be more simple than Java and ActiveX programs, however.

Q I ran a useful Java program on a Web page. Can I run it on my system without the browser?

A Under most circumstances, no. Java programs typically are developed to run on a Web page or to run from the command line. A program can be written so that it works in both ways, but most of the programs you will find in a directory such as developer.com do not include this functionality. You'll learn much more about the different types of Java programs during Hour 4, "Understanding How Java Programs Work."

Q If Java programs are platform-independent, why are some Java programs such as SunSoft Java WorkShop only available for specific systems?

A Java programs might be limited to specific systems such as PC compatibles because the programs include the use of non-Java programming for some features. For example, a Java program might use a program written in C++ to take advantage of an existing C++ program's capabilities.

Q Is there a print edition of *JavaWorld*?

A At present, *JavaWorld* is distributed strictly through the World Wide Web. However, several newsstand magazines are available that cover the language, including *Java Report*, *Dr. Dobb's Journal*, and others.

Q Can a Java program I run on a Web page give my computer a virus?

A Because of general security restrictions that prevent Web programs from reading, writing, or modifying files, there's no way for a virus to be transmitted from a Java program on a Web page to your system unless you gave the program full permission to access the hard drive on your system. Java programs you download and run from the command line have the same risk of viruses as any program you download. If you're using programs received over the Internet, you need to acquire a good antivirus program and use it regularly.

Quiz

If your mind hasn't taken a vacation by this point in the hour, test your knowledge of this chapter with the following questions.

Questions

1. How did object-oriented programming get its name?

    (a) Programs are considered to be a group of objects working together.

    (b) People often object because it's hard to master.

    (c) Its parents named it.

2. Which of the following isn't a part of Java's security?

    (a) Web programs cannot run programs on the user's computer.

    (b) The identity of a program's author is verified.

    (c) Java windows are labeled as Java windows.

3. What is a program's capability to handle more than one task called?

    (a) Schizophrenia

    (b) Multiculturalism

    (c) Multithreading

Answers

1. a. It's also abbreviated as OOP.

2. b. ActiveX programs verify the author of the program, but this security method is not implemented with Java.

3. c. This also is called multitasking, but the term *multithreading* is used in conjunction with Java because an independently running part of a program is called a thread.

Activities

Before unpacking your luggage, you can explore the topics of this hour more fully with the following activities:

3

- Use the developer.com directory at `http://www.developer.com` to find out what card games have been developed using Java.
- Find the sample Java programs by searching Sun's official Java site and download one of them to your computer.

When solutions can be provided for the activities in this book, they'll be presented on the book's Web site at `http://www.prefect.com/java24`.

Hour 4

Understanding How Java Programs Work

An important distinction to make in Java programming is where your program is supposed to be running. Some programs are intended to work on your computer; you type in a command or click an icon to start them up. Other programs are intended to run as part of a World Wide Web page. You encountered several examples of this type of program during the previous hour's whirlwind vacation.

Java programs that run locally on your own computer are called *applications*. Programs that run on Web pages are called *applets*. During this hour, you'll learn why that distinction is important, and the following topics will be covered:

- How applications work
- Organizing an application
- Sending arguments to an application
- How applets work

- The required parts of an applet
- Sending parameters to an applet
- Using HTML tags to put an applet on a page

Creating an Application

Although Java has become well-known because it can be used in conjunction with World Wide Web pages, you also can use it to write any type of computer program. The BigDebt program you wrote during Hour 2, "Writing Your First Program," is an example of a Java application.

To try out another program, use your word processor to open up a new file and enter everything from Listing 4.1. Remember not to enter the line numbers and colons along the left side of the listing; these items are used to make parts of programs easier to describe in the book. When you're done, save the file as Root.java, making sure to save it in text-only or plain ASCII text format.

LISTING 4.1 THE FULL TEXT OF Root.java

```
1: class Root {
2:     public static void main(String[] arguments) {
3:         int number = 225;
4:         System.out.println("The square root of "
5:             + number
6:             + " is "
7:             + Math.sqrt(number) );
8:     }
9: }
```

Before you can test out this application, you need to compile it with the javac compiler tool. While in the same folder as the Root.java file, compile it by entering the following at a command line:

```
javac Root.java
```

If you have entered Listing 4.1 without any typos, including all punctuation and every word capitalized as shown, it should compile without any errors. The javac compiler responds to a successful compilation by not responding with any message at all.

You run Java applications in the same way you would run any program that's installed on your computer. Because they require the use of the java interpreter to run, the most common way you'll run a Java program is probably by typing a command like the following at a command-line prompt:

```
java DrumMachine
```

This command would cause the `java` interpreter to look for a Java program called `DrumMachine.class` in the current folder. If it found one, the interpreter would start running it. To run the `Root` application, type the following at a command line:

```
java Root
```

The output should resemble the following:

OUTPUT   `The square root of 225 is 15.0`

When you run a Java application, the interpreter looks for a `main()` block and starts handling Java statements at that point. If your program does not have a `main()` block, as most applets do not, the interpreter will respond with an error.

Sending Arguments to Applications

Because Java applications are usually run from a command line, you can send information to applications at the same time you run them. The following example uses the `java` interpreter to run an application called `DisplayTextFile.class`, and it sends two extra items of information to the application: `readme.txt` and `/p`:

```
java DisplayTextFile readme.txt /p
```

The extra information you can send to a program is called an *argument*. The first argument, if there is one, is provided one space after the name of the application. Each additional argument is also separated by a space.

If you want to include a space inside an argument, you must put quotation marks around the argument, as in the following:

```
java DisplayTextFile readme.txt /p "Page Title"
```

This example runs the `DisplayTextFile` program with three arguments: `readme.txt`, `/p`, and `Page Title`. The quotation marks prevent `Page` and `Title` from being treated as separate arguments.

You can send as many arguments as you want to a Java application. In order to do something with them, however, you have to write some statements in the application to handle them.

To see how arguments work in an application, create a new file in your word processor called `NewRoot.java`. Enter the text of Listing 4.2 into the file and save it when you're done. Compile the program with the `javac` compiler tool, correcting any errors that are caused by typos.

LISTING 4.2   THE FULL TEXT OF NewRoot.java

```
 1: class NewRoot {
 2:     public static void main(String[] arguments) {
 3:         int number = 0;
 4:         if (arguments.length > 0)
 5:             number = Integer.parseInt( arguments[0] );
 6:         System.out.println("The square root of "
 7:             + number
 8:             + " is "
 9:             + Math.sqrt(number) );
10:     }
11: }
```

This program is similar to the Root program except for lines 3–5. Don't worry about the specific statements used in these lines; they make use of some advanced features. What's important to note is what these lines are accomplishing: If an argument is sent to the NewRoot program when it is run, the argument is stored in the number variable.

To try it out, use the Java interpreter with a command such as the following:

```
java NewRoot 169
```

This command causes the output to report that the square root of 169 is 13.0. Try the program several times with different numbers.

Arguments are a useful way to customize the performance of a program. They are often used to configure a program so it runs a specific way. Java applications use arguments, but applets use a different way to receive information as they are run.

Applet Basics

Applets—programs that can run on World Wide Web pages—were the things that made Java a computer magazine cover subject upon its release. Applets put a spotlight on the ways that Java was different and remarkable. Before Java, World Wide Web pages were a combination of text, images, and forms that used gateway programs running on the computer that hosted the pages. These gateway programs required special access to the Web page server machine, so most Web users did not have the ability to use them. Writing them required even more expertise.

In contrast, programmers of all skill levels can write Java applets, and you'll write several during the span of these 24 hours. You can test them with any Web browser that handles Java programs, and put one on a Web page without requiring any special access from a Web provider. The Java programs you toured during the previous hour were all applets. Their structure differs from applications in several important ways, and they are designed specifically for presentation on the World Wide Web.

Because the applets you'll write in this book use Java 2, these applets must be run with a browser that supports this version of the language. During Hour 13, "Learning How Applets Work," you'll learn how to use the Java Plug-in with current browsers so that they can run all Java 2 applets. All applets also can be tested with the `appletviewer` tool that is included with the Java Development Kit.

As stated previously, applets do not have a `main()` block as applications do. Applets have several different sections that are handled depending on what is happening in the applet. These sections are detailed fully during Hour 13. Two of the sections are the `init()` block statement and the `paint()` block. `init()` is short for initialization, and it is used to set up anything that needs to be set up as an applet first runs. The `paint()` block is used to display anything that should be displayed.

To see an applet version of the `Root` application, create a new file in your word processor and call it `RootApplet.java`. Enter the code in Listing 4.3, and save it when you're done.

LISTING 4.3 THE FULL TEXT OF `RootApplet.java`

```
 1: import java.awt.*;
 2:
 3: public class RootApplet extends com.sun.java.swing.JApplet {
 4:     int number;
 5:
 6:     public void init() {
 7:         number = 225;
 8:     }
 9:
10:     public void paint(Graphics screen) {
11:         super.paint (screen);
12:         Graphics2D screen2D = (Graphics2D) screen;
13:         screen2D.drawString("The square root of " +
14:             number +
15:             " is " +
16:             Math.sqrt(number), 5, 50);
17:     }
18: }
```

4

Compile this file with the javac compiler tool by typing the following at a command line:

```
javac RootApplet.java
```

This program contains a lot of the same statements as the Java application that did the same thing. The main difference is in how it is organized—the main() block has been replaced with an init() block and a paint() block.

 The sample programs in this hour are provided primarily to introduce you to the way Java programs are structured. Some aspects of these programs will be introduced fully later, so don't feel like you're falling behind. The main purpose of this hour is to get the programs to compile and see how they function when you run them.

Unlike applications, compiled Java applets cannot be tested using the java interpreter tool. You have to put them on a Web page and view that page in one of two ways:

- Use a Web browser that can handle Java 2 applets by using Sun's Java Plug-in, which requires special configuration of the Web page. You'll learn how to do this during Hour 13.
- Use the appletviewer tool that comes with the Java Development Kit.

To create a Web page that can display the RootApplet program, return to your word processor and create a new file. Enter Listing 4.4 in that file and save it as RootApplet.html.

LISTING 4.4   THE FULL TEXT OF RootApplet.html

```
1: <applet code="RootApplet.class" height=100 width=300>
2: </applet>
```

This Web page contains the bare minimum needed to display a Java applet on a Web page. The <APPLET> tag is used to specify that a Java program is being put on the page, the code attribute provides the name of the applet, and the height and width attributes describe the size of the applet's display area. These items will be described in detail during Hour 13.

For now, use the appletviewer tool included with Java Development Kit to take a look at this page. Type the following at the command line:

```
appletviewer RootApplet.html
```

Figure 4.1 shows what the applet looks like using `appletviewer`.

If you're using a beta version of the JDK and can't produce the same output as Figure 4.1, type the following at a command line:

```
appletviewer -J-Djava2d.font.usePlatformfont=true RootApplet.html
```

FIGURE 4.1

The `RootApplet` *applet displayed with the* `appletviewer` *tool.*

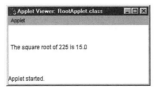

The square root of 225 is 15.0

Sending Parameters to Applets

Java applets are never run from the command line, so you can't specify arguments the way you can with applications. Applets use a different way to receive information at the time the program is run. This information is called *parameters*, and you can send parameters through the HTML page that runs the applet. You have to use a special HTML tag for parameters called <PARAM>.

Load the file `RootApplet.java` back into your word processor. The `init()` block of the program should resemble the following:

```
public void init() {
    number = 225;
}
```

Replace these three lines with the following statements:

```
public void init() {
    String parameter = getParameter("NUMBER");
        if (parameter != null)
            number = Integer.parseInt(parameter);
}
```

When you're done, the code of `RootApplet.java` should be the same as Listing 4.5.

LISTING 4.5 THE MODIFIED TEXT OF `RootApplet.java`

```
1: import java.awt.*;
2:
3: public class RootApplet extends com.sun.java.swing.JApplet {
4:     int number;
5:
```

continues

LISTING 4.5 CONTINUED

```
 6:     public void init() {
 7:         String parameter = getParameter("NUMBER");
 8:         if (parameter != null)
 9:             number = Integer.parseInt(parameter);
10:     }
11:
12:     public void paint(Graphics screen) {
13:         super.paint(screen);
14:         Graphics2D screen2D = (Graphics2D) screen;
15:         screen2D.drawString("The square root of " +
16:             number +
17:             " is " +
18:             Math.sqrt(number), 5, 50);
19:     }
20: }
```

Save the file and then compile it by typing the following at the command line:

```
javac RootApplet.java
```

Before you can try out this change, you need to modify the Web page `RootApplet.html` so that it sends a parameter. Load the page into your word processor and add a line between the `<APPLET>` line and the `</APPLET>` line, so that the code resembles the following:

```
<applet code="RootApplet.class" height=100 width=300>
<param name="NUMBER" value=196>
</applet>
```

Save the file when you're done, and load the page using `appletviewer` again. The output should resemble Figure 4.2. Change the value of the `value` attribute in the `RootApplet.html` file and run the program again. Try this several times, and you'll see that your program is now flexible enough to handle any number.

FIGURE 4.2

The modified `RootApplet` *program displayed with* `appletviewer`.

You can use as many parameters as needed to customize the operation of an applet, as long as each has a different `name` attribute specified along with the `<PARAM>` tag.

Workshop: Viewing the Code Used to Run Applets

As a brief workshop to better familiarize yourself with the <APPLET> tag and how it can be used to alter the performance of an applet, visit this book's World Wide Web site at http://www.prefect.com/java24.

Visit this site by using either the current version of Netscape Navigator or Microsoft Internet Explorer. Go to the section of the site labeled "Hour 4 Showcase," and you'll be given a guided tour through several working examples of applets. These applets were written with Java version 1.02, so they can be run with any browser that supports Java.

On each of the pages in the Hour 4 Showcase, you can use a pull-down menu command to view the HTML tags that were used to create the page. With Navigator, the command is View, Page Source, and with Internet Explorer, the command is View, Source. Compare the parameters that are used with each applet to the way the applet runs.

Appendix B, "This Book's Web Site," describes other things you can find on the book's site. The Web site is intended as a complement to the material covered in this book and a way to find out about corrections, revisions, or other information that makes this 24 hours more productive.

4

Summary

During this hour, you got a chance to create both a Java application and an applet. These two types of programs have several important differences in the way they function and the way they are created.

The next several hours will continue to focus on applications as you become more experienced as a Java programmer. Applications are quicker to test because they don't require you to create a Web page to view them; they can be easier to create as well. The last several hours of the book focus on applets, however, because that's the area where beginning programmers are most likely to want to put their skills to work.

Q&A

Q Can a single Java program be both an applet and an application?

A It is possible to make a program serve as both applet and application, but it's often an unwieldy solution unless the program is simple. An applet could be set up to run as an application also by including a main() block in the applet, but you would not be able to use the init() block or paint() block in the automatic fashion in which they are used in an applet. Most programs are written as either an application or as an applet, rather than attempting to do both.

Q **Do all arguments sent to a Java application have to be strings?**

A Java makes all arguments into strings for storage when an application runs. When you want to use one of these arguments as an integer or some other non-string type, you have to convert the value. You'll learn how to do this during the coming hours.

Q **I get errors when I try to load `RootApplet.html` into either Netscape Navigator or Microsoft Internet Explorer. What's the problem?**

A In most cases, the problem is that the browser isn't equipped to run Java 2 applets. The two browsers have built-in support for Java 1.02, the first widely available version of the language. Netscape Navigator also offers partial support for Java 1.1. Sun is introducing the Java Plug-in that will make it possible for both leading browsers to support 2 applets, but it only will work if the Web page containing the applet is equipped to work with the plug-in. When you're in doubt about why an applet won't work in a browser, try loading it with the `appletviewer` tool included with the Java Development Kit. If it works in `appletviewer`, the problem is with the browser rather than your Java applet.

Q **Why don't Java applets require the same kind of special access as gateway programs?**

A Java applets don't have the same access requirements because they don't pose the same risk to a Web site provider. Gateway programs don't have any kind of security in place to prevent the program from attempting to do harmful things to the machine presenting the Web page. Java applets, on the other hand, have strict restrictions to prevent them from being used to write harmful programs. Also, Java programs do not run on the Web site's machine—they run on the system of the person viewing the page. This means that the Web site's machine will not slow down due to numerous people running a Java applet on a page.

Quiz

Test your knowledge of the material covered in this chapter by answering the following questions.

Questions

1. Which type of Java program can be run by the `java` interpreter tool?

    (a) Applets

    (b) Applications

    (c) None

2. What special HTML tag is used to put a Java program onto a Web page?

  (a) <APPLET>

  (b) <PROGRAM>

  (c) <RUN>

3. If you get into a fight with someone over the way to send information to a Java application, what are you doing?

  (a) Struggling over strings

  (b) Arguing about arguments

  (c) Feudin' for functionality

Answers

1. b. Applications are run with the interpreter tool, and Web pages containing applets can be run with the `appletviewer` tool as well as Java-capable World Wide Web browsers.

2. a. The <APPLET> tag is used along with the <PARAM> tag to send parameters to the applet. You'll learn about a second tag that can be used to present applets during Hour 13, "Learning How Applets Work."

3. b. Can't we all get along?

Activities

If you'd like to apply your acumen of applets and applications, the following activities are suggested:

- Check out developer.com's Java directory at `http://www.developer.com` and use the search term `Marquee` to see links and descriptions to all of the applets that have been written to display text in a marquee sign format. Each of these applets use parameters to modify the text that is displayed.

- Write a Java applet that can handle a parameter named X and a parameter named Y. Display the two numbers in a `drawString()` statement like the one in the `RootApplet` program.

To see a Java program that implements the second activity, visit the book's Web site at `http://www.prefect.com/java24`.

PART II

Learning the Basics of Programming

Hour

Hour 5

Storing and Changing Information in a Program

In Hour 2, "Writing Your First Program," you used a *variable*, a special storage place that is used to hold information. The information stored in variables can be changed as your program runs, which is why they're called variables. Your first program stored an integer number in a variable called debt. Integers are only one of the types of information that can be stored in variables. Variables also can hold characters, lines of text, floating-point numbers, and other things.

Variables are the main way that a computer remembers something as it runs a program. The BigDebt program used the debt variable to tell the computer that the National Debt increases by $446 million per day. The computer needed to remember that fact a little later so a minute's worth of debt increase could be calculated. During this hour, you'll learn more about using variables in your Java programs.

The following topics will be covered during this hour:

- Creating variables
- The different types of variables
- Storing values into variables
- Using variables in mathematical expressions
- Putting one variable's value into another variable
- Increasing and decreasing a variable's value

Statements and Expressions

Computer programs are a set of instructions that tell the computer what to do. Each of these instructions is called a statement. The following example from a Java program is a statement:

```
int HighScore = 400000;
```

You can use brackets to group a set of statements together in a Java program. These groupings are called *block statements*. Consider the following portion of a program:

```
1: public static void main(String[] arguments) {
2:     int a = 3;
3:     int b = 4;
4:     int c = 8 * 5;
5: }
```

Lines 2–4 of this example are a block statement. The opening bracket on Line 1 denotes the beginning of the block, and the closing bracket on Line 5 denotes the end of the block.

Some statements are called *expressions* because they involve a mathematical expression. Line 4 in the preceding example is an expression because it sets the value of the c variable equal to 8 multiplied by 5. You'll be working with several different types of expressions throughout the coming sections.

Assigning Variable Types

In a Java program, variables are created with a statement that must include two things:

- The name of the variable
- The type of information the variable will store

To see the different types of variables and how they are created, load the word processor you're using to write programs and set it up to start a new file. You will be creating a program called Variable.

Give your new file the name Variable.java and start writing the program by entering the following lines:

```
class Variable {
    public static void main(String[] arguments) {
        // Coming soon: variables
    }
}
```

Go ahead and save these lines before making any changes.

Integers and Floating-Point Numbers

So far, the Variable program has a main() block with only one statement in it—the comment line Coming soon: variables. Delete the comment line and enter the following statement in its place:

```
int tops;
```

This statement creates a variable named tops. This statement does not specify a value for tops, so the variable is an empty storage space for the moment. The int text at the beginning of the statement designates tops as a variable that will be used to store integer numbers. You can use the int type to store most of the nondecimal numbers you will need in your computer programs. It can hold any integer from –2.14 billion to 2.14 billion.

Create a blank line after the int tops; statement and add the following statement:

```
float gradePointAverage;
```

This statement creates a variable with the name gradePointAverage. The float text stands for floating-point numbers. Floating-point variables are used to store numbers that might contain a decimal point.

A floating-point variable could be used to store a grade point average such as 2.25, to pick a number that's dear to my heart. It also could be used to store a number such as 0, which is the percentage chance of getting into a good graduate school with that grade point average, despite my really good cover letter and a compelling written recommendation from my parole officer.

Characters and Strings

Because all the variables you have dealt with so far are numeric, you might have the mistaken impression that all variables are used with numbers. You can also use variables to store text. Two types of text can be stored as variables: characters and strings. A *character* is a single letter, number, punctuation mark, or other symbol. Most of the things you can use as characters are shown on your computer's keyboard. A *string* is a group of characters.

Your next step in creating the `Variable` program is to create a `char` variable and a `string` variable. Add these two statements after the line `float gradePointAverage;`:

```
char key = 'C';
String productName = "Orbitz";
```

When you are using character values in your program, such as in the preceding example, you must put single quotation marks on both sides of the character value being assigned to a variable. You must surround string values with double quotation marks. These quotation marks are needed to prevent the character or string from being confused with a variable name or other part of a statement. Take a look at the following statement:

```
String productName = Orbitz;
```

This statement might look like a statement that tells the computer to create a string variable called `productName` and give it the text value of `Orbitz`. However, because there are no quotation marks around the word `Orbitz`, the computer is being told to set the `productName` value to the same value as a variable named `Orbitz`.

After adding the `char` and `String` statements, your program should resemble Listing 5.1. Make any changes that are needed and be sure to save the file. This program does not produce anything to display, but you should compile it with the `javac` compiler tool to make sure it was created correctly.

LISTING 5.1 THE `Variable` PROGRAM

```
1: class Variable {
2:     public static void main(String[] arguments) {
3:         int tops;
4:         float gradePointAverage;
5:         char key = 'C';
6:         String productName = "Orbitz";
7:     }
8: }
```

The last two variables in the Variable program use the = sign to assign a starting value when the variables are created. You can use this option for any variables you create in a Java program. For more information, see the section called "Storing Information in Variables."

> Although the other variable types are all lowercase letters (int, float, char), the capital letter is required in the word String when creating string variables. A string in a Java program is somewhat different than the other types of information you will use in variables. You'll learn about this distinction in Hour 6, "Using Strings to Communicate."

Other Numeric Variable Types

The variables you have been introduced to so far will be the main ones you use during this book and probably for most of your Java programming. There are a few other types of variables you can use in special circumstances.

You can use three other variable types with integers. The first, byte, can be used for integer numbers that range from –128 to 127. The following statement creates a variable called escapeKey with an initial value of 27:

```
byte escapeKey = 27;
```

The second, short, can be used for integers that are smaller in size than the int type. A short integer can range from –32,768 to 32,767, as in the following example:

```
short roomNumber = 222;
```

The last of the special numeric variable types, long, is typically used for integers that are too big for the int type to hold. A long integer can be of almost any size; if the number has five commas or less when you write it down, it can fit into a long. Some six-comma numbers can fit as well.

Except for times when your integer number is bigger than 2.14 billion or smaller than –2.14 billion, you won't need to use any of these special variable types very often. If they're muddling your understanding of variable types, concentrate on int and float. Those types are the ones you'll be using most often.

The boolean Variable Type

Java has a special type of variable that can only be used to store the value true or the value false. This type of variable is called a boolean. At first glance, a boolean variable might not seem particularly useful unless you plan to write a lot of computerized true-or-false quizzes. However, `boolean` variables will be used in a variety of situations in your programs. The following are some examples of questions that `boolean` variables can be used to answer:

- Has the user pressed a key?
- Is the game over?
- Is this the first time the user has done something?
- Is the bank account overdrawn?
- Have all ten images been displayed onscreen?
- Can the rabbit eat Trix?

The following statement is used to create a `boolean` variable called `gameOver`:

```
boolean gameOver = false;
```

This variable has the starting value of `false`, and a statement such as this one could be used in a game program to indicate that the game isn't over yet. Later on, when something happens to end the game (such as the destruction of all of the player's acrobatic Italian laborers), the `gameOver` variable can be set to `true`. Although the two possible `boolean` values—`true` and `false`—look like strings in a program, you should not surround them with quotation marks. Hour 7, "Using Conditional Tests to Make Decisions," describes `boolean` variables more fully.

Boolean numbers are named for George Boole, who lived from 1815 to 1864. Boole, a Irish mathematician who was mostly self-taught until late adulthood, invented Boolean algebra, a fundamental part of computer programming, digital electronics, and logic. One imagines that he did pretty well on true-false tests as a schoolchild.

Naming Your Variables

Variable names in Java can begin with a letter, underscore character (_),or a dollar sign ($). The rest of the name can be any letters or numbers, but you cannot use blank spaces. You can give your variables any names you like under those rules, but you should be consistent in how you name variables. This section outlines the generally recommended naming method for variables.

Java is case-sensitive when it comes to variable names, so you must always capitalize variable names in the same way throughout a program. For example, if the gameOver variable is used as GameOver somewhere in the program, the GameOver statement will cause an error when you compile the program.

First, the name you give a variable should describe its purpose in some way. The first letter should be lowercase, and if the variable name has more than one word, make the first letter of each subsequent word a capital letter. For instance, if you wanted to create an integer variable to store the all-time high score in a game program, you could use the following statement:

```
int allTimeHighScore;
```

You can't use punctuation marks or spaces in a variable name, so neither of the following would work:

```
int all-TimeHigh Score;
int all Time High Score;
```

If you tried to use these names in a program, the Java compiler would respond with an error.

Storing Information in Variables

You can put a value into a variable at the same time that you create the variable in a Java program. You also can put a value in the variable at any time later in the program.

To set up a starting value for a variable upon its creation, use the equal sign (=). The following is an example of creating a floating-point variable called pi with the starting value of 3.14:

```
float pi = 3.14;
```

All variables that store numbers can be set up in a similar fashion. If you're setting up a character or a string variable, quotation marks must be placed around the value as shown previously.

You also can set one variable equal to the value of another variable if they both are of the same type. Consider the following example:

```
int mileage = 300;
int totalMileage = mileage;
```

First, an integer variable called `mileage` is created with a starting value of 300. In the second line, an integer variable called `totalMileage` is created with the same value as `mileage`. Both variables will have the starting value of 300. In future hours, you will learn ways to convert one variable's value to the type of another variable.

> If you do not give a variable a starting value, you must give it a value before you try to use it. If you don't, when you attempt to compile your program, the `javac` compiler will respond with an error message such as the following:
>
> ```
> WarGame.java:7: Variable warships may not have been
> →initialized.
>                     warships = warships + 10;
>                     ^
>
> 1 error
> ```

Workshop: Using Expressions

As you worked on a particularly unpleasant math problem in school, did you ever complain to a higher power, protesting that you would never use this knowledge in your life? Sorry to break this to you, but all your teachers were right: Those math skills are going to be used in your computer programming.

That's the bad news. The good news is that the computer will do any of the math you ask it to do. As mentioned earlier in this hour, any instructions you give a computer program involving math are called expressions. Expressions will be used frequently in your computer programs. You can use them for tasks such as the following:

- Changing the value of a variable
- Counting the number of times something has happened in a program
- Using a mathematical formula in a program

As you write computer programs, you will find yourself drawing on your old math lessons as you use expressions. Expressions can use addition, subtraction, multiplication, division, and modulus division.

To see expressions in action, return to your word processor and close the `Variable.java` file if it is still open. Create a new file and save it as `Elvis.java`. The `Elvis` program creates a fictional person whose weight loss and gain can be tracked with mathematical expressions. Instead of adding statements to the program piece-by-piece, enter the full text of Listing 5.2 into the word processor. Each part of the program will be discussed in turn.

LISTING 5.2 THE Elvis PROGRAM

```
 1: class Elvis {
 2:     public static void main(String[] arguments) {
 3:         int weight = 250;
 4:         System.out.println("Elvis weighs " + weight);
 5:         System.out.println("Elvis visits all-you-can-eat rib joint.");
 6:         System.out.println("Elvis throws Thanksgiving luau.");
 7:         weight = weight + 10;
 8:         System.out.println("Elvis now weighs " + weight);
 9:         System.out.println("Elvis discovers aerobics.");
10:         weight = weight - 15;
11:         System.out.println("Elvis now weighs " + weight);
12:         System.out.println("Elvis falls into washing machine during "
13:             + "shrink cycle.");
14:         weight = weight / 3;
15:         System.out.println("Elvis now weighs " + weight);
16:         System.out.println("Oops! Elvis clones himself 12 times.");
17:         weight = weight + (weight * 12);
18:         System.out.println("The 13 Elvii now weigh " + weight);
19:     }
20: }
```

When you're done, save the file and use the `javac` tool to compile the program. In the same folder as the `Elvis.java` file, type the following at a command line to compile the Elvis program:

```
javac Elvis.java
```

If it compiles without any errors, you will not see any output; `javac` only responds if something goes wrong. If you do see error messages, check the line number that is listed in the error message to look for typos. Correct any typos you find and compile the program.

Next, run the program by typing the following at a command line:

```
java Elvis
```

Listing 5.3 shows the output for this program.

LISTING 5.3 THE OUTPUT OF THE Elvis PROGRAM

```
Elvis weighs 250
Elvis visits all-you-can-eat rib joint.
Elvis throws Thanksgiving luau.
Elvis now weighs 260
Elvis discovers aerobics.
Elvis now weighs 245
```

continues

LISTING 5.3   CONTINUED

```
Elvis falls into washing machine during shrink cycle.
Elvis now weighs 81
Oops! Elvis clones himself 12 times.
The 13 Elvii now weigh 1053
```

As in the other programs you have created, the `Elvis` program uses a `main()` block statement for all of its work. This statement can be broken into the following five sections:

1. Lines 3–4: The initial weight of Elvis is set to 250.
2. Lines 5–8: Elvis gains weight.
3. Lines 9–11: Elvis loses weight.
4. Lines 12–15: Elvis reduces in size dramatically.
5. Lines 16–18: Elvis multiplies.

Line 3 creates the `weight` variable and designates it as an integer variable with `int`. The variable is given the initial value `250`, and it is used throughout the program to monitor Elvis' weight.

The next line is similar to several other statements in the program:

```
System.out.println("Elvis weighs " + weight);
```

The `System.out.println()` command displays a string that is contained within the parenthesis marks. In the preceding line, the text `Elvis weighs` is displayed, followed by the value of the `weight` variable. There are numerous `System.out.println()` statements in the program. If you're still unclear about how these statements work, look at each of them in Listing 5.2 and compare them to the corresponding lines in Listing 5.3.

All About Operators

Four different mathematical expressions are used in the `Elvis` program to add weight to Elvis, subtract weight from Elvis, divide it, and finish it off with some multiplication. Each of these expressions uses symbols (+, -, *, /, and %) called *operators*. You will be using these operators to crunch numbers throughout your Java programs.

An additional expression in Java uses the + sign, as in Line 7 of your program:

```
weight = weight + 10;
```

This line sets the `weight` variable equal to its current value plus 10. Because the `weight` was set to `250` when it was created, Line 7 changes `weight` to `260`.

A subtraction expression uses the - sign, as in Line 10:

```
weight = weight - 15;
```

This expression sets the `weight` variable equal to its current value minus 15. The `weight` variable is now equal to 245.

A division expression uses the / sign, as in Line 14:

```
weight = weight / 3;
```

The `weight` variable is set to its current value divided by 3 and rounded down because `weight` is an integer. The `weight` variable is now equal to 81.

There's another expression you can use to find the remainder of a division. When the value of the `weight` variable was divided by 3 in Line 14, a remainder of 2 was discarded in order for `weight` to remain as an integer value. To find a remainder from an expression, use the % operator. You could use the following statement to find the remainder of 245 divided by 3:

```
remainder = 245 % 3;
```

A multiplication expression uses the * sign. Line 17 uses a multiplication expression as part of a more complicated statement:

```
weight = weight + (weight * 12);
```

The `weight * 12` part of the expression multiplies `weight` by 12. The full statement takes the current value of `weight` and adds it to `weight` multiplied by 12. This example shows how more than one expression can be combined in a statement. The result is that `weight` becomes 1,053—in other words, 81 + (81 * 12).

Incrementing and Decrementing a Variable

One thing you will often need to do is to change the value of a variable by 1. Because this task is so common, there are special, simplified ways to accomplish it in your Java programs. You can increase the value by 1, which is called *incrementing* the variable, or decrease the value by 1, which is *decrementing* the variable. You use special operators for each of these tasks.

To increment the value of a variable by 1, you can use the ++ operator, as in the following statement:

```
x++;
```

This statement adds 1 to the value stored in the x variable.

To decrement the value of a variable by 1, use the - - operator:

```
y--;
```

This statement reduces y by 1.

You also can put the increment and decrement operators in front of the variable name, as in the following statements:

```
++x;
--y;
```

Putting the operator in front of the variable name is called *prefixing*, and putting it after the name is called *postfixing*. You doubtlessly have many cherished memories of grade school language classes when you learned about prefixes such as "pre-", "extra-", and "de-". A prefixed operator is like a prefix in a word—both come first. Postfixed operators lag behind. (If your memories of those classes are less-than-cherished, you must not have sat behind Mary Beth Farkas.)

Although it might seem redundant for Java to include both prefixed and postfixed operators, the difference becomes important when you use the increment and decrement operators inside an expression.

Consider the following statements:

```
int x = 3;
int answer = x++ * 10;
```

What does the answer variable equal after these statements are handled? You might expect it to equal 40—3 is incremented by 1, which equals 4, and then 4 is multiplied by 10.

However, answer is set to 30. The reason is that the postfixed operator was used instead of the prefixed operator.

When a postfixed operator is used on a variable inside an expression, the variable's value won't change until the expression has been completely evaluated.

The opposite is true of prefixed operators. If one is used on a variable inside an expression, the variable's value changes before the expression is evaluated.

Now consider the following statements:

```
int x = 3;
int answer = ++x * 10;
```

This does result in the answer variable being equal to 40. The prefixed operator causes the value of the x variable to be changed before the expression is evaluated.

At this point, you might be ready to say, "Prefixing, postfixing, incrementing, decrementing—let's call the whole thing off!" It's easy to get a little exasperated with the ++ and -- operators, because they're not as straightforward as many of the concepts you'll encounter in this book.

There's some good news in this regard: You don't need to use the increment and decrement operators in your own programs. You can achieve the same results by using the + and - operators. Increment and decrement are useful shortcuts, but taking the longer route in an expression is fine, too.

> During Hour 1, "Becoming a Programmer," the name of the C++ programming language was described as a joke you'd understand later. Now that you've been introduced to the increment operator ++, you have all the information you need to figure out why C++ has two plus signs instead of just one. If you're still having trouble, C++ adds new features and functionality to the C programming language in the same way that the ++ operator adds 1 to a variable. Just think: After you work through all 24 hours of this book, you'll be able to tell jokes that are incomprehensible to more than 99 percent of the world's population.

Operator Precedence

When you are using an expression with more than one operator, you need to know what order the computer will use as it works out the expression. Consider the following statement:

```
x = y * 3 + 5;
```

Unless you know what order the computer will use when working out the math in this expression, you cannot be sure what the x variable will be set to. If y is equal to 10 and multiplication occurs before addition, x will equal 35. If y equals 10 and addition occurs before multiplication, x will equal 80.

The following order is used when working out an expression:

- Incrementing and decrementing take place first.
- Multiplication, division, and modulus division occur next.
- Addition and subtraction follow.
- Comparisons take place next.
- The equal sign = is used to set a variable's value.

Comparisons will be discussed during Hour 7. The rest has been described during this hour, so you should be able to figure out the result of the following statements:

```
int x = 5;
int number = x++ * 6 + 4 * 10 / 2;
```

These statements set the `number` variable equal to 50.

How does the computer come up with this total? First, the increment operator is handled, and x++ sets the value of the x variable to 6. However, make note of the fact that the ++ operator is postfixed after x in the expression. This means that the expression is evaluated with the original value of x.

Because the original value of x is used before the variable is incremented, the expression becomes the following:

```
int number = 5 * 6 + 4 * 10 / 2;
```

Now, multiplication and division are handled from left to right. First, 5 is multiplied by 6, 4 is multiplied by 10, and that result is divided by 2 (`4 * 10 / 2`). The expression becomes the following:

```
int number = 30 + 20;
```

This expression results in the `number` variable being set to 50.

If you want an expression to be evaluated in a different order, you can use parentheses to group parts of an expression that should be handled first. For example, the expression `x = 5 * 3 + 2;` would normally cause x to equal 17 because multiplication is handled before addition. However, look at a modified form of that expression:

```
x = 5 * (3 + 2);
```

In this case, the expression within the parentheses is handled first, so the result equals 25. You can use parentheses as often as needed in a statement.

Summary

Now that you have been introduced to variables and expressions, you can give a wide range of instructions to your computer in a program. Programs that you write can accomplish many of the same tasks as a calculator by handling sophisticated mathematical equations with ease. Manipulating numbers is only one element of variable use. You also can handle characters, strings of characters, and special `true` or `false` values called `boolean` variables. The next hour will expand your knowledge of `String` variables and how they are used.

Q&A

Q Is a line in a Java program the same thing as a statement?

A No. Although the programs you will create in this book put one statement on each line, this is done to make the programs easier to understand; it's not required. The Java compiler does not consider lines, spacing, or other formatting issues when compiling a program. The compiler just wants to see semicolons at the end of each statement. You can put more than one statement on a line, although this is not generally recommended.

Q Is there a reason to set up a variable without giving it a value right away?

A For many of the simple programs you will be creating in the first several hours, no. However, there are many circumstances in which it makes more sense to give a variable a value at some point later in the program. One example would be a calculator program. The variable that stores the result of a calculation will not be needed until a user tries out the program's calculator buttons. You would not need to set up an initial value when a `result` variable is created.

Q What's the specific range for the `long` variable type?

A In Java, a `long` integer variable can be anything from –9,223,372,036,854,775,808 to 9,223,372,036,854,775,807. This range ought to give your mathematical expressions plenty of breathing room when you can't use `int`, which has a range of –2,147,483,648 to 2,147,483,647.

Q Why should the first letter of a variable name be lowercase, as in `gameOver`?

A It makes the variable easier to spot among all of the other elements of a Java program. Also, by following a consistent style in the naming of variables, you eliminate errors that can occur when you use a variable in several different places in a program. The style of naming used in this book has become popular since Java's release.

Q Can two variables have the same letters but different capitalization, as in `highScore` and `HighScore`?

A Each of the differently capitalized names would be treated as its own variable, so it's possible to use the same name twice in this way. However, it seems likely to cause a lot of confusion when you or someone else is attempting to figure out how the program works. It also increases the likelihood of using the wrong variable name somewhere in your program, which is an error that will not be caught during compilation. Errors like that make it into the finished product and are called *logic errors*. They must be caught by an attentive programmer during testing.

Quiz

Test your knowledge of variables, expressions, and the rest of the information in this hour by answering the following questions.

Questions

1. What do you call a group of statements that are contained with an opening bracket and a closing bracket?

    (a) A block statement

    (b) Groupware

    (c) Bracketed statements

2. A `boolean` variable is used to store `true-or-false` values.

    (a) True

    (b) False

    (c) No, thanks. I already ate.

3. What characters cannot be used to start a variable name?

    (a) A dollar sign

    (b) Two forward slash marks (//)

    (c) A letter

Answers

1. a. The grouped statements are called a *block statement* or a *block*.

2. a. `true` and `false` are the only answers a `boolean` variable can store.

3. b. Variables can start with a letter, dollar sign ($), or an underscore character (_). If you started a variable name with two slash marks, the rest of the line would be ignored because the slash marks are used to start a comment line.

Activities

You can review the topics of this hour more fully with the following activities:

- Expand the `Elvis` program to track the weight if it were incremented upward by one pound for three straight days.

- Create a short Java program that uses an x integer and a y integer and displays the result of x squared plus y squared.

To see Java programs that implement these activities, visit the book's Web site at `http://www.prefect.com/java24`.

Hour 6

Using Strings to Communicate

In the film *The Piano*, Holly Hunter portrays Ada, a young Scottish woman who marries badly. A mute since the age of 6, Ada can only express herself fully by playing her prized possession, a piano. Like Ada, your computer programs are capable of quietly doing their work and never stopping for a chat—or piano recital—with humans. However, if *The Piano* teaches us anything, it is that communication ranks up there with food, water, and shelter as essential needs. (It also teaches us that Harvey Keitel has a lot of body confidence, but that's a matter for another book.)

Java programs don't have access to a piano. They use strings as the primary means to communicate with users. *Strings* are collections of text—letters, numbers, punctuation, and other characters. During this hour, you will learn all about working with strings in your Java programs. The following topics will be covered:

- Using strings to store text
- Displaying strings in a program

- Including special characters in a string
- Pasting two strings together
- Including variables in a string
- Some uses for strings
- Comparing two strings
- Determining the length of a string
- Changing a string to upper- or lowercase

Storing Text in Strings

Strings are a common feature in computer programming because they provide a way to store text and present it to users. The most basic element of a string is a character. A *character* is a single letter, number, punctuation mark, or other symbol.

In Java programs, a character is one of the types of information that can be stored in a variable. Character variables are created with the char type in a statement such as the following:

```
char keyPressed;
```

This statement creates a variable named keyPressed that can store a character. When you create character variables, you can set them up with an initial value, as in the following:

```
char quitKey = '@';
```

Note that the value of the character must be surrounded by single quotation marks. If it isn't, the javac compiler tool will respond with an error when the program is compiled.

A string is a collection of characters. You can set up a variable to hold a string value by using the String text and the name of the variable, as in the following statement:

```
String fullName = "Ada McGrath Stewart";
```

This statement creates a string variable called fullName and stores the text Ada McGrath Stewart in it, which is the full name of Hunter's pianist. A string is denoted with double quotation marks around the text in a Java statement. These quotation marks will not be included in the string itself.

Unlike the other types of variables you have used—int, float, char, boolean, and so on—the name of the String type is capitalized. The reason for this is that strings are somewhat different than the other variable types in Java. Strings are a special resource called an object, and the types of all objects are capitalized. You'll be learning about objects during Hour 10, "Creating Your First Object." The important thing to note during this hour is that strings are different than the other variable types, and because of this difference, String is capitalized when strings are used in a statement.

Displaying Strings in Programs

The most basic way to display a string in a Java program is with the System.out. println() statement. This statement takes any strings and other variables inside the parentheses and displays them. The following statement displays a line of text to the system output device, which is the computer's monitor:

```
System.out.println("Silence affects everyone in the end.");
```

The preceding statement would cause the following text to be displayed:

```
Silence affects everyone in the end.
```

Displaying a line of text on the screen is often called printing, which is what println() stands for—"print this line." You can use the System.out.println() statement to display text within double quotation marks and also to display variables, as you will see. Put all material you want to be displayed within the parentheses.

Using Special Characters in Strings

When a string is being created or displayed, its text must be enclosed within double quotation marks to indicate the beginning and end of the string. These quotation marks are not displayed, which brings up a good question: What if you want to display double quotation marks?

In order to display them, Java has created a special code that can be put into a string: \". Whenever this code is encountered in a string, it is replaced with a double quotation mark. For example, examine the following:

```
System.out.println("Jane Campion directed \"The Piano\" in 1993.");
```

This code is displayed as the following:

```
Jane Campion directed "The Piano" in 1993.
```

You can insert several special characters into a string in this manner. The following list shows these special characters; note that each is preceded by a backslash (\).

Special characters	Display
\'	Single quotation mark
\"	Double quotation mark
\\	Backslash
\t	Tab
\b	Backspace
\r	Carriage return
\f	Formfeed
\n	Newline

The newline character causes the text following the newline character to be displayed at the beginning of the next line. Look at this example:

```
System.out.println("Music by\nMichael Nyman");
```

This statement would be displayed as the following:

```
Music by
Michael Nyman
```

Pasting Strings Together

When you use the System.out.println() statement and handle strings in other ways, you will sometimes want to paste two strings together. You do this by using the same operator that is used to add numbers: +.

The + operator has a different meaning in relation to strings. Instead of trying to do some math, it pastes two strings together. This action can cause strings to be displayed together, or it can make one big string out of two smaller ones. *Concatenation* is a word used to describe this action, because it means to link two things together. You'll probably see this term in other books as you build your programming skills, so it's worth knowing. However, pasting is the term used here to describe what happens when one string and another string decide to get together. Pasting sounds like fun. Concatenating sounds like something that should never be done in the presence of an open flame.

The following statement uses the + operator to display a long string:

```
System.out.println("\"\'The Piano\' is as peculiar and haunting as any" +
    " film I've seen.\"\n\t-- Roger Ebert, \'Chicago Sun-Times\'");
```

Instead of putting this entire string on a single line, which would make it harder to understand when you look at the program later, the + operator is used to break up the text over two lines of the program's Java text file. When this statement is displayed, it will appear as the following:

```
"'The Piano' is as peculiar and haunting as any film I've seen."
    -- Roger Ebert, 'Chicago Sun-Times'
```

Several special characters are used in the string: \", \', \n, and \t. To better familiarize yourself with these characters, compare the output with the System.out.println() statement that produced it.

Using Other Variables with Strings

Although you can use the + operator to paste two strings together, as demonstrated in the preceding section, you will use it more often to link strings and variables. Take a look at the following:

```
int length = 121;
char rating = 'R';
System.out.println("Running time: " + length + " minutes");
System.out.println("Rated " + rating);
```

This code will be displayed as the following:

```
Running time: 121 minutes
Rated R
```

This example displays a unique facet about how the + operator works with strings. It can cause variables that are not strings to be treated just like strings when they are displayed. The variable length is an integer set to the value 121. It is displayed between the strings Running time: and minutes. The System.out.println() statement is being asked to display a string plus an integer plus another string. This statement works because at least one part of the group is a string. The Java language offers this functionality to make displaying information easier.

One thing you might want to do with a string is paste something to it several times, as in the following example:

```
String searchKeywords = "";
searchKeywords = searchKeywords + "drama ";
searchKeywords = searchKeywords + "romance ";
searchKeywords = searchKeywords + "New Zealand";
```

This code would result in the searchKeywords variable being set to drama romance New Zealand. The first line creates the searchKeywords variable and sets it to be an empty string, because there's nothing between the double quotation marks. The second line sets the searchKeywords variable equal to its current string plus the string drama added to the end. The next two lines add romance and New Zealand in the same way.

As you can see, when you are pasting more text at the end of a variable, the name of the variable has to be listed twice. Java offers a shortcut to simplify this process a bit: the += operator. The += operator combines the functions of the = and + operators. With strings, it is used to add something to the end of an existing string. The searchKeywords example can be shortened by using +=, as shown in the following code:

```
String searchKeywords = "";
searchKeywords += "drama ";
searchKeywords += "romance ";
searchKeywords += "New Zealand";
```

This code produces the same result: searchKeywords is set to drama romance New Zealand.

Advanced String Handling

In addition to creating strings, pasting them together, and using them with other types of variables, there are several different ways you can examine a string variable and change its value. These advanced features are possible because strings are objects in the Java language. Working with strings develops skills you'll be using to work with other objects later.

Comparing Two Strings

One thing you will be testing often in your programs is whether one string is equal to another. You do this by using equals() in a statement with both of the strings, as in this example:

```
String favorite = "piano";
String guess = "ukelele";
System.out.println("Is Ada's favorite instrument a " + guess + "?");
System.out.println("Answer: " + favorite.equals(guess));
```

This example uses two different string variables. One, favorite, is used to store the name of Ada's favorite instrument: a piano. The other, guess, is used to store a guess as to what her favorite might be. The guess is that Ada prefers the ukelele.

The third line displays the text Is Ada's favorite instrument a followed by the value of the guess variable and then a question mark. The fourth line displays the text Answer: and then contains something new:

```
favorite.equals(guess)
```

This part of the statement is known as a method. A *method* is a way to accomplish a task in a Java program. This method's task is to determine if one string, favorite, has the same value as another string, guess. If the two string variables have the same value, the text true will be displayed. If not, the text false will be displayed. The following is the output of this example:

```
Is Ada's favorite instrument a ukelele?
Answer: false
```

Determining the Length of a String

It also can be useful at times to determine the length of a string in characters. You do this by using the length() method. This method works in the same fashion as the equals() method, except that only one string variable is involved. Look at the following example:

```
String cinematographer = "Stuart Dryburgh";
int nameLength = cinematographer.length();
```

This example sets nameLength, an integer variable, equal to 15. The cinematographer.length() method counts the number of characters in the string variable called cinematographer, and this count is assigned to the nameLength integer variable.

Changing a String's Case

Because computers take everything literally, it's easy to confuse them. Although a human would recognize that the text *Harvey Keitel* and the text *HARVEY KEITEL* are referring to the same thing, most computers would disagree. For instance, the equals() method discussed previously in this hour would state authoritatively that *Harvey Keitel* is not equal to *HARVEY KEITEL*.

To get around some of these obstacles, Java has methods that display a string variable as all uppercase letters (toUpperCase()) or all lowercase letters (toLowerCase()). The following example shows the toUpperCase() method in action:

```
String baines = "Harvey Keitel";
String change = baines.toUpperCase();
```

This code sets the string variable change equal to the baines string variable converted to all uppercase letters—HARVEY KEITEL, in other words. The toLowerCase() method works in the same fashion but returns an all-lowercase string value.

Note that the toUpperCase() method does not change the case of the string variable it is called on. In the preceding example, the baines variable still will be equal to Harvey Keitel.

Workshop: Presenting Credits

In *The Piano*, Ada McGrath Stewart was thrown into unfamiliar territory when she moved from Scotland to New Zealand to marry a stranger who didn't appreciate her ivory tickling. You might have felt similarly lost with some of the topics introduced during this hour.

As a workshop to reinforce the string handling features that have been covered, you will write a Java program to display credits for a feature film. You have three guesses as to the movie chosen, and if you need a hint, it starts with *The* and ends with a musical instrument that can be used to express the repressed passion of attractive mutes.

Load the word processor you're using to write Java programs and create a new file called Credits.java. Enter the text of Listing 6.1 into the word processor and save the file when you're done.

LISTING 6.1 THE Credits PROGRAM

```
 1: class Credits {
 2:     public static void main(String[] arguments) {
 3:         // set up film information
 4:         String title = "The Piano";
 5:         int year = 1993;
 6:         String director = "Jane Campion";
 7:         String role1 = "Ada";
 8:         String actor1 = "Holly Hunter";
 9:         String role2 = "Baines";
10:         String actor2 = "Harvey Keitel";
11:         String role3 = "Stewart";
12:         String actor3 = "Sam Neill";
13:         String role4 = "Flora";
14:         String actor4 = "Anna Paquin";
15:         // display information
16:         System.out.println(title + " (" + year + ")\n" +
17:                 "A " + director + " film.\n\n" +
18:                 role1 + "\t" + actor1 + "\n" +
19:                 role2 + "\t" + actor2 + "\n" +
20:                 role3 + "\t" + actor3 + "\n" +
21:                 role4 + "\t" + actor4);
22:     }
23: }
```

Before you attempt to compile the program with the javac tool, look over the program and see whether you can figure out what it's doing at each stage. Here's a breakdown of what's taking place:

- Line 1 gives the Java program the name `Credits`.
- Line 2 begins the `main()` block statement in which all of the program's work gets done.
- Line 3 is a comment statement explaining that you're going to set up the film's information in subsequent lines.
- Lines 4–14 set up variables to hold information about the film, its director, and its stars. One of the variables, `year`, is an integer. The rest are string variables.
- Line 15 is another comment line for the benefit of humans like us examining the program.
- Lines 16–21 are one long `System.out.println()` statement. Everything between the first parenthesis on Line 16 and the last parenthesis on Line 21 is displayed on-screen. The newline special character (\n) causes the text after it to be displayed at the beginning of a new line. The tab special character (\t) inserts tab spacing in the output. The rest are either text or string variables that should be shown.
- Line 22 ends the `main()` block statement.
- Line 23 ends the program.

Attempt to compile the program by going to the folder that contains `Credits.java` and typing this command:

```
javac Credits.java
```

If you do not see any error messages, the program has compiled successfully, and you can run it with the following command:

```
java Credits
```

If you do encounter error messages, correct any typos you find in your version of the `Credits` program and try again to compile it.

Listing 6.2 shows the output of the `Credits` program: a rundown of the film, year of release, director, and the four lead performers from *The Piano*. Be glad that you didn't have to present the credits for an ensemble film. A program detailing Robert Altman's *Short Cuts*, the 1993 film with more than 25 lead characters, could hog an hour of typing alone.

LISTING 6.2 THE OUTPUT OF THE `Credits` PROGRAM

```
The Piano (1993)
A Jane Campion film.

Ada      Holly Hunter
Baines   Harvey Keitel
Stewart  Sam Neill
Flora    Anna Paquin
```

If this hour's trivia related to *The Piano* and the films of director Jane Campion has sparked your curiosity, or if you just dig quiet women in braids, visit the following World Wide Web sites:

- Magnus Hjelstuen's unofficial *The Piano* Web site, with cast descriptions, storyline discussion, and comprehensive details about his favorite movie can be found at `http://www.fys.uio.no/~magnushj/Piano/`.
- The Internet Movie Database, a voluminous and searchable database of movies, TV shows, actors, directors, and other related topics can be found at `http://www.imdb.com`.

Summary

Once your version of `Credits` works like the one shown in Listing 6.2, give yourself some credit, too. You're writing longer Java programs and dealing with more sophisticated issues each hour. Like variables, strings are something you'll use every time you sit down to write a program.

At the beginning of *The Piano*, Holly Hunter's Ada lost her piano when her new husband refused to make his Maori laborers carry it home. Luckily for you, the ability to use strings in your Java programs cannot be taken away by an insensitive spouse or anyone else. You'll be using strings in many ways to communicate with users.

Q&A

Q In addition to `System.out.println()`, what are some other ways to display strings in Java programs?

A Strings can be displayed using different means in Java programs that run on World Wide Web pages and in programs that have a graphical user interface. Web-page Java programs, which are called applets, rely on a method called `drawString()` to display text. Hour 13, "Learning How Applets Work," covers several programming features that are specific to applet programming. Programs that have a graphical user interface display strings by putting them into a text-entry field or displaying them as a label next to some other part of the program's window.

Q How can I set the value of a string variable to be blank?

A A pair of double quotation marks without any text between them is considered to be an empty string. You can set a string variable equal to this upon its creation or in other parts of your programs. The following code creates a new string variable called adaSays and sets it to nothing:

```
String adaSays = "";
```

Q **Is there a way to make the text in one `println()` statement start right at the end of the text in the preceding `println()` statement? I don't want the second `println()` statement to start at the beginning of a new line, but it always does.**

A Java automatically starts each `System.out.println()` statement on its own new line, so the only way to prevent this is to use a statement that includes all of the text you want to display, or use the `System.out.print()` statement, which displays a string without ending it with a newline character automatically. The `Credits` program from the workshop has an example of a `println()` statement that includes several different lines of output. Take a look at it and see whether it fits what you want to do.

Q **If the + operator is used with strings to link up two different strings, can you add the numeric value of one string to the value of another?**

A You can use the value of a `String` variable as an integer only by using a method that converts the string's value into a numeric form. This procedure is called *casting* because it recasts existing information, in this case a string, as a different type of information. You'll learn about casting during Hour 11, "Describing What Your Object Is Like."

Q **Is it necessary to use += instead of + when adding some text to a string variable?**

A Not at all. The += operator is strictly for the benefit of programmers who want to use it as a shortcut. If you're more comfortable using the + operator when pasting some added text to a string variable, you ought to stick with it. The time and convenience you can gain by using += will be lost pretty quickly if it causes you to make errors in your program.

Q **Isn't there some kind of == operator that can be used to determine if two strings have the same value, as in `daughter == "Flora"`?**

A As you will discover during the next hour, "Using Conditional Tests to Make Decisions, " the == operator can be used with all of the variable types except for strings. The reason for the difference is that strings are objects. Java treats objects differently than other types of information, so special methods are necessary to determine whether one string is equal to another.

Q Do all methods in Java display `true` or `false` in the same way that the `equals()` method does in relation to strings?

A Methods have different ways of making a response after they are used. When a method sends back a value, as the `equals()` method does, this is called *returning* a value. The `equals()` method is set to return a Boolean value. Other methods might return a string, an integer, another type of variable, or nothing at all.

Quiz

The following questions will test your knowledge of the care and feeding of a string.

Questions

1. My friend concatenates. Should I report him to the authorities?

    (a) No. It's only illegal during the winter months.

    (b) Yes, but not until I sell my story to *Hard Copy* first.

    (c) No. All he's doing is pasting two strings together in a program.

2. Why is the word `String` capitalized while `int` and others are not?

    (a) `String` is a full word, but `int` ain't.

    (b) Like all objects in Java, `String` has a capitalized name.

    (c) Poor quality control at Sun Microsystems.

3. Which of the following characters will put a single quote in a string?

    (a) `<QUOTE>`

    (b) `\'`

    (c) `'`

Answers

1. c. Concatenation is just another word for pasting, joining, melding, or otherwise connecting two strings together. It uses the + and += operators.

2. b. The types of objects available in Java are all capitalized, which is the main reason variable names have a lowercase first letter. It makes it harder to mistake them for objects.

3. b. The single backslash is what begins one of the special characters that can be inserted into strings.

Activities

You can review the topics of this hour more fully with the following activities:

- Write a short Java program called Favorite that puts the code from this hour's "Comparing Two Strings" section into the main() block statement. Test it out to make sure it works as described and says that Ada's favorite instrument is not the ukelele. Then, change the initial value of the guess variable from ukelele to piano. See what happens.

- Modify the Credits program so that the names of the director and all performers are displayed entirely in uppercase letters.

To see Java programs that implement these activities, visit the book's Web site at http://www.prefect.com/java24.

Hour 7

Using Conditional Tests to Make Decisions

Writing a computer program has been compared to telling a household robot what to do. You provide the computer a list of instructions, called *statements*, and these instructions are followed to the letter. You can tell the computer to work out some unpleasant mathematical formulas, and it will work them out for you. Tell it to display some information, and it will dutifully respond.

However, there are times when you need the computer to be more selective about what it does. For example, if you have written a program to balance your checkbook, you might want the computer to display a warning message if your account is overdrawn. The warning could be something along the lines of `Hear that bouncing noise? It's your checks`. The computer should display this message only if your account is overdrawn. If it isn't, the message would be both inaccurate and emotionally upsetting.

The way to accomplish this task in a Java program is to use a statement called a conditional. *Conditionals* cause something to happen in a program only if a specific condition is met. During this hour, you'll learn how to use three different types of conditional statements: if, else, and switch. The following topics will be covered:

- Testing to see whether conditions are met
- Using the if statement for basic conditional tests
- Using other statements in conjunction with if
- Testing whether one value is greater than or less than another
- Testing whether two values are equal or unequal
- Using else statements as the opposite of if statements
- Chaining several conditional tests together
- Using the switch statement for complicated conditional tests
- Creating complicated tests with the ternary operator

Testing a Condition

Country star Kenny Rogers sang with the hippie-rock group The First Edition in the late 60s, and one of the group's singles hit the top 5 in 1968: *Just Dropped In (To See What Condition My Condition Was In)*. During this hour, you'll be dropping in to check the condition of several things in your Java programs using the conditional statements if, else, switch, case, and break. You also will be using several conditional operators: ==, !=, <, > and ?.

if Statements

If you want to test a condition in a Java program, the most basic way is with an if statement. As you learned previously, the boolean variable type is used to store only two possible values: true or false. The if statement works along the same lines, testing to see whether a condition is true or false and taking action only if the condition is true.

You use if along with a condition to test, as in the following statement:

```
if (account < 0.01)
    System.out.println("Hear that bouncing noise? It's your checks");
```

Although this code is listed on two lines, it's one statement. The first part uses if to determine whether the account variable is less than 0.01 by using the < operator. The second part displays the text Hear that bouncing noise? It's your checks.

The second part of an `if` statement will be run only if the first part is true. In the preceding example, if the `account` variable has a value of `0.01` (1 cent) or higher, the `println` statement will be ignored. Note that the condition you test with an `if` statement must be surrounded by parentheses, as in `(account < 0.01)`.

> If you're not sure why `if (account < 0.01)` is not a statement on its own, note that there is no semicolon at the end of the line. In Java programs, semicolons are used to show where one statement ends and the next one begins. In the preceding example, the semicolon does not appear until after the `println` portion of the statement. If you put a semicolon after the `if` portion, as in `if (account < 0.01);`, you'll cause a logic error in your program that can be hard to spot. Take care regarding semicolons when you start using the `if` statement.

The less than operator, <, is one of several different operators you can use with conditional statements. You'll become more familiar with the `if` statement as you use it with some of the other operators.

Less Than and Greater Than Comparisons

In the preceding section, the < operator is used the same way it was used in math class: as a less-than sign. There also is a greater-than conditional operator: >. This operator is used in the following statements:

```
if (elephantWeight > 780)
    System.out.println("This elephant is too fat for your tightrope "
        + "act.");
if (elephantTotal > 12)
    cleaningExpense = cleaningExpense + 150;
```

The first `if` statement tests whether the value of the `elephantWeight` variable is greater than 780. The second `if` statement tests whether the `elephantTotal` variable is greater than 12.

One thing to learn about `if` statements is that they often cause nothing to happen in your programs. If the preceding two statements are used in a program where `elephantWeight` is equal to 600 and `elephantTotal` is equal to 10, the rest of the `if` statements will be ignored. It's as though you are giving an order to a younger sibling who is subject to your whims: "Tyler, go to the store. If they have Everlasting Gobstopper candy, buy some for me. If not, do nothing and await further orders."

There will be times when you will want to determine whether something is less than or equal to something else. You can do this with the <= operator, as you might expect; use the >= operator for greater-than-or-equal-to tests. Here's an example:

```
if (account <= 0)
    System.out.println("Hear that bouncing noise? It's your checks");
```

This revision of the checkbook example mentioned previously should be a bit easier to understand. It tests whether account is less than or equal to the value 0 and taunts the user if it is.

Equal and Not Equal Comparisons

Another condition to check on in a program is equality. Is a variable equal to a specific value? Is one variable equal to the value of another? These questions can be answered with the == value, as in the following statements:

```
if (answer == rightAnswer)
    studentGrade = studentGrade + 10;
if (studentGrade == 100)
    System.out.println("Congratulations — a perfect score!");
```

> The operator used to conduct equality tests has two equal signs: ==. It's very easy to confuse this operator with the = operator, which is used to give a value to a variable. Always use two equal signs in a conditional statement.

You also can test inequality—whether something is not equal to something else. This is accomplished with the != operator, as shown in the following example:

```
if (number != 8675309)
    jennyNumber = false;
if (answer != rightAnswer)
    score = score - 5;
```

You can use the == and != operators with every type of variable except for one: strings. To see whether one string has the value of another, use the equals() method described during Hour 6, "Using Strings to Communicate."

Organizing a Program with Block Statements

Up to this point, all of the if statements have been followed with a single instruction, such as the println() method. In many cases, you will want to do more than one action in response to an if statement. To do this, you'll use the squiggly bracket marks { and } to create a block statement.

Block statements are statements that are organized as a group. Previously, you have seen how block statements are used to mark the beginning and end of the main() block of a Java program. Each statement within the main() block is handled when the program is run. Listing 7.1 is an example of a Java program with a block statement used to denote the main() block. The block statement begins with the opening bracket { on Line 2 and ends with the closing bracket } on Line 11. Load your word processor and enter the text of Listing 7.1 as a new file.

LISTING 7.1   A JAVA PROGRAM USING A main() BLOCK STATEMENT

```
 1: class Game {
 2:     public static void main(String[] arguments) {
 3:         int total = 0;
 4:         int score = 7;
 5:         if (score == 7)
 6:             System.out.println("You score a touchdown!");
 7:         if (score == 3)
 8:             System.out.println("You kick a field goal!");
 9:         total = total + score;
10:         System.out.println("Total score: " + total);
11:     }
12: }
```

Save this file as Game.java and compile it with the javac compiler tool. When you run the program, the output should resemble Listing 7.2.

LISTING 7.2   THE OUTPUT OF THE Game PROGRAM

```
You score a touchdown!
Total score: 7
```

You also can use block statements in conjunction with if statements to make the computer do more than one thing if a conditional statement is true. The following is an example of an if statement that includes a block statement:

```
if (playerScore > 9999) {
    playerLives++;
    System.out.println("Extra life!");
    difficultyLevel = difficultyLevel + 5;
}
```

The brackets are used to group all statements that are part of the if statement. If the variable playerScore is greater than 9,999, three things will happen:

- The value of the playerLives variable increases by one (because the increment operator ++ is used).
- The text Extra life! is displayed.
- The value of the difficultyLevel variable is increased by 5.

If the variable playerScore is not greater than 9,999, nothing will happen. All three statements inside the if statement block will be ignored.

if...else Statements

There are times when you want to do something if a condition is true and do something else if the condition is false. You can do this by using the else statement in addition to the if statement, as in the following example:

```
if (answer == correctAnswer) {
    score += 10;
    System.out.println("That's right. You get 10 points.");
}
else {
    score -= 5;
    System.out.println("Sorry, that's wrong. You lose 5 points.");
}
```

The else statement does not have a condition listed alongside it, unlike the if statement. Generally, the else statement is matched with the if statement that immediately comes before it in a Java program. You also can use else to chain several if statements together, as in the following example:

```
if (grade == 'A')
    System.out.println("You got an A. Great job!");
else if (grade == 'B')
    System.out.println("You got a B. Good work!");
else if (grade == 'C')
    System.out.println("You got a C. You'll never get into a good "
        + "college!");
else
    System.out.println("You got an F. You'll do well in Congress!");
```

By putting together several different if and else statements in this way, you can handle a variety of conditions. In the preceding example, a specific message is sent to A students, B students, C students, and future legislators.

switch Statements

The if and else statements are good for situations with only two possible conditions, but there are times when you have more than two options that need to be considered.

With the preceding grade example, you saw that `if` and `else` statements can be chained to handle several different conditions.

Another way to do this is to use the `switch` statement. You can use it in a Java program to test for a variety of different conditions and respond accordingly. In the following example, the grade example has been rewritten with the `switch` statement to handle a complicated range of choices:

```
switch (grade) {
    case 'A':
        System.out.println("You got an A. Great job!");
        break;
    case 'B':
        System.out.println("You got a B. Good work!");
        break;
    case 'C':
        System.out.println("You got a C. You'll never get into a good "
            + "college!");
        break;
    default:
        System.out.println("You got an F. You'll do well in Congress!");
}
```

The first line of the `switch` statement specifies the variable that will be tested—in this example, `grade`. Then the `switch` statement uses the { and } brackets to form a block statement.

Each of the `case` statements checks the test variable from `switch` against a specific value. In this example, there are `case` statements for values of A, B, and C. Each of these has one or two statements that follow it. When one of these `case` statements matches the variable listed with `switch`, the computer handles the statements after the `case` statement until it encounters a `break` statement.

For example, if the `grade` variable has the value of B, the text You got a B. Good work! will be displayed. The next statement is `break`, so no other part of the `switch` statement will be considered. The `break` statement tells the computer to break out of the `switch` statement.

The `default` statement is used as a catch-all if none of the preceding `case` statements is true. In this example, it will occur if the `grade` variable does not equal A, B, or C. You do not have to use a `default` statement with every `switch` block statement you use in your programs. If it is omitted, nothing will happen if none of the `case` statements has the correct value.

One thing you may want to do with switch is to make each case statement represent a range of values. As an example, in a grading program, you might want to use an integer called numberGrade and test for case numberGrade > 89:. Unfortunately, this isn't possible in Java, because each case statement must refer to a single value. You'll have to use a series of if statements or if...else statements when you aren't working with a bunch of different one-value conditions.

The Conditional Operator

The most complicated conditional statement is one that you might not find reasons to use in your applications: the ternary operator. If you find it too confusing to implement in your own programs, take heart: You can use other conditionals to accomplish the same thing.

You can use the ternary operator when you want to assign a value or display a value based on a conditional test. For example, in a video game, you might need to set the numberOfEnemies variable based on whether the skillLevel variable is greater than 5. One way to do this is with an if...else statement:

```
if (skillLevel > 5)
    numberOfEnemies = 10;
else
    numberOfEnemies = 5;
```

A shorter way to do this is to use the ternary operator, which is ?. A ternary operator has five parts:

- The condition to test, surrounded by parentheses, as in (skillLevel > 5)
- A question mark (?)
- The value to use if the condition is true
- A colon (:)
- The value to use if the condition is false

To use the ternary operator to set the value of numberOfEnemies based on skillLevel, you could use the following statement:

```
numberOfEnemies = ( skillLevel > 5) ? 10 : 5;
```

You also can use the ternary operator to determine what information to display. Consider the example of a program that displays the text Mr. or Ms. depending on the value of the gender variable. You could do this action with another if...else statement:

```
if (gender.equals("male"))
    System.out.print("Mr.");
else
    System.out.print("Ms.");
```

A shorter method is to use the ternary operator to accomplish the same thing, as in the following:

```
System.out.print( (gender.equals("male")) ? "Mr." : "Ms." );
```

The ternary operator can be useful, but it's also the hardest element of conditional tests in Java to understand. Feel free to use the longer if and else statements if you want.

Workshop: Watching the Clock

This hour's workshop gives you another look at each of the conditional tests you can use in your programs. For this project, you will use Java's built-in timekeeping feature, which keeps track of the current date and time, and present this information in sentence form.

Run the word processor you're using to create Java programs and give a new document the name ClockTalk.java. This program is long, but most of it consists of long conditional statements. Type the full text of Listing 7.3 into the word processor and save the file when you're done.

LISTING 7.3 THE FULL TEXT OF ClockTalk.java

```
 1: import java.util.*;
 2:
 3: class ClockTalk {
 4:     public static void main(String[] arguments) {
 5:         // get current time and date
 6:         Calendar now = Calendar.getInstance();
 7:         int hour = now.get(Calendar.HOUR_OF_DAY);
 8:         int minute = now.get(Calendar.MINUTE);
 9:         int month = now.get(Calendar.MONTH) + 1;
10:         int day = now.get(Calendar.DAY_OF_MONTH);
11:         int year = now.get(Calendar.YEAR);
12:
13:         // display greeting
14:         if (hour < 12)
15:             System.out.println("Good morning.\n");
16:         else if (hour < 17)
17:             System.out.println("Good afternoon.\n");
18:         else
19:             System.out.println("Good evening.\n");
```

continues

LISTING 7.3   CONTINUED

```
20:
21:            // begin time message by showing the minutes
22:            System.out.print("It's");
23:            if (minute != 0) {
24:                System.out.print(" " + minute + " ");
25:                System.out.print( (minute != 1) ? "minutes" :
26:                    "minute");
27:                System.out.print(" past");
28:            }
29:
30:            // display the hour
31:            System.out.print(" ");
32:            System.out.print( (hour > 12) ? (hour - 12) : hour );
33:            System.out.print(" o'clock on ");
34:
35:            // display the name of the month
36:            switch (month) {
37:                case (1):
38:                    System.out.print("January");
39:                    break;
40:                case (2):
41:                    System.out.print("February");
42:                    break;
43:                case (3):
44:                    System.out.print("March");
45:                    break;
46:                case (4):
47:                    System.out.print("April");
48:                    break;
49:                case (5):
50:                    System.out.print("May");
51:                    break;
52:                case (6):
53:                    System.out.print("June");
54:                    break;
55:                case (7):
56:                    System.out.print("July");
57:                    break;
58:                case (8):
59:                    System.out.print("August");
60:                    break;
61:                case (9):
62:                    System.out.print("September");
63:                    break;
64:                case (10):
65:                    System.out.print("October");
66:                    break;
67:                case (11):
```

```
68:                         System.out.print("November");
69:                     break;
70:                 case (12):
71:                         System.out.print("December");
72:             }
73:
74:             // display the date and year
75:             System.out.println(" " + day + ", " + year + ".");
76:     }
77: }
```

Save the file when you're done, and attempt to compile it by entering javac ClockTalk.java at the command line. Correct any typos that cause error messages to occur during the attempted compilation. After the program compiles correctly, look over lines 13–75 before going over the description of the program. See whether you can get a good idea about what is taking place in each of these sections and how the conditional tests are being used.

With the exception of lines 6–11, the ClockTalk program contains material that has been covered up to this point. After a series of variables are set up to hold the current date and time, a series of if or switch conditionals are used to determine what information should be displayed.

This program contains several uses of System.out.println() to display strings, and it also includes a similar statement: System.out.print(). The difference between these two statements is that println() ends the string with a newline character, and print() does not. You'll see why print() is needed when you view the output of the program.

Lines 6–11 refer to a Calendar variable called now. The Calendar variable type is capitalized, just as String is capitalized in a program that uses strings. The reason for the capitalization is that Calendar is an object.

You'll learn how to create and work with objects during Hour 10, "Creating Your First Object." For this hour, focus on what's taking place in lines 6–11 rather than how it's happening.

The ClockTalk program is made up of the following sections:

- Line 1 enables your program to use a class that is needed to track the current date and time: java.util.Calendar.

- Lines 3–4 begin the ClockTalk program and its main() statement block.

- Line 6 creates a Calendar objcct called now that contains the current date and time of your system. The now object will change each time you run this program (unless, of course, the physical laws of the universe are altered and time stands still).

- Lines 7–11 create variables to hold the hour, minute, month, day, and year. The values for these variables are pulled from the Calendar object, which is the storehouse for all of this information. These variables are used in the subsequent sections as the program displays information.

- Lines 14–19 display one of three possible greetings: Good morning., Good afternoon., or Good evening. The greeting to display is selected based on the value of the hour variable.

- Lines 22–28 display the current minute along with some accompanying text. First, the text It's is displayed in line 22. If the value of minute is equal to 0, lines 24–26 are ignored because of the if statement in line 23. This statement is necessary because it would not make sense for the program to tell someone that it's 0 minutes past an hour. Line 24 displays the current value of the minute variable. A ternary operator is used in lines 25–26 to display either the text minutes or minute, depending on whether minute is equal to 1. Finally, in line 27 the text past is displayed.

- Lines 30–33 display the current hour by using another ternary operator. This ternary conditional statement in line 32 causes the hour to be displayed differently if it is larger than 12, which prevents the computer from stating things like 15 o'clock.

- Lines 35–72, almost half of the program, are a long switch statement that displays a different name of the month based on the integer value stored in the month variable.

- Lines 74–75 finish off the display by showing the current date and the year.

- Lines 76–77 close out the main() statement block and then the entire ClockTalk program.

When you run this program, the output should resemble the following code, with changes based on the current date and time. For example, if today's date is 7-6-1998 and the time is 11:30 a.m., your program would display the following text:

```
Good morning.
It's 30 minutes past 11 o'clock on July 6, 1998.
```

Run the program several times to see how it keeps up with the clock. If the time doesn't match the time on your computer, the Java interpreter might be using the wrong time zone to determine the current time. When the interpreter does not know the default time zone to use, it uses Greenwich Time instead.

The following example sets the current time zone:

```
TimeZone tz = TimeZone.getTimeZone("EST");
TimeZone.setDefault(tz);
```

The setDefault() method should be used before any calendar or other date-related items are created.

The first statement creates a TimeZone object called tz. The text EST is sent as an argument to the getTimeZone() method, and this causes TimeZone to be set up for Central Standard Time.

The second statement sets the time zone by calling the setDefault() method of the TimeZone class. If you're having trouble finding the right time zone arguments, the following statements show how to display all valid ones:

```
String[] ids = TimeZone.getAvailableIDs();
for (int i = 0; i < ids.length; i++)
    System.out.println(ids[i].toString());
```

The ClockTalk program uses the Gregorian calendar system that has been used throughout the Western world for many years to determine the date and time. It was introduced in 1582 when Pope Gregory XIII moved the Julian calendar system forward 10 days—turning Oct. 5, 1582, into Oct. 15, 1582. This was needed because the calendar was moving out of alignment with the seasons due to discrepancies in the Julian system. Changes introduced with version 1.1 of the Java language made it possible to create other calendar systems for use with Java programs. Check Developer.Com's Java directory at http://www.developer.com or other Java programming resources for these as they become available.

Summary

Now that you can use conditional statements, the overall intelligence of your Java programs has improved greatly. You programs can now evaluate information and use it to react differently in different situations, even if information changes as the program is running. They can decide between two or more alternatives based on specific conditions.

Using the if statement and other conditionals in programming also promotes a type of logical thinking that can reap benefits in other aspects of your life. ("*If* she's attractive, I'll take her to an expensive restaurant, *else* we're using my two-for-one Taco Barn burrito coupon.") Programming a computer forces you to break down a task into a logical set of steps to undertake and decisions that must be made, and it provides interesting insight.

One thing that conditional statements do not offer insight about is the thinking of the lyricist who penned *Just Dropped In (To See What Condition My Condition Was In)*. There may be no rational explanation for lyrics such as, "I tred on a cloud, I fell eight miles high. Told my mind I'm gonna sky. I just dropped in to see what condition my condition was in."

Q&A

Q **The `if` statement seems like the one that's most useful. Is it possible to use only `if` statements in programs and never use the others?**

A It's possible to do without `else` or `switch`, and many programmers never use the ternary operator `?`. However, `else` and `switch` often are beneficial to use in your programs because they make them easier to understand. A set of `if` statements chained together can become unwieldy.

Q **An `if` statement is described as either a single statement or as a conditional statement followed by another statement to handle if the condition is true. Which is it?**

A The point that might be confusing is that `if` statements and other conditionals are used in conjunction with other statements. The `if` statement makes a decision, and the other statements do work based on the decision that is made. The `if` statement combines a conditional statement with one or more other types of Java statements, such as statements that use the `println()` method or create a variable.

Q **In the `ClockTalk` program, why is 1 added to `Calendar.MONTH` in order to get the current month value?**

A This is necessary because of a quirk in the way that the `Calendar` class represents months. Instead of numbering them from 1 to 12 as you might expect, `Calendar` numbers months beginning with 0 in January and ending with 11 in December. Adding 1 causes months to be represented numerically in a more understandable manner.

Q **During this hour, opening and closing brackets { and } are not used with an `if` statement if it is used in conjunction with only one statement. Isn't it mandatory to use brackets?**

A No. Brackets can be used as part of any `if` statement to surround the part of the program that's dependent on the conditional test. Using brackets is a good practice to get into because it prevents a common error that might take place when you revise the program. If you add a second statement after an `if` conditional and don't add brackets, unexpected errors will occur when the program is run.

Q **Will the Java compiler `javac` catch the error when a = operator is used with a conditional instead of a ==?**

A Often it will not, and it results in a real doozy of a logic error. These errors only show up when a program is being run and can be discovered only through observation and testing. Because the = operator is used to assign a value to a variable, if you use `name = "Fernando"` in a spot in a program where you mean to use `name`

== "Fernando", you could wipe out the value of the name variable and replace it with Fernando. When the value stored in variables changes unexpectedly, the result is subtle and unexpected errors that you must debug.

Q Does break have to be used in each section of statements that follow a case?

A You don't have to use break. If you do not use it at the end of a group of statements, all of the remaining statements inside the switch block statement will be handled, regardless of the case value they are being tested with.

Q What's the difference between System.out.println() and System.out.print()?

A The println() statement displays a line of text and ends the line with a newline character. The newline character has the same behavior as the carriage return key on a manual typewriter. It causes the next text to begin displaying at the left-most edge of the next line. The print() statement does not use a newline character, making it possible to use several print() statements to display information on the same line.

Quiz

The following questions will see what condition your knowledge of conditions is in.

Questions

1. Conditional tests result in either a true or false value. Which variable type does this remind you of?

    (a) None. They're unique.

    (b) The long variable type.

    (c) The boolean type.

2. Which statement is used as a catch-all category in a switch block statement?

    (a) default

    (b) otherwise

    (c) onTheOtherHand

3. What's a conditional?

    (a) The thing that repairs messy split ends and tangles after you shampoo.

    (b) Something in a program that tests whether a condition is true or false.

    (c) The place where you confess your sins to a neighborhood religious figure.

Answers

1. c. The `boolean` variable type can only equal `true` or `false`, making it similar to conditional tests.

2. a. `default` statements will be handled if none of the other `case` statements matches the `switch` variable.

3. b. The other descriptions are conditioner and confessional.

Activities

To improve your conditioning in terms of Java conditionals, review the topics of this hour with the following activities:

- Remove the `break` statement from one of the lines in the `ClockTalk` program, and then compile it and see what happens when you run it. Try it again with a few more `break` statements removed.

- Create a short program that stores a value of your choosing from 1 to 100 in an integer variable called `grade`. Use this `grade` variable with a conditional statement to display a different message for all A, B, C, D, and F students. Try it first with an `if` statement, and then try it with a `switch` statement.

To see Java programs that implement these activities, visit the book's Web site at `http://www.prefect.com/java24`.

Hour **8**

Repeating an Action with Loops

One of the punishments schoolchildren find most annoying is writing something over and over again on paper. For particularly heinous offenses such as subject-verb disagreement, the child might be asked to repeat the phrase numerous times on the chalkboard.

In one of his frequent trips to the board, cartoon problem child Bart Simpson had to write, "I will not trade pants with others" dozens of times. This kind of punishment might work on children, but it definitely would fail on a computer. They can repeat a task with ease.

As you might expect, every one of Bart Simpson's chalkboard punishments has been documented on the World Wide Web. Visit `http://www.ncf.carleton.ca/~co378/HomePage.Chalk.html` to see the list.

Computer programs are ideally suited to do the same thing over and over again because of loops. A *loop* is a statement or set of statements that will be repeated in a program. Some loops are set to occur a fixed number of times. Others can loop indefinitely. In the Java programs that you write, you will find many circumstances in which a loop is useful. You can use them to wait until a specific thing has taken place, such as a user clicking on a button. You also can use them to cause the computer to wait and do nothing for a brief period, such as in an animation program.

To create and control loops, you use a *loop statement*. A loop statement causes a computer program to return to the same place more than once. If the term seems unusual to you, think of what a stunt plane does when it loops: It completes a circle and returns to the place where it started the loop. There are three loop statements in Java: `for`, `do`, and `while`. These loop statements are often interchangeable in a program because each can be made to work like the others. The choice to use a loop statement in a program often depends on personal preference, but it's beneficial to learn how all three work. You frequently can simplify a loop section of a program by choosing the right statement.

The following topics are covered during this hour:

- Using the `for` loop
- Using the `while` loop
- Using the `do...while` loop
- Exiting a loop prematurely
- Naming a loop

for Loops

The most complex of the loop statements is `for`. The `for` loop is often used in cases where you want to repeat a section of a program a fixed number of times. It also can be used if the number of times the loop should be repeated is variable. The following is an example of a `for` loop:

```
for (int number = 0; number < 1000; number++) {
    if (number % 12 == 0)
        System.out.println("#: " + number);
}
```

This loop displays every number from 0 to 999 that is evenly divisible by 12.

Every for loop has a variable that is used to determine when the loop should begin and end. This variable often is called the *counter*. The counter in the preceding loop is number.

The example illustrates the three parts of a for statement:

- The initialization section: In the first part, the number variable is initialized with a value of 0.

- The conditional section: In the second part, there is a conditional test like one you might use in an if statement. The test is number < 1000.

- The change section: The third part is a statement that changes the value of the number variable by using the increment operator.

In the initialization section, you can set up the counter variable you want to use in the for statement. You can create the variable inside the for statement, as the number variable was created in the preceding example, or you can create the variable elsewhere in the program. In either case, the variable should be given a starting value in this section of the for statement. The variable will have this value when the loop starts.

The conditional section contains a test that must remain true for the loop to continue looping. Once the test is false, the loop will end. In this example, the loop will end when the number variable is no longer smaller than 1,000.

The last section of the for statement contains a Java statement that changes the value of the counter variable in some way. This statement is handled each time the loop goes around. The counter variable has to change in some way or the loop will never end. For instance, in this example, number is incremented by 1 using the increment operator ++ in the change section. If number were not changed, it would stay at its original value, 0, and the conditional number < 1000 would always be true.

The statements inside the bracket marks, { and }, also are executed during each trip through the loop. The bracketed area is usually where the main work of the loop takes place, although some loops do all of their work in the change section.

The preceding example has the following statement within the { and } marks:

```
if (number % 12 == 0)
        System.out.println("#: " + number);
```

This statement will be executed 1,000 times. The loop starts by setting the number variable equal to 0. It then adds 1 to number before each pass through the loop and stops looping when number is no longer less than 1,000. Every time number is evenly divisible by 12, the number is displayed next to the text #: .

An unusual term you might hear in connection with loops is iteration. An *iteration* is a single trip through a loop. The counter variable that is used to control the loop is often called an *iterator*.

As you have seen with if statements, a for loop does not require brackets if it contains only a single statement. This is shown in the following example:

```
for (int p = 0; p < 500; p++)
    System.out.println("I will not trade pants with others.");
```

This loop will display the text I will not trade pants with others. 500 times. Although brackets are not required around a single statement inside a loop, you can use them, if desired, as a way of making the program easier to understand.

Each section of a for loop is set off from the other sections with a semicolon (;). A for loop can have more than one variable set up during the initialization section and more than one statement in the change section, as in the following:

```
for (i = 0, j = 0; i * j < 1000; i++, j += 2) {
    System.out.println(i + " * " + j + " = " i * j);
}
```

These multiple statement sections of the for loop are set off by commas, as in i = 0, j = 0. This loop will display a list of equations where the i variable is multiplied by the j variable. The i variable increases by 1 and the j variable increases by 2 during each trip through the loop. Once i multiplied by j is no longer less than 1,000, the loop will end.

Sections of a for loop can be empty. An example of this would be if the counter variable has already been created with an initial value in another part of the program, as in the following:

```
for ( ; displayCount < endValue; displayCount++) {
    // loop statements would be here
}
```

while Loops

The while loop does not have as many different sections to set up as does the for loop. The only thing it needs is a conditional test, which accompanies the while statement. The following is an example of a while loop:

```
while ( gameLives > 0) {
    // the statements inside the loop go here
}
```

Because many Java statements end with a semicolon, an easy mistake to make is putting a semicolon at the end of a `for` statement, as in the following:

```
for (int i = 0; i < 100; i++); {
    value = value + i;
}
```

In this example, the semicolon puts the statement in the brackets, `value = value + i;`, outside of the loop. As a result, nothing will happen as the `for` loop is handled. The program will compile without any errors, but you won't get the results you expect when it runs.

8

This loop will continue repeating until the `gameLives` variable is no longer greater than 0. The `while` statement tests the condition at the beginning of the loop, before any statements of the loop have been handled.

When a program reaches the `while` statement for the first time, if the tested condition is `false`, the statements inside the loop will be ignored. If the `while` condition is `true`, the loop goes around once and tests the `while` condition again. If the tested condition never changes inside the loop, the loop will keep looping indefinitely.

do...while Loops

The do...while loop is similar in function to the `while` loop, but the conditional test goes in a different place. The following is an example of a do...while loop:

```
do {
    // the statements inside the loop go here
} while ( gameLives > 0 );
```

Like the previous `while` loop, this loop will continue looping until the `gameLives` variable is no longer greater than 0. The do...while loop is different because the conditional test is conducted after the statements inside the loop instead of before them.

When the do loop is reached for the first time as a program runs, the statements between the do and the `while` are handled automatically. Then the `while` condition is tested to determine whether the loop should be repeated. If the `while` condition is `true`, the loop goes around one more time. If the condition is `false`, the loop ends. Something must happen inside the do and `while` statements that changes the condition tested with `while`, or the loop will continue indefinitely. The statements inside a do...while loop always will be handled at least once.

If you're still confused about the difference between a `while` loop and a `do...while` loop, engage in a little role playing and pretend you're a teenager who wants to borrow your father's car. If you are a teenager with a case of car envy, all the better. There are two strategies that you can take:

1. Borrow the car first and tell Dad later that you did it.
2. Ask Dad before you borrow the car.

Strategy 1 has an advantage over Strategy 2 because you get to use the car once even if Dad doesn't want to let you use it. The `do...while` loop is like Strategy 1 because something happens once even if the loop condition is `false` the first time `while` is encountered. The `while` loop is like Strategy 2 because nothing will happen unless the `while` condition at the beginning is `true`. It all depends on the situation in your program.

> Sams makes no warranties express nor implied that your father will be happy if you borrow his car without telling him first.

Exiting a Loop

The normal way to exit a loop is for the condition that is tested to become `false`. This is true of all three types of loops in Java: `for`, `while`, and `do...while`. However, there might be times when you want a loop to end immediately, even if the condition being tested is still `true`. You can do this with a `break` statement, as shown in the following code:

```
while (index <= 1000) {
    index = index + 5;
    if (index == 400)
        break;
    System.out.println("The index is " + index);
}
```

This loop will continue looping until the value of the `index` variable is greater than `1,000`. However, a special case causes the loop to end even if the `index` variable is less than or equal to `1,000`: If `index` equals `400`, the loop ends immediately.

Another special-circumstance statement you can use inside a loop is `continue`. The `continue` statement causes the loop to exit its current trip through the loop and start over at the first statement of the loop. Consider the following loop:

```
while (index <= 1000) {
    index = index + 5;
```

```
    if (index == 400)
        continue;
    System.out.println("The index is " + index);
}
```

The statements will be handled normally unless the value of index equals 400. In that case, the continue statement causes the loop to go back to the while statement instead of proceeding normally to the System.out.println() statement. Because of the con- tinue statement, the loop will never display the following text:

```
The index is 400
```

You can use the break and continue statements with all three kinds of Java loop state- ments.

Naming a Loop

Like other statements in Java programs, loops can be put inside of each other. The fol- lowing shows a for loop inside of a while loop:

```
while ( totalCoconuts < 100) {
    for ( int count = 0; count < 10; count++) {
        totalCoconuts = totalCoconuts + count;
        if (totalCoconuts > 400)
            break;
    }
}
```

The break statement will cause the for loop to end if the totalCoconuts variable equals 400 or greater. However, there might be a case where you want to break out of both loops for some reason. To make this possible, you have to give the outer loop—the while statement—a name. To name a loop, put the name on the line before the beginning of the loop and follow it with a colon (:).

Once the loop has a name, you can use the name after the break or continue statement to indicate to which loop the break or continue statement applies. Note that although the name of the loop is followed by a colon at the spot where the loop begins, the colon is not used with the name in a break or continue statement. The following example repeats the previous one with the exception of one thing: If the totalCoconuts variable equals 400 or more, both loops are ended.

```
coconutLoop:
while ( totalCoconuts < 100) {
    for ( int count = 0; count < 10; count++) {
        totalCoconuts = totalCoconuts + count;
        if (totalCoconuts > 400)
```

```
                    break coconutLoop;
        }
    }
```

Workshop: Teaching Your Computer a Lesson

This hour's workshop provides evidence that you cannot punish your computer in the same way that Bart Simpson is punished at the beginning of each episode of *The Simpsons*. Pretend you're a teacher and the computer is the kid who contaminated your morning cup of coffee with Thorium 230. Even if you're the most strident liberal, you realize that the computer must be taught a lesson—it's not acceptable behavior to give the teacher radiation poisoning. Your computer must be punished, and the punishment is to display the same sentence over and over again.

The Repeat program will use a loop statement to handle a System.out.println() statement again and again. Once the computer has been dealt this punishment for 25,000 sentences or one minute, whichever comes first, it can stop running and think about the error of its ways.

> A topic of heated debate here at Sams concerns whether the punishment is severe enough. Thorium is a silver-white metal that has a half-life of 80,000 years. Some scientists believe that it is as toxic as plutonium, and, if it finds a home in someone's liver, bone marrow, or lymphatic tissue, Thorium 230 can cause cancer, leukemia, or lung cancer. A student who irradiates a teacher probably should receive three hours of in-school detention, at least.

Use your word processor to create a new file called Repeat.java. Enter the text in Listing 8.1 and save the file when you're done.

LISTING 8.1   THE FULL SOURCE CODE OF Repeat.java

```
 1: import java.util.*;
 2:
 3: class Repeat {
 4:     public static void main(String arguments[]) {
 5:         String sentence = "Thorium 230 is not a toy.";
 6:         int count = 0;
 7:         Calendar start = Calendar.getInstance();
 8:         int startMinute = start.get(Calendar.MINUTE);
 9:         int startSecond = start.get(Calendar.SECOND);
10:         start.roll(Calendar.MINUTE, true);
11:         int nextMinute = start.get(Calendar.MINUTE);
```

```
12:         int nextSecond = start.get(Calendar.SECOND);
13:         while (count < 50000) {
14:             System.out.println(sentence);
15:             GregorianCalendar now = new GregorianCalendar();
16:             if (now.get(Calendar.MINUTE) >= nextMinute)
17:                 if (now.get(Calendar.SECOND) >= nextSecond)
18:                     break;
19:             count++;
20:         }
21:         System.out.println("\nI wrote the sentence " + count
22:             + " times.");
23:         System.out.println("I have learned my lesson.");
24:     }
25: }
```

The following things are taking place in this program:

- Line 1: The import statement makes the java.util group of classes available to this program. You're going to use one of these classes, Calendar, in order to keep track of time while the program is running.

- Lines 3 and 4: The Repeat class is declared, and the main() block of the program begins.

- Lines 5 and 6: The sentence variable is set up with the text of the punishment sentence, and the count variable is created with a value of 0.

- Line 7: Using the Calendar class, which keeps track of time-related information, the start variable is created with the current time as its value.

- Lines 8 and 9: The get() method of the Calendar class is used to retrieve the current minute and second and store them in the variables startMinute and startSecond.

- Line 10: The Calendar roll() method is used to roll the value of the start variable one minute forward in time.

- Lines 11 and 12: The get() method is used again to retrieve the minute and second for start and store them in the variables nextMinute and nextSecond.

- Line 13: The while statement begins a loop using the count variable as the counter. When count hits 50,000, the loop will end.

- Line 14: The punishment text, stored in the string variable sentence, is displayed.

- Line 15: Using the Calendar class, the now variable is created with the current time.

- Lines 16–18: Using one if statement inside of another, the program tests to see if one minute has passed by comparing the current minute and second to the values of nextMinute and nextSecond. If it has passed, break ends the while loop.

- Line 19: The } marks the end of the while loop.
- Lines 20–22: The computer displays the number of times it repeated the punishment sentence and claims to be rehabilitated.
- Lines 24 and 25: The main() block of the program and the program are closed out with } marks.

Compile the program with the javac compiler tool and then give it a try by typing the following at the command line:

```
java Repeat
```

Run this program several times to see how many sentences are displayed in a minute's time. The Repeat program is an excellent way to see whether your computer is faster than mine. During the testing of this workshop program, Repeat usually displayed from 13,300 to 14,400 sentences in a minute's time. If your computer displays the sentence more times than mine does, don't just send me your condolences. Buy more of my books so I can upgrade.

> Although many of the programs you will write in this book will work under an older version of the Java Development Kit such as 1.0.2, the Repeat program will not compile successfully unless you use a version of the Kit that's 1.1 or greater. This program uses features of the Calendar class that were introduced with version 1.1 of the Java language. Sun Microsystems encourages the use of new features like this because they make improvements on the language. For example, the updated Calendar class is part of Sun's effort to enable programmers to use different calendar systems in Java programs.

Summary

The information presented in this chapter is information you will be coming back to again and again and again when you write programs. Loops are a fundamental part of most programming languages. In several of the hours to come, you'll get a chance to manipulate graphics so you can produce animated effects. You couldn't do this without loops.

Q&A

Q Should the counter variable used in a for loop be created inside the for statement or before the loop begins?

A The only time the counter should be created outside of the `for` loop, or any other loop for that matter, is when it needs to be used in another part of the program. A variable that is created in a loop or other kind of block statement only exists inside that block. You can't use the value in any other part of the program. This is good programming practice because it makes it harder to misuse variables—you can't set their value in one part of the program and use them somewhere else incorrectly. The concept of a variable existing in one part of a program and not existing anywhere else is called *scope*, and it's covered fully during Hour 11, "Describing What Your Object Is Like."

Q **The term *initialization* has been used in several places. What does it mean?**

A It means to give something an initial value and set it up. When you create a variable and assign a starting value to it, you are initializing the variable.

Q **If a loop never ends, how does the program stop running?**

A Usually in a program where a loop does not end, something else in the program is set up to stop execution in some way. For example, a loop could continue indefinitely while the program waits for the user to click a button labeled `Quit`. However, if a program isn't working correctly, one bug you'll run into during testing is a loop that cannot be stopped. This bug is called an *infinite loop* because the program will loop happily forever. If one of the Java programs you run from the command line is stuck in an infinite loop, press Ctrl+C.

Quiz

The following questions will test your knowledge of loops. In the spirit of the subject matter, repeat each of these until you get them right.

Questions

1. What must be used to separate each section of a `for` statement?

    (a) Commas

    (b) Semicolons

    (c) Off-duty police officers

2. Which statement causes a program to go back to the statement that began a loop and then keep going from there?

    (a) `continue`

    (b) `next`

    (c) `skip`

3. When it comes to borrowing a car from your father, what lesson did you learn during this hour?

    (a) Don't even think about it.

    (b) Speak softly and carry a big stick.

    (c) It's better to beg forgiveness than to ask permission.

Answers

1. b. Commas are used to separate things within a section, but semicolons separate sections.

2. a. `continue` skips to the next go-round of the loop. (`break` ends a loop entirely.)

3. c.

Activities

If your head isn't going in circles from all this looping, review the topics of this hour with the following activities:

- Modify the `Repeat` program so that it uses a `for` loop instead of a `while` loop and compare the efficiency of each approach.

- Write a short program using loops that finds the first 400 prime numbers.

To see Java programs that implement these activities, visit the book's Web site at `http://www.prefect.com/java24`.

PART III

Moving Into Advanced Topics

Hour

HOUR 9

Storing Information with Arrays

No one benefits more from the development of the computer than Santa Claus. For centuries, humankind has put an immense burden on him to gather and process information. Old St. Nick has to keep track of the following things:

- Naughty children
- Nice children
- Gift requests
- Homes with impassable chimneys
- Women who want more from Santa than Mrs. Claus is willing to let him give
- Countries that shoot unidentified aircraft first and ask questions later

Computers must have been a great boon at the North Pole because they are ideal for the storage, categorization, and study of information.

The most basic way that information is stored in a computer program is by putting it into a variable. However, this method is limited to relatively simple usage. If Santa had to give each naughty child his or her own variable name, he'd be working on the program for the next 12 holiday seasons at least, to say nothing of the effect on his jolly disposition or his carpal tunnel nerves. The list of naughty children is an example of a collection of similar information. Each child's name is a string of text or some kind of Santa Information System ID number. In order to keep track of a list of this kind, you can use arrays.

Arrays are groups of related variables that share the same type. You can have arrays of any type of information that can be stored as a variable. Arrays can be used to keep track of more sophisticated types of information than a single variable, but they are almost as easy to create and manipulate as variables are.

The following topics will be covered during this hour:

- Creating an array
- Definition of an array's dimension
- Giving a value to an array element
- Changing the information in an array
- Making multidimensional arrays
- Sorting an array

Creating Arrays

Arrays are variables that are grouped together under a common name. The term should be familiar to you, though the meaning might not be so clear—think of a salesman showing off his array of fabulous cleaning products or a game show with a dazzling array of prizes. Like variables, arrays are created by stating the type of the variable being organized into the array and the name of the array. The difference lies in the addition of the square bracket marks [and].

You can create arrays for any type of information that can be stored as a variable. For example, the following statement creates an array of string variables:

```
String[] naughtyChild;
```

Here are a few more examples:

```
int[] reindeerWeight;
boolean[] hostileAirTravelNations;
```

Java is flexible about where the square brackets are placed when an array is being created. You can put them after the variable name instead of after the variable type, as in the following:

```
String niceChild[];
```

To make arrays easier for humans to spot in your programs, you probably should stick to one style rather than switching back and forth, though Java allows both styles of usage.

9

The previous examples create arrays, but they do not store any values in them initially. To do this, you must either use the new statement along with the variable type or store values in the array within { and } marks. You also must specify how many different items will be stored in the array. Each item in an array is called an *element*. The following statement creates an array and sets aside space for the values that it will hold:

```
int[] elfSeniority = new int[250];
```

This example creates an array of integers called elfSeniority. The array has 250 elements in it that can be used to store the number of months that each of Santa's elves has been employed at the Pole. If the rumors are true and Santa runs a union shop, this information is extremely important to keep track of.

When you create an array with the new statement, you must specify the number of elements. Each element of the array is given an initial value when it is set up with new; the value depends on the type of the array. All numeric arrays have the value 0, char arrays have the value '\0', and Boolean arrays have the value false. A string array and all other objects are created with the initial value of null.

For arrays that are not extremely large, you can set up their initial values at the same time you create them. The following example creates an array of strings and gives them initial values:

```
String[] reindeerNames = { "Dasher", "Dancer", "Prancer", "Vixen",
    "Comet", "Cupid", "Donder", "Blitzen" };
```

The information that should be put into elements of the array is put between { and } brackets, and commas separate each element. The number of elements in the array is not specified in the statement because it is set to the number of elements in the comma-separated list. Each element of the array in the list must be of the same type. The preceding example uses a string for each of the reindeer names.

Once the array is created, you cannot make more space and add another variable to the array. Even if you recall the most famous reindeer of all, you couldn't add "Rudolph" as the ninth element of the `reindeerNames` array. The `javac` compiler won't let poor Rudolph join in any `reindeerNames`.

Using Arrays

You use arrays in a program as you would use any variable, except for the element number between the square brackets next to the array's name. Once you refer to the element number, you can use an array element anywhere a variable could be used. The following statements all use arrays that already have been defined in this hour's examples:

```
elfSeniority[193] += 1;
niceChild[94287612] = "Max";
if ( hostileAirTravelNations[currentNation] == true)
    sendGiftByMail();
```

An important thing to note about arrays is that the first element of an array is numbered 0 instead of 1. This means that the highest number is one less than you might expect. For example, consider the following statement:

```
String[] topGifts = new String[10];
```

This statement creates an array of string variables that are numbered from 0 to 9. If you referred to a `topGifts[10]` somewhere else in the program, you would get an error message like the following when you run the program:

```
java.lang.ArrayIndexOutOfBoundsException:
        at SantaGifts.main(SantaGifts.java:4);
```

Like all of the error messages Java generates, this one's a bit hard to decipher. The key thing to note is the part that mentions an exception, because *exceptions* are another word for errors in Java programs. This exception is an "array out of bounds" error, which means that a program tried to use an array element that doesn't exist within its defined boundaries.

If you want to check the upper limit of an array during a program so you can avoid going beyond that limit, use a variable called `length` that is associated with each array that is created. The `length` variable is an integer that returns the number of elements an array can hold. The following example creates an array and then reports its length:

```
String[] reindeerNames = { "Dasher", "Dancer", "Prancer", "Vixen",
    "Comet", "Cupid", "Donder", "Blitzen", "Rudolph" };
System.out.println("There are " + reindeerNames.length + " reindeer.");
```

In this example, the value of `reindeerNames.length` is 9, which means that the highest element number you can specify is 8.

Multidimensional Arrays

The arrays you have been introduced to thus far in the hour all have one dimension; a line of numbers ranging from 0 to the largest element number is used to refer to an array. But some types of information require more dimensions to adequately store as arrays. An example would be the (x,y) coordinate system that's a staple in any math class. If you needed to store a list of x and y coordinates that have a point marked on them, you could use a two-dimensional array. One dimension of the array could store the x coordinate, and the other dimension could store the y coordinate.

To create an array that has two dimensions, you must use an additional set of square brackets when creating and using the array. Consider the following:

```
boolean[][] selectedPoint = new boolean[50][50];
selectedPoint[4][13] = true;
selectedPoint[7][6] = true;
selectedPoint[11][22] = true;
```

This example creates an array of Boolean values called selectedPoint. The array has 50 elements in its first dimension and 50 elements in its second dimension, so there are 2,500 individual array elements that can hold values (50 multiplied by 50). When the array is created, each element is given the default value of false. Three elements are then given the value of true: a point at the (x,y) position of (4,13), one at (7,6), and one at (11,22).

Arrays can have as many dimensions as you need, but keep in mind that they take up a lot of memory if they're extremely large. Creating the 50 by 50 selectedPoint array was equivalent to creating 2,500 individual variables.

Sorting an Array

When you have grouped a bunch of similar items together into an array, one of the things you can easily do is rearrange items. The following statements switch the values of two elements in an integer array called numbers:

```
int temp = numbers[5];
numbers[5] = numbers[6];
numbers[6] = temp;
```

These statements result in numbers[5] and numbers[6] trading values with each other. The integer variable called temp is used as a temporary storage place for one of the values being swapped.

The most common reason to rearrange elements of an array is to sort them into a specific order. *Sorting* is the process of arranging a list of related items into a set order. An example would be sorting a list of numbers from lowest to highest.

Santa Claus, the world's biggest user of lists, might want to use sorting to rearrange the order of gift recipients according to last name. This order could determine who receives gifts first on Christmas Eve, with people such as Alan Alda and Adam Arkin raking in their Yuletide plunder much earlier than alphabetical unfortunates such as Dweezil Zappa and Jim Zorn. (As someone whose last name begins with "C," I'm not necessarily opposed to this practice.)

Sorting an array is easy in Java because the `Arrays` class does all of the work for you. `Arrays`, which is part of the `java.util` group of classes, can rearrange arrays of all variable types as well as strings.

To use the `Arrays` class in a program to sort an array, undertake the following steps:

- Use the `import java.util.*;` statement to make all of the `java.util` classes available in the program.
- Create the array.
- Use the `sort()` method of the `Arrays` class to rearrange an array.

An array of variables that is sorted by the `Arrays` class will be rearranged into ascending numerical order. This will be easy to see with an array of numbers such as `float` values. Characters and strings will be arranged according to the alphabet, with the first letters such as A, B, and C coming first, and the last letters such as X, Y, and Z coming last.

Listing 9.1 contains a short program that sorts five names. Enter this with your word processor and save the file as `Name.java`.

LISTING 9.1 THE FULL SOURCE CODE OF `Name.java`

```
 1: import java.util.*;
 2:
 3: class Name {
 4:     public static void main(String arguments[]) {
 5:         String names[] = { "Akbar", "Umberto", "Percival",
 6:             "Zemo", "Diego" };
 7:         System.out.println("The original order:");
 8:         for (int i = 0; i < names.length; i++)
 9:             System.out.println(i + ": " + names[i]);
10:         Arrays.sort(names);
11:         System.out.println("The new order:");
12:         for (int i = 0; i < names.length; i++)
13:             System.out.println(i + ": " + names[i]);
14:     }
15: }
```

After you have created this source file, compile it at a command line by entering `javac Name.java`. This Java program displays a list of five names in their original order, sorts the names, and then redisplays the list.

The following output is produced:

```
The original order:
0: Akbar
1: Umberto
2: Percival
3: Zemo
4: Diego
The new order:
0: Akbar
1: Diego
2: Percival
3: Umberto
4: Zemo
```

When you're working with strings and the basic types of variables such as integers and floating-point numbers, you only can sort them by ascending order using the `Arrays` class. You can write code to do your own sorts by hand, if you desire a different arrangement of elements during a sort or you want better efficiency than the `Arrays` class provides.

> There are numerous sorting techniques that have been created for use in computer programs. The `Arrays` class uses a technique called a "tuned quicksort" that was described in a 1993 software development industry publication. Different techniques have their own names, including the heap sort, tree sort, and bubble sort.

Workshop: Array of Prizes Indeed

Watch the syndicated game show *Wheel of Fortune* for any length of time and you'll be surprised at how predictable the contestants are. In the years that this show has been one of the world's most successful television programs, fortune seekers have worked the puzzle-solving process into an exact science. *Wheel* contestants typically guess the same letters when they are starting out on a puzzle: R, S, T, L, and N. In the final round, when these letters and the vowel E are given to the players right away, they usually choose four other letters: C, D, M, and the vowel O. The reason for this predictability is that these are the letters that appear most often in English words. The contestants are stifling their desire for spontaneity in order to better their chances to win a trip to Bermuda, cash, and a Yamaha Waverunner.

In case you're unfamiliar with the show, *Wheel of Fortune* is a game in which three contestants try to guess the letters of a phrase, name, quote, or other memorable item. If they get a letter right and it's a consonant, they win the amount of money they spun on a big wheel. To re-create the experience, play Hangman with some of your friends in front of a studio audience, hand out random amounts of money when someone guesses a letter in the secret word or phrase, and give the winner a new Ford Explorer.

Your Java workshop during this hour will test the most-common-letter theory by looking at as many different phrases and expressions as you care to type. An array will be used to count the number of times that each letter appears. When you're done, the program will present each letter and the number of times it appears in the phrases you entered. It also will present some clues about which letters to avoid entirely unless you suspect that a puzzle's answer is the Aztec priest-ruler Quetzalcoatl or the fire god Xiuhtecuhtle.

Open up a new file in your word processor and call it Wheel.java. Enter Listing 9.2 and save the file when you're done.

LISTING 9.2   THE FULL SOURCE CODE OF Wheel.java

```
 1: class Wheel {
 2:     public static void main(String arguments[]) {
 3:         String phrase[] = {
 4:             "A STITCH IN TIME SAVES NINE",
 5:             "DON'T EAT YELLOW SNOW",
 6:             "JUST DO IT",
 7:             "EVERY GOOD BOY DOES FINE",
 8:             "I WANT MY MTV",
 9:             "HOW 'BOUT THEM COWBOYS",
10:             "PLAY IT AGAIN, SAM",
11:             "FROSTY THE SNOWMAN",
12:             "ONE MORE FOR THE ROAD",
13:             "HOME FIELD ADVANTAGE",
14:             "VALENTINE'S DAY MASSACRE",
15:             "GROVER CLEVELAND OHIO",
16:             "WONDERFUL WORLD OF DISNEY",
17:             "COAL MINER'S DAUGHTER",
18:             "WILL IT PLAY IN PEORIA"
19:         };
20:         int[] letterCount = new int[26];
21:         for (int count = 0; count < phrase.length; count++) {
22:             String current = phrase[count];
23:             char[] letters = current.toCharArray();
24:             for (int count2 = 0;  count2 < letters.length; count2++) {
```

```
25:                     char lett = letters[count2];
26:                     if ( (lett >= 'A') & (lett <= 'Z') ) {
27:                         letterCount[lett - 'A']++;
28:                     }
29:                 }
30:             }
31:         for (char count = 'A'; count <= 'Z'; count++) {
32:             System.out.print(count + ": " +
33:                     letterCount[count - 'A'] +
34:                     "\t");
35:         }
36:         System.out.println();
37:     }
38: }
```

9

After you compile the file and run it, the output should resemble Listing 9.3.

LISTING 9.3 OUTPUT OF THE Wheel PROGRAM

```
A: 22  B: 3   C: 5   D: 13  E: 28  F: 6   G: 5   H: 8   I: 18  J: 1
K: 0   L: 13  M: 10  N: 19  O: 27  P: 3   Q: 0   R: 13  S: 15  T: 19
U: 4   V: 7   W: 9   X: 0   Y: 10  Z: 0
```

The following things are taking place in the Wheel program:

- Lines 1 and 2: The Wheel program and the main() block of the program begin.

- Lines 3–19: Phrases are stored in a string array called phrase. Every phrase between the { on line 3 and the } on line 19 will be stored in its own element of the array, beginning with A STITCH IN TIME SAVES NINE in phrase[0].

- Line 20: An integer array called letterCount is created with 26 elements. This array will be used to store the number of times each letter appears. The order of the elements is from A to Z. letterCount[0] will store the count for letter A, letterCount[1] will store the count for B, and so on up to letterCount[25] for Z.

- Line 21: A for loop is begun that cycles through the phrases stored in the phrase array. The phrase.length variable is used in the for statement to end the loop after the last phrase is reached.

- Line 22: A string variable named current is created and set with the value of the current element of the phrase array.

- Line 23: A character array that stores all of the characters in the current phrase is created.

- Line 24: A `for` loop is begun that cycles through the letters of the current phrase. The `letters.length` variable is used to end the loop after the last letter is reached.

- Line 25: A character variable called `lett` is created with the value of the current letter. In addition to their text value, characters have a numeric value. Because elements of an array are numbered, the numeric value of each character will be used to determine its element number.

- Lines 26–28: An `if` statement is used to weed out all characters that are not part of the alphabet, such as punctuation and spaces. An element of the `letterCount` array is increased by 1, depending on the numeric value of the current character, which is stored in `lett`. The numeric values of the alphabet range from 65 for `'A'` to 90 for `'Z'`. Because the `letterCount` array begins at 0 and ends at 25, `'A'` (65) is subtracted from `lett` to determine which array element to increase.

- Line 29: One pass through the inner `for` loop ends, and the loop returns to line 24 to get the next letter in the current phrase, if there is one.

- Line 30: One pass through the outer `for` loop ends, and the loop returns to line 21 to get the next phrase, if there is one.

- Line 31: A `for` loop is used to cycle through the alphabet from `'A'` to `'Z'`.

- Lines 32–34: The current letter is displayed, followed by a semicolon and the number of times the letter appeared in the phrases stored in the `phrase` array. The `\t` inserts a Tab character.

- Line 35: One pass through the `for` loop ends, and the loop returns to line 31 to get the next character in the alphabet, unless `'Z'` has been reached.

- Lines 36–38: A blank line is displayed, followed by the end of the program's `main()` block and the end of the program.

This workshop project shows how two nested `for` loops can be used to cycle through a group of phrases one letter at a time. Java attaches a numeric value to each character; this value is easier to use than the character inside arrays.

The numeric values associated with each of the characters from 'A' to 'Z' are those used by the ASCII character set. ASCII is a standard method of arranging and numbering letters, numbers, punctuation, and other symbols that can be represented by a computer. The ASCII character set is part of Unicode, the full character set supported by the Java language. Unicode includes support for more than 60,000 different characters used in the world's written languages.

Using the `length` variable makes it possible for you to add as many phrases as desired within the { and } marks. The letters in each of the new phrases you add will be analyzed, and you can build up a better idea of what it takes to make a small fortune in 30 minutes on television.

Summary

Arrays make it possible to store complicated types of information in a program and manipulate that information. They're ideal for anything that can be arranged in a list and can be accessed easily using the loop statements that you learned about during Hour 8, "Repeating an Action with Loops."

The information processing needs of Santa Claus possibly have outgrown arrays. There are more children being manufactured each year, and the gifts they want are increasing in complexity and expense. Tickle Me Elmo alone created a logistical nightmare for him in Christmas 1996. Your programs are likely to use arrays to store information that is unwieldy to work with through variables, even if you're not making any lists or checking them twice.

Q&A

Q Do arrays have to begin with an element 0, or could they range from a higher minimum number to a higher maximum number, such as 65 to 90?

A No, but it is more efficient to do so because it takes up less memory in the computer to store arrays that begin with 0. You can use arrays of a higher index number simply by referring to the numbers you want to use. For example, if you created a `for` loop that cycled from array element 65 to element 90, you could disregard any other element numbers. However, there still will be array elements numbered from 0 to 64 taking up space in memory, even if you don't use them for anything.

Q Why are some errors called exceptions?

A The significance of the term is that a program normally runs without any problems, and the exception signals an exceptional circumstance that must be dealt with. Exceptions are warning messages that are sent from within a Java program. The Java language uses the term *error* specifically to describe error conditions that take place within the interpreter running a program.

Q In a multidimensional array, is it possible to use the `length` variable to measure different dimensions other than the first?

A You can test any dimension of the array. For the first dimension, use `length` with the name of the array, as in `x.length`. Subsequent dimensions can be measured by using `length` with the `[0]` element of that dimension. Consider an array called `data` that was created with the following statement:

```
int[][][] data = new int[12][13][14];
```

The dimensions of this array can be measured by using the `data.length` variable for the first dimension, `data[0].length` for the second, and `data[0][0].length` for the third.

Q Can the `length` variable be set to increase or decrease the size of an array after it has been created?

A There's no way to modify the size of an array after it has been created; `length` is strictly used to find out an array's upper boundary.

Quiz

If the brain were an array, you could test its `length` by answering each of the following questions about arrays.

Questions

1. What types of information are arrays best suited for?

    (a) Lists

    (b) Pairs of related information

    (c) Trivia

2. What variable can be used to check the upper boundary of an array?

    (a) `top`

    (b) `length`

    (c) `limit`

3. Who is the famous Aztec priest-ruler?

    (a) Quisp

    (b) Quetzalcoatl

    (c) Quichelorraine

Answers

1. a. Lists that contain nothing but the same type of information—strings, numbers, and so on—are well suited for storage in arrays.

2. b.

3. b. It's also the name of a god of learning and civilization who is depicted as an approaching storm whose winds kick up dust before the rain comes.

9

Activities

To give yourself an array of experiences to draw from later, you can expand your knowledge of this hour's topics with the following activities:

- Create a program that uses a multidimensional array to store student grades. The first dimension should be a number for each student, and the second dimension should be for each student's grades. Display the average of all the grades earned by each student and an overall average for every student.

- Write a program that stores the first 400 prime numbers in an array.

To see Java programs that implement these activities, visit the book's Web site at `http://www.prefect.com/java24.`.

HOUR 10

Creating Your First Object

One of the more fearsome items of jargon that you'll encounter during these 24 hours is *object-oriented programming*. This is a complicated term for an elegant way of describing what a computer program is and how it works. Before object-oriented programming, computer programs were usually described under the simplest definition you've learned in this book: sets of instructions that are listed in a file and handled in some kind of reliable order. Whether the program is big or small, the programmer's job is largely the same—write instructions for each thing the computer must do. By thinking of a program as a collection of objects instead, you can figure out the tasks a program must accomplish and assign the tasks to the objects where they best belong.

During this hour, the following topics will be covered:

- Understanding objects
- How attributes describe an object
- What determines how objects behave

- Combining objects
- Inheriting from other objects
- Creating an object
- Converting objects and other information

How Object-Oriented Programming Works

The programs you create with Java can be thought of as objects just like any other objects in the world, such as nails, skateboards, Liquid Paper, glue, or *60 Minutes* cohost Morley Safer. An object is made up of smaller objects—in the case of Mr. Safer, two legs, two arms, a torso, a head, and a reporter's notebook. Each object has things that make it different from other objects. Morley's legs are long and angular; they bend in the middle and end in feet. His arms end in hands and are shorter than the legs. Each object also has specific jobs it has to do. Morley's legs are used for movement and support, and his arms are used to grab things, take notes, and hail taxicabs. If you break down computer programs in the same way you have broken down Morley Safer, you are engaging in object-oriented programming. It's a much less complicated concept than it originally sounds.

In object-oriented programming, an object contains two things: attributes and behavior. *Attributes* are things that describe the object and show how it is different from other objects. *Behavior* is what an object does.

You create objects in Java by using a class as a template. The *class* is a master copy of the object that is consulted to determine which attributes and behavior an object should have. The term class should be familiar to you because every Java program you have written thus far has been called a class. Every program you create with Java will be a class because each one could be used as a template for the creation of new objects. As an example, any Java program that uses strings is using the String class. This class contains attributes that determine what a String object is and behavior that controls what String objects can do.

With object-oriented programming, any computer program is a group of objects that work together to get something done. Some simple programs may seem as though they consist of only one object—the class file. However, even those programs are using other objects to get their work done.

Objects in Action

Consider the case of a dice-rolling program. Rolling a six-sided die is a simple thing to do in the real world—you toss a cube and check the uppermost side of the cube when it stops rolling. When you make a computer do the same thing, you can think of the die as an object. In fact, during Hour 21, "Playing Games with Java," you will be using a `Die` object as you teach the computer to play the dice-rolling game called craps.

A `Die` object could consist of the following:

- A behavior to roll the die and figure out the result
- An attribute to store the result of a die roll

When you compare a six-sided die in the real world to a `Die` object in a computer program, it might seem odd to ask the `Die` object to roll itself. Dice don't roll themselves in the real world. However, objects in object-oriented programming work for themselves whenever possible. This quality makes them more useful because you can incorporate them in other programs without having as many things to teach them. If a `Die` object did not know how to roll itself, for instance, every time you used that `Die` object somewhere you would have to create behavior to roll it.

For another example of object-oriented programming, consider the autodialer program that Matthew Broderick's character used in *WarGames* to find computers he could hack into. If you're unfamiliar with the term, an *autodialer* is software that uses a modem to dial a series of phone numbers in sequence. The purpose of such a program is to find other computers that answer their own phones, so you can call them up later to see what they are.

Using an autodialer today practically guarantees you'll be on a first-name basis with your local phone company. In the early 80s, it was a good way to be rebellious without actually leaving the house. David Ladyman (Broderick) used his autodialer to look for a video game company's private computer system. He wanted to play the new game on which they were working. Instead, Ladyman found a secret government computer that could play everything from chess to global thermonuclear war.

An autodialer, like any computer program, can be thought of as a group of objects that work together. It could be broken down into the following:

- A `Modem` object, which knows how to make the modem dial a number and how to report when another computer system has answered a call
- A `Monitor` object, which keeps track of what numbers were called and which ones were successful and can save this information for inspection later

Each object exists independently of the other. The Modem object does its job without requiring any help from the Monitor object.

One of the advantages of having a completely independent Modem object is that it could be used in other programs that need modem functionality. If Broderick's character returns to hacking in *WarGames 1998* after a bitter divorce from Ally Sheedy's character, he could use the Modem object as part of an elaborate ATM fraud scheme.

Another reason to use self-contained programs such as objects is that they are easier to debug. Computer programs quickly become unwieldy in size. If your program is just one big list of instructions, you can't change one part without making sure it won't damage the performance of other parts that are dependent on it. If you're debugging something like a Modem object, though, you know it's not dependent on anything else. You can focus on making sure the Modem object does the job it's supposed to do and holds the information that it needs to do its job.

For these reasons, object-oriented programming is becoming the norm in many areas of software development. Learning an object-oriented language like Java as your first programming language can be an advantage in some ways because you're not unlearning the habits of other styles of programming. The main disadvantage is that an object-oriented language can be more challenging to learn that a non-object-oriented language such as Visual Basic.

What Objects Are

As stated, objects are created by using a class of objects as a guideline. The following is an example of a class:

```
public class Dog {
}
```

Any object created from this class can't do anything because it doesn't have any attributes or behavior yet. You need to add those or this class that won't be terribly useful. You could expand the class into the following:

```
public class Dog {
    String name;

    public void speak() {
        System.out.println("Arf! Arf!");
    }
}
```

The Dog class now should be recognizable to you because it looks a lot like the programs you wrote during Hours 1 through 9. The Dog class begins with a class statement, as your programs have, except that it has a `public` statement alongside it. The `public` statement means that the class is available for use by the public—in other words, by any program that wants to use `Dog` objects.

The first part of the `Dog` class creates a string variable called `name`. This variable is an attribute of the object; the name is one of the things that distinguishes a dog from other dogs. The second part of the `Dog` class is a method called `speak()`. This method has one statement, a `System.out.println()` statement that displays the text, `Arf! Arf!`

If you wanted to use a `Dog` object in a program, you would create the object much like you would create a variable. You could use the following statement:

```
Dog firstDog = new Dog();
```

This statement creates a `Dog` object called `firstDog`. You can now use the object in the program; you can set its variables and call its methods. To set the value of the `name` variable of the `firstDog` object, you could use the following statement:

```
firstDog.name = "Checkers";
```

To make this dog speak by calling the `speak()` method, you could use the following code:

```
firstDog.speak();
```

Like a well-trained pet, the `Dog` object would respond to this statement by displaying the text, `Arf! Arf!`

Understanding Inheritance

The final selling point to object-oriented programming is called inheritance. *Inheritance* is the way one object can inherit behavior and attributes from other objects that are similar to it.

When you start creating objects for use in other programs, you will find that some new objects you want are a lot like other objects that have already been developed. For example, if David Ladyman does not run afoul of the law because of his ATM scheme, he might want to create an object that can handle error correction and other advanced modem features that weren't around back in 1983 when *WarGames* was released.

Ladyman could create a new `ErrorCorrectionModem` object by copying the statements of the `Modem` object and revising them. However, if most of the behavior and attributes of `ErrorCorrectionModem` are the same as those of `Modem`, this is a lot of unnecessary work. It also means that Ladyman will have to maintain two separate programs if something needs to be changed or debugged later. Through inheritance, a programmer can create a new class of objects by defining only how it is different from an existing class. Ladyman could make ErrorCorrectionModem inherit from Modem, and all he would have to write are the things that make error-correction modems different than previous modems.

The way a class of objects inherits from another class is through the extends statement. The following is a skeleton of an ErrorCorrectionModem class that inherits from the Modem class:

```
class ErrorCorrectionModem extends Modem {
    // program goes here
}
```

Building an Inheritance Hierarchy

Inheritance enables a variety of related classes to be developed without a lot of redundant work. Inheritance can be passed down from one class to another class to another class. This system of classes is called a class hierarchy, and all of the standard classes you can use in your Java programs are part of a hierarchy.

Understanding a hierarchy is easier if you understand what subclasses and superclasses are. A class that inherits from another class is called a *subclass,* and the class that is inherited from is called a *superclass.*

In the preceding *WarGames* example, the Modem class is the superclass of the ErrorCorrectionModem class, and ErrorCorrectionModem is the subclass of Modem. A class can have more than one class that inherits from it in the hierarchy—another subclass of Modem could be ISDNModem, since ISDN modems have behavior and attributes that make them different from error-correcting modems. If there were a subclass of ErrorCorrectionModem such as InternalErrorCorrectionModem, it would inherit from all classes above it in the hierarchy—both ErrorCorrectionModem and Modem. These inheritance relationships are shown in Figure 10.1.

The programs you write as you are learning about Java won't use complicated class hierarchies. However, the classes that are part of the standard Java language make full use of inheritance. Understanding it is essential to making the most of the classes that are part of the Java language. You'll learn more about inheritance during Hour 12, "Making the Most of Existing Objects."

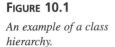

FIGURE 10.1

An example of a class hierarchy.

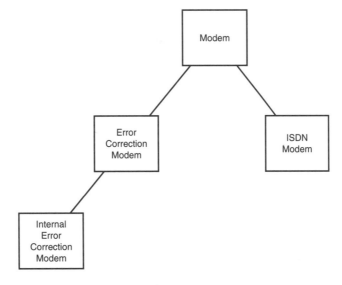

Converting Objects and Simple Variables

One of the most common tasks you'll need to accomplish in Java is to convert information from one form into another. There are several types of conversions you can do:

- Converting an object into another object.
- Converting a simple variable into another type of variable.
- Using an object to create a simple variable.
- Using a simple variable to create an object.

Simple variables are the basic data types you learned about during Hour 5, "Storing and Changing Information in a Program." These types include int, float, char, long, and double.

When using a method or an expression in a program, you must use the right type of information that's expected by these methods and expressions. A method that expects a string object must receive a string object, for instance. If you used a method that takes a single integer argument and you sent it a floating-point number instead, an error would occur when you attempted to compile the program.

Converting information into a new form in a program is called *casting*. Casting produces a new value that is a different type of variable or object than its source. You don't actually change the value of a variable or object when it is cast. Instead, a new variable or object is created in the format you need.

There is one area in which Java is less particular: strings. When a method such as `System.out.println()` requires a string argument, you can use the + operator to combine several different types of information in that argument. As long as one of the things being combined is a string, the combined argument will be converted into a string. This makes the following statements possible:

```
float sentence = 17.5F;
System.out.println("My sentence has been reduced to "
    + sentence + "years.");
```

The terms *source* and *destination* are useful when discussing the concept of casting. The source is some kind of information in its original form—whether its a variable or an object. The destination is the converted version of the source in its new form.

Casting Simple Variables

With simple variables, casting occurs most commonly between numeric variables such as integers and floating-point numbers. There's one type of variable that cannot be used in any casting: Boolean values.

To cast information into a new format, you precede it with the new format surrounded by parenthesis marks. For example, if you wanted to cast something into a `long` variable, you would precede it with `(long)`.

The following statements cast a `float` value into an `int`:

```
float source = 7.06F;
int destination = (int)source;
```

In a variable cast where the destination holds larger values than the source, the value is converted easily. An example is when a `byte` is cast into an `int`. A `byte` holds values from –128 to 127, while an `int` holds values from –2.1 million to 2.1 million. No matter what value the `byte` variable holds, there's plenty of room for it in a new `int` variable.

You sometimes can use a variable in a different format without casting it at all. For example, `char` variables can be used as if they were `int` variables. Also, `int` variables can be used as if they were `long` variables, and anything can be used as a `double`.

In most cases, because the destination provides more room than the source, the information is converted without changing its value. The main exceptions occur when an `int` or `long` variable is cast to a `float`, or a `long` is cast into a `double`.

> A character can be used as an `int` variable because each character has a corresponding numeric code that represents its position in the character set. As an example, if the variable `k` has the value 67, the cast `(char)k` produces the character value `C` because the numeric code associated with a capital `C` is 67, according to the ASCII character set. The ASCII character set is part of the Unicode character standard adopted by the Java language.

When you are converting information from a larger variable type into a smaller type, you must explicitly cast it with statements such as the following:

```
int xNum = 103;
byte val = (byte)xNum;
```

Casting is used to convert an integer value called `xNum` into a `byte` variable called `val`. This is an example where the destination variable holds a smaller range of values than the source variable. A `byte` holds integer values ranging from -128 to 127, and an `int` holds a much larger range of integer values: -2.14 billion to 2.14 billion.

When the source variable in a casting operation has a value that isn't allowed in the destination variable, Java will change the value in order to make the cast fit successfully. This can produce unexpected results if you're not expecting the change.

Casting Objects

Objects can be cast into other objects as long as the source and destination are related by inheritance. One class must be a subclass of the other.

Some objects do not require casting at all. An object can be used where any of its superclasses are expected. For example, because all objects in Java are subclasses of the `Object` class, you can use any object as an argument when an `Object` is expected.

You also can use an object where one of its subclasses is expected. However, because subclasses usually contain more information than their superclasses, you might lose some of this information. If the object doesn't have a method that the subclass would contain, an error will result if that missing method is used in the program.

To use an object in the place of one of its subclasses, you must cast it explicitly with statements such as the following:

```
Window win = new Window();
Frame top = new (Frame)win;
```

This casts a `Window` object called `win` into a `Frame` object. You won't lose any information in the cast, but you gain all the methods and variables the subclass defines.

Converting Simple Variables to Objects and Back

One thing you can't do is cast an object to a simple variable or a simple variable to an object. These types of information are too different in Java for them to be substituted for each other.

Instead, there are classes in the java.lang package for each of the simple variable types: Boolean, Byte, Character, Double, Float, Integer, Long, and Short. All of these classes are capitalized, which serves as a reminder that they are objects rather than simple variable types.

Using class methods defined in each of these classes, you can create an object using a variable's value as an argument. The following statement creates an Integer object with the value 5309:

```
Integer suffix = new Integer(5309);
```

After you have created an object like this, you can use it like any other object. When you want to use that value again as a simple variable, the class has methods for this also. For example, to get an int value from the preceding suffix object, the following statement can be used:

```
int newSuff = suffix.intValue(); // returns 5309
```

One of the most commonplace casts from an object to a variable is when you have a string that should be used in a numeric way. This is done by using the parseInt() method of the Integer class, as in the following example:

```
String count = "25";
int myCount = Integer.parseInt(count);
```

This converts a string with the text 25 into an integer with the value 25.

Workshop: Creating an Object

To see a working example of classes and inheritance, you will create classes that represent two types of objects: dogs and Morley Safer. Dogs will be handled by the Dog class, and Mr. Safer will be handled by the MorleySafer class.

For the sake of simplicity, the workshop will focus on a few simple attributes and behavior for these objects:

- Each object should have a name and be able to remember it.
- Each object should snore when it sleeps.

- Each object should speak in an accurate way. Although dogs and Morley Safer can remember their own names and snore in the same manner, they do not speak in the same manner.

The first two things are shared between dogs and Morley Safer. Because of this, the behavior and attributes can be put into a class that is the superclass of both the `Dog` and `MorleySafer` classes. Call this class `Mammal`. Using your word processor, create a new file and save it as `Mammal.java`. Enter Listing 10.1 and save the file.

LISTING 10.1 THE FULL TEXT OF `Mammal.java`

```
1: public class Mammal {
2:     String name;
3:
4:     public void sleep() {
5:         System.out.println("ZZZZ ZZZZZZ ZZZZ");
6:     }
7: }
```

Compile this file with the `javac` compiler tool to produce a file called `Mammal.class`. Although you cannot run this program with the interpreter, you will be able to use it in other classes. You now have a `Mammal` class that can handle both of the things that the `Dog` and `MorleySafer` classes have in common. By using the `extends` statement when you are creating the `Dog` and `MorleySafer` classes, you can make each of them a subclass of `Mammal`.

Start a new file in your word processor and save it as `Dog.java`. Enter Listing 10.2 and then save and compile the file.

LISTING 10.2 THE FULL TEXT OF `Dog.java`

```
1: public class Dog extends Mammal {
2:     public void speak() {
3:         System.out.println("Arf! Arf!");
4:     }
5: }
```

Create a third file with your word processor, and save it as `MorleySafer.java`. Enter Listing 10.3 and then save and compile the file when you're done.

LISTING 10.3 THE FULL TEXT OF MorleySafer.java

```
1: public class MorleySafer extends Mammal {
2:     public void speak() {
3:         System.out.println("Can I ask you a few questions about "
4:             + "your 1987 tax statement?");
5:     }
6: }
```

Once you have compiled all three of these files with the javac compiler tool, you will have three class files: Mammal.class, Dog.class, and MorleySafer.class. However, you cannot run any of these class files at the command line with the java interpreter tool because they do not have main() blocks. You need to create a short Java program to test out the class hierarchy you have just built.

Return to your word processor and create a new file called Speak.java. Enter Listing 10.4.

LISTING 10.4 THE FULL TEXT OF Speak.java

```
1: class Speak {
2:     public static void main(String[] arguments) {
3:         Dog doggie = new Dog();
4:         MorleySafer morley = new MorleySafer();
5:         doggie.name = "Cujo";
6:         morley.name = "Morley Safer";
7:         System.out.println("First we'll get the dog to speak:");
8:         doggie.speak();
9:         System.out.println("Now it's Morley's turn to speak:");
10:         morley.speak();
11:         System.out.println("Time for both to sleep:");
12:         doggie.sleep();
13:         morley.sleep();
14:     }
15: }
```

Save and compile the file when you're done. When you run it, the output should resemble the following:

OUTPUT
```
First we'll get the dog to speak:
Arf! Arf!
Now it's Morley's turn to speak:
Can I ask you a few questions about your 1987 tax statement?
Time for both to sleep:
ZZZZ ZZZZZZ ZZZZ
ZZZZ ZZZZZZ ZZZZ
```

Note the following statements in this program:

- Lines 3 and 4: Two new objects are created, a Dog object called doggie and a MorleySafer object called morley.

- Line 5: The name variable of the Dog object doggie is set to Cujo.

- Line 6: The name variable of the MorleySafer object morley is set to Morley Safer.

- Line 8: The speak() method of the doggie object is called. Looking at the speak() method of the Dog class of objects, you can see that it displays the text, Arf! Arf!.

- Line 10: The speak() method of the morley object is called, resulting in the display of the following text: Can I ask you a few questions about your 1987 tax statement?

- Lines 12 and 13: The sleep() methods of doggie and then morley are called. If you look at the Dog class or the MorleySafer class, you won't find a sleep() method. However, because Dog and MorleySafer both inherit from the Mammal class, you should look there to see if it has a sleep() method that could have been inherited by its subclasses. The Mammal class does have a sleep() method, so the snoring text, ZZZZ ZZZZZZ ZZZZ, is displayed twice.

Summary

After creating your first class of objects and arranging several classes into a hierarchy, you ought to be more comfortable with the term *object-oriented programming*. You will be learning more about object behavior and attributes in the next two hours as you start creating more sophisticated objects.

Terms such as *program*, *class*, and *object* will make more sense as you have more experience with object-oriented development. It's a concept that takes some time to get used to. Once you have mastered it, you'll find that it's an effective way to design, develop, and debug computer programs.

Q&A

Q Can classes inherit from more than one class?

A It's possible with some programming languages but not Java. Multiple inheritance is a powerful feature, but it also makes object-oriented programming a bit harder to use and to learn. Java's developers decided to limit inheritance to one superclass for any class, although a class can have numerous subclasses. One way to compensate for this limitation is to inherit methods from a special type of class called an interface. You'll learn more about interfaces during Hour 14, "Creating a Threaded Applet."

Q **Why are object-oriented programs easier to debug?**

A Object-oriented programs enable you to focus on a smaller part of a computer program when figuring out where an error is happening. Because a related group of tasks is handled by the same object, you can focus on that object if the tasks aren't being performed correctly. You don't have to worry about any other parts of the program.

Q **When would you want to create a class that isn't `public`?**

A The main time you would not want to make a class of objects available to other programs is when the class is strictly for the use of one program you're writing. If you're creating a game program and your `ReloadGun` class of objects is highly specific to the game you're writing, it could be a `private` class. To keep a class from being `public`, leave off the `public` statement in front of `class`.

Quiz

The following questions will test your knowledge of objects and the programs that use them.

Questions

1. What statement is used to enable one class to inherit from another class?

    (a) `inherits`

    (b) `extends`

    (c) `handitover`

2. Why are compiled Java programs saved with the `.class` file extension?

    (a) Java's developers think it's a classy language.

    (b) It's a subtle tribute to the world's teachers.

    (c) Every Java program is a class.

3. What are the two things that make up an object?

    (a) Attributes and behavior

    (b) Commands and data files

    (c) Spit and vinegar

Answers

1. b. The `extends` statement is used because the subclass is an extension of the attributes and behavior of the superclass and of any superclasses above that in the class hierarchy.

2. c. Your programs will always be made up of at least one main class and any other classes that are needed.

3. a. In a way, b is also true because commands are comparable to behavior, and data files are analogous to attributes.

Activities

If you don't object, you can `extends` your knowledge of this hour's topics with the following activity:

- Create a few more classes of objects to go under the `Mammal` class alongside `Dog` and `MorleySafer`. Add classes for ducks, horses, *60 Minutes* correspondent Mike Wallace, and owls that do not snore. By creating an `Owl` class that inherits from `Mammal` and putting a new `sleep()` method in `Owl`, you can create your own special snoring statement for that creature.

To see Java programs that implement this activity, visit the book's Web site at `http://www.prefect.com/java24`.

10

Hour 11

Describing What Your Object Is Like

As you learned during last hour's introduction to object-oriented programming, an object is a way of organizing a program so that it has everything it needs to accomplish a task. Objects need two things to do their jobs: attributes and behavior.

Attributes are the information stored within an object. They can be variables such as integers, characters, Boolean values, or even other objects. Behavior is the groups of statements used to handle specific jobs within the object. Each of these groups is called a *method*.

Up to this point, you have been working with the methods and variables of objects without knowing it. Any time your statement had a period in it that wasn't a decimal point or part of a string, chances are an object was involved. You'll see this during this coming hour as the following topics are covered:

- Creating variables for an object
- Creating variables for a class

- Using methods with objects and classes
- Calling a method in a statement
- Returning a value with a method
- Creating constructor methods
- Sending arguments to a method
- Using this to refer to an object
- Creating new objects
- Putting one object inside another

For the purposes of this hour's examples, you'll be looking at a class of objects called Virus whose sole purpose in life is to reproduce in as many places as possible—much like some of my college classmates. A Virus has several different things it needs in order to do its work, and these will be implemented as the behavior of the class. The information that's needed for the methods will be stored as attributes.

The example in this hour will not teach actual virus writing, though it might provide some insight into how virus programs work as they wreak havoc on the file systems of the computer-loving world. This publisher had scheduled *Sams' Teach Yourself Virus Programming in a Three-Day Weekend* for spring of this year, but the book has been postponed because the author's hard drive was unexpectedly erased on Michaelangelo's birthday.

Creating Variables

The attributes of an object represent any variables needed in order for the object to function. These variables could be simple data types such as integers, characters, and floating-point numbers, or they could be arrays or objects of classes such as String or Graphics. An object's variables can be used throughout its program, in any of the methods the object includes. You create variables immediately after the class statement that creates the class and before any methods.

One of the things that a Virus object needs is a way to indicate that a file already has been infected. Some computer viruses change the field that stores the time a file was last modified; for example, a virus might move the time from 13:41:20 to 13:41:61. Because no normal file would be saved on the 61st second of a minute, the time is a sign that the file was infected. The Virus object will use 86 as the seconds field of a file's modification time because "86 it" is slang that means to throw something away—exactly the kind of unpleasant antisocial connotation we're going for. The value will be stored in an integer variable called newSeconds.

The following statements begin a class called `Virus` with an attribute called `newSeconds` and two other attributes:

```
public class Virus {
    public int newSeconds = 86;
    public String author = "Sam Snett";
    int maxFileSize = 30000;
```

All three variables are attributes for the class: `newSeconds`, `maxFileSize`, and `author`.

Putting a statement such as `public` in a variable declaration is called *access control*, because it determines how other classes can use that variable—or if they can use it at all.

The `newSeconds` variable has a starting value of `86`, and the statement that creates it has `public` as the first part of the statement. Making a variable `public` makes it possible to modify the variable from another program that is using the `Virus` object. If the other program attaches special significance to the number `92`, for instance, it can change `newSeconds` to that value. If the other program creates a `Virus` object called `influenza`, it could set that object's `newSeconds` variable with the following statement:

```
influenza.newSeconds = 92;
```

In the `Virus` class, the `author` variable also is `public`, so it can be changed freely from other programs. The other variable, `maxFileSize`, can only be used within the class itself.

When you make a variable in a class `public`, the class loses control over how that variable is used by other programs. In many cases, this might not be a problem. For example, the `author` variable can be changed to any name or pseudonym that identifies the author of the virus, and the only restriction is aesthetic. The name might eventually be used on court documents if you're prosecuted, so you don't want to pick a dumb one. *The State of Ohio v. LoveHandles* doesn't have the same ring to it as *Ohio v. April Mayhem*.

Restricting access to a variable keeps errors from occurring if the variable is set incorrectly by another program. With the `Virus` class, if `newSeconds` is set to a value of 60 or less, it won't be reliable as a way to tell that a file is infected. Some files might be saved with that number of seconds regardless of the virus, and they'll look infected to `Virus`. If the `Virus` class of objects needs to guard against this problem, you need to do these two things:

- Switch the variable from `public` to `protected` or `private`, two other statements that provide more restrictive access.
- Add behavior to change the value of the variable and report the value of the variable to other programs.

A `protected` variable only can be used in the same class as the variable, any subclasses of that class, or by classes in the same package. A *package* is a group of related classes that serve a common purpose. An example is the `java.util` package, which contains classes that offer useful utility functions such as date and time programming and file archiving. When you use the `import` statement in a Java program with an asterisk, as in `import java.util.*;`, you are making the classes of a package available for use in that program.

A `private` variable is restricted even further than a `protected` variable—it only can be used in the same class. Unless you know that a variable can be changed to anything without affecting how its class functions, you probably should make the variable `private` or `protected`.

The following statement makes `newSeconds` a `private` variable:

```
private int newSeconds = 86;
```

If you want other programs to use the `newSeconds` variable in some way, you'll have to create behavior that makes it possible. This task will be covered later in the hour.

There is another type of access control: The lack of any `public`, `private`, or `protected` statement when the variable is created.

In the programs you have created prior to this hour, you didn't specify any of these statements. When no access control is specified, the variable is available to be used by any classes in the same package. This often is called default or package access, although there are no statements used to declare it specifically when creating a variable.

Creating Class Variables

When you create an object, it has its own version of all variables that are part of the object's class. Each object created from the Virus class of objects has its own version of the `newSeconds`, `maxFileSize`, and `author` variables. If you modified one of these variables in an object, it would not affect the same variable in another Virus object.

There are times when an attribute has more to do with an entire class of objects than a specific object itself. For example, if you wanted to keep track of how many Virus objects were being used in a program, it would not make sense to store this value repeatedly in each Virus object. Instead, you can use a class variable to store this kind of information. You can use this variable with any object of a class, but only one copy of the variable exists for the whole class. The variables you have been creating for objects thus far can be called *object variables*, because they are tied to a specific object. *Class variables* refer to a class of objects as a whole.

Both types of variables are created and used in the same way, except that `static` is used in the statement that creates class variables. The following statement creates a class variable for the `Virus` example:

```
static int virusCount = 0;
```

Changing the value of a class variable is no different than changing an object's variables. If you have a `Virus` object called `tuberculosis`, you could change the class variable `virusCount` with the following statement:

```
tuberculosis.virusCount++;
```

Because class variables apply to an entire class instead of a specific object, you can use the name of the class instead:

```
Virus.virusCount++;
```

Both statements accomplish the same thing, but there's an advantage to using the name of the class when working with class variables. It shows immediately that `virusCount` is a class variable instead of an object's variable, because you can't refer to object variables using the name of a class. If you always use object names when working with class variables, you won't be able to tell whether they are class or object variables without looking carefully at the source code of the class.

11

Creating Behavior with Methods

Attributes are the way to keep track of information about a class of objects, but they don't actually take any action. For a class to actually do the things it was created to do, you must create behavior. Behavior describes all of the different sections of a class that accomplish specific tasks. Each of these sections is called a *method*.

You have been using methods throughout your programs up to this point without knowing it, including two in particular: `println()` in Java applications and `drawString()` in applets. These methods display text onscreen. Like variables, methods are used in connection with an object or a class. The name of the object or class is followed by a period and the name of the method, as in `screen.drawString()` or `Integer.parseInt()`.

Declaring a Method

You create methods with a statement that looks similar to the statement that begins a class. Both can take arguments between parentheses after their names, and both use { and } marks at the beginning and end. The difference is that methods can send back a value after they are handled. The value can be one of the simple types such as integers or Boolean values, or it can be a class of objects. If a method should not return any value, use the statement `void`.

The System.out.println() method might seem confusing because it has two periods instead of one. This is because two classes are involved in the statement—the System class and the PrintStream class. The System class has a variable called out that is a PrintStream object. println() is a method of the PrintStream class. The System.out.println() statement means, in effect, "Use the println() method of the out variable of the System class." You can chain together references to variables and methods in this way.

The following is an example of a method the Virus class can use to infect files:

```
public boolean infectFile(String filename) {
    boolean success = false;
    // file-infecting statements would be here
    return success;
}
```

The infectFile() method is used to add a virus to a file. This method takes a single argument, a string variable called filename, and this variable represents the file that should be attacked. The actual code to infect a file is omitted here due to the author's desire to stay on the good side of the U.S. Secret Service. The only thing you need to know is that if the infection is a success, the success variable is set to a value of true.

By looking at the statement that begins the method, you can see boolean preceding the name of the method, infectFile. This statement signifies that a boolean value will be sent back after the method is handled. The return statement is what actually sends a value back. In this example, the value of success is returned.

When a method returns a value, you can use the method as part of an assignment statement. For example, if you created a Virus object called malaria, you could use statements such as these:

```
if (malaria.infectFile(currentFile))
    System.out.println(currentFile + " has been infected!");
else
    System.out.println("Curses! Foiled again!");
```

Any method that returns a value can be used anywhere a value or variable could be used in a program.

Earlier in the hour, you switched the newSeconds variable to private to prevent it from being set by other programs. However, because you're a virus writer who cares about people, you still want to make it possible for newSeconds to be used if it is used correctly. The way to do this is to create public methods in the Virus class that read the value of newSeconds or write a new value to newSeconds. These new methods should be public, unlike the newSeconds variable itself, so they can be called by other programs. The new methods will be able to work with newSeconds because they are in the same class as the variable.

Consider the following two methods:

```
public int getSeconds() {
    return newSeconds;
}

public void setSeconds(int newValue) {
    if (newValue > 60)
        newSeconds = newValue;
}
```

The getSeconds() method is used to send back the current value of newSeconds. The getSeconds() method is necessary because other programs can't even look at a private variable such as newSeconds. The getSeconds() method does not have any arguments, but it still must have parentheses after the method name. Otherwise, when you were using getSeconds in a program, the method would look no different than a variable.

The setSeconds() method takes one argument, an integer called newValue. This integer contains the value that a program wants to change newSeconds to. If newValue is greater than 60, the change will be made. The setSeconds() method has void preceding the method name, so it does not return any kind of value.

In this example, the Virus class controls how the newSeconds variable can be used by other classes. This process is called *encapsulation*, and it's a fundamental concept of object-oriented programming. The better your objects are able to protect themselves against misuse, the more useful they will be when you use them in other programs.

Similar Methods with Different Arguments

As you have seen with the setSeconds() method, you can send arguments to a method to affect what it does. Different methods in a class can have different names, but methods also can have the same name if they have different arguments.

Two methods can have the same name if they have a different number of arguments, or the specific arguments are of different variable types. For example, it might be useful for the Virus class of objects to have two tauntUser() methods. One could have no arguments at all and would deliver a generic taunt. The other could specify the taunt as a string argument. The following statements could implement these methods:

```
void tauntUser() {
    System.out.println("The problem is not with your set, but "
        + "with yourselves.");
}
```

```
void tauntUser(String taunt) {
    System.out.println(taunt);
}
```

Constructor Methods

When you want to create an object in a program, the new statement is used, as in the following example:

```
Virus typhoid = new Virus();
```

This statement creates a new Virus object called typhoid. When you use the new statement, a special method of that object's class is called. This method is called a *constructor*, because it handles the work required to create the object. The purpose of a constructor is to set up any variables and other things that need to be established for the object to function properly.

Constructor methods are defined like other methods, except that they cannot return a value as other methods do. The following are two constructor methods for the Virus class of objects:

```
public Virus() {
    author = "Ignoto";
    maxFileSize = 30000;
}

public Virus(String name, int size) {
    author = name;
    maxFileSize = size;
}
```

Like other methods, constructors can use the arguments they are sent as a way to define more than one constructor in a class. In this example, the first constructor would be called when a new statement such as the following is used:

```
Virus mumps = new Virus();
```

The other constructor could be called only if a string and an integer were sent as arguments with the new statement, as in this example:

```
Virus rubella = new Virus("April Mayhem", 60000);
```

If you don't include any constructor methods in a class, it will inherit a single constructor method with no arguments from its superclass. There also might be other constructor methods that it inherits, depending on the superclass used.

In any class, there must be a constructor method that has the same number and type of arguments as the new statement that's used to create objects of that class. In the example of the Virus class, which has Virus() and a Virus(String name, int size) constructors, you only could create Virus objects with two different types of new statements: one without arguments and one with a string and an integer as the only two arguments.

Class Methods

Like class variables, class methods are a way to provide functionality associated with an entire class instead of a specific object. Use a class method when the method does nothing that affects an individual object of the class. One example that you have used in a previous hour was the parseInt() method of the Integer class. This method is used to convert a string to a variable of the type int, as in the following:

```
int time = Integer.parseInt(timeText);
```

To make a method into a class method, use static in front of the method name, as in the following:

```
static void showVirusCount() {
    System.out.println("There are " + virusCount + " viruses.");
}
```

The virusCount class variable was used earlier to keep track of how many Virus objects have been created by a program. The showVirusCount() method is a class method that displays this total, and it should be called with a statement such as the following:

```
Virus.showVirusCount();
```

Variable Scope Within Methods

When you create a variable or an object inside a method in one of your classes, it is usable only inside that method. The reason for this is the concept of *variable scope*. Scope is the section in which a variable exists in a program. If you go outside of the part of the program defined by the scope, you can no longer use the variable.

The { and } statements in a program define the boundaries for a variable. Any variable created within these marks cannot be used outside of them. For example, consider the following statements:

```
if (numFiles < 1) {
    String warning = "No files remaining.";
}
System.out.println(warning);
```

This example does not work correctly because the warning variable was created inside the brackets of the if block statement. Those brackets define the scope of the variable. The warning variable does not exist outside of the brackets, so the System.out.println() method cannot use it as an argument.

11

When you use a set of brackets inside another set of brackets, you'll need to pay attention to the scope of the variables with which you are working. Take a look at the following example:

```
if (infectedFiles < 5) {
    int status = 1;
    if (infectedFiles < 1) {
        boolean firstVirus = true;
        status = 0;
    } else {
        firstVirus = false;
    }
}
```

In this example the status variable can be used anywhere, but the firstVirus variable will cause a compiler error. Because firstVirus is created within the scope of the if (infectedFiles < 1) statement, it doesn't exist inside the scope of the else statement that follows.

To fix the problem, firstVirus must be created outside both of these blocks so that its scope includes both them. One solution would be to create firstVirus at the same time that status is created.

Rules that enforce scope make programs easier to debug because scope limits the area in which a variable can be used. This reduces one of the most common errors that can crop up in many programming languages: the same variable being used two different ways in different parts of a program. By enforcing restrictive rules for a variable's scope, the Java language makes it more difficult to misuse a variable.

The concept of scope applies to methods also, because they are defined by an opening bracket and closing bracket. A variable created inside a method cannot be used in other methods. You only can use a variable in more than one method if it was created as an object variable or class variable after the class statement at the beginning of the program.

Putting One Class Inside Another

Although a Java program sometimes is called a class, there are many occasions when a program requires more than one class to get its work done. A multiclass program consists of a main class and any helper classes that are needed. These helper classes earn their name by helping the main class do its work.

An example might be a Java applet that displays a scrolling headline as part of its graphical user interface. The headline could be an independent object in the program, just like other interface elements such as buttons and scroll bars. It makes sense to put the headline into its own class rather than including its variables and methods in the `applet` class.

When you divide a program into multiple classes, there are two ways to define the helper classes.

One way is to define each class separately, as in the following example:

```
public class WreakHavoc {
    String author = "Ignoto";

    public void infectFile() {
        VirusCode vic = new VirusCode(1024);
    }
}

class VirusCode {
    int vSize;

    VirusCode(int size) {
        vSize = size;
    }
}
```

In this example, the `VirusCode` class is being used as a helper of the `WreakHavoc` class. Helper classes often will be defined in the same `.java` source file as the class they're assisting. When the source file is compiled, multiple class files will be produced. The preceding example would produce the files `WreakHavoc.class` and `VirusCode.class`.

If more than one class is defined in the same source file, only one of the classes can be `public`. The other classes should not have `public` in their class statements. Also, the name of the source file should match the name of the `public` class. In the preceding example, the name should be `WreakHavoc.java`.

When creating a main class and a helper class, you also can put the helper inside the main class. When this is done, the helper class is called an *inner class*.

An inner class is placed within the opening bracket and closing bracket of another class.

```
public class WreakMoreHavoc {
    String author = "Ignoto";

    public void infectFile() {
        VirusCode vic = new VirusCode(1024);
    }
```

```
class VirusCode {
    int vSize;

    VirusCode(int size) {
        vSize = size;
    }
}
}
```

An inner class can be used in the same manner as any other kind of helper class. The main difference—other than its location—is what happens after the compiler gets through with these classes. Inner classes do not get the name indicated by their class statement. Instead, the compiler gives them a name that includes the name of the main class.

In the preceding example, the compiler produces WreakHavoc.class and WreakHavoc$VirusCode.class.

> This section illustrates one of the simplest examples of how an inner class can be defined and used. Inner classes are an advanced feature of Java that you won't encounter often as you first learn the language. The functionality they offer can be accomplished by using helper classes defined separately from a main class, and that's the best course to take as you're starting out in programming.

Using the this Keyword

Because you can refer to variables and methods in other classes along with variables and methods in your own classes, the variable you're referring to can become confusing in some circumstances. One way to make things a little clearer is with the this statement. The this statement is a way to refer in a program to the program's own object.

When you are using an object's methods or variables, you put the name of the object in front of the method or variable name, separated by a period. Consider these examples:

```
Virus chickenpox = new Virus();
chickenpox.name = "LoveHandles";
chickenpox.setSeconds(75);
```

These statements create a new Virus object called chickenpox, set the name variable of chickenpox, and then call the setSeconds() method of chickenpox.

There are times in a program when you need to refer to the current object—in other words, the object represented by the program itself. For example, inside the Virus class, you might have a method that has its own variable called author:

```
void public checkAuthor() {
    String author = null;
}
```

A variable called author exists within the scope of the checkAuthor() method, but it isn't the same variable as an object variable called author. If you wanted to refer to the current object's author variable, you have to use the this statement, as in the following:

```
System.out.println(this.author);
```

By using this, you make it clear to which variable or method you are referring. You can use this anywhere in a class that you would refer to an object by name. If you wanted to send the current object as an argument in a method, for example, you could use a statement such as the following:

```
verifyData(this);
```

In many cases, the this statement will not be needed to make it clear that you're referring to an object's variables and methods. However, there's no detriment to using this any time you want to be sure you're referring to the right thing.

Workshop: Using Class Methods and Variables

11

At the insistence of every attorney and management executive in the Macmillan family of computer publishers, the workshop for this hour will not be the creation of a working virus program. Instead, you'll create a simple Virus object that can do only one thing: Count the number of Virus objects that a program has created and report the total.

Load your word processor and create a new file called Virus.java. Enter Listing 11.1 into the word processor and save the file when you're done.

LISTING 11.1   THE FULL TEXT OF Virus.java

```
 1: public class Virus {
 2:     static int virusCount = 0;
 3:
 4:     public Virus() {
 5:         virusCount++;
 6:     }
 7:
 8:     static int getVirusCount() {
 9:         return virusCount;
10:     }
11: }
```

Compile the file and return to your word processor. To test out this new Virus class, you need to create a second class that can create Virus objects.

The VirusLook class is a simple application that creates Virus objects and then counts the number of objects that have been created with the getVirusCount() class method of the Virus class.

Open up a new file with your word processor and enter Listing 11.2. Save the file as VirusLook.java when you're done.

LISTING 11.2 THE FULL TEXT OF VirusLook.java

```
 1: class VirusLook {
 2:     public static void main(String[] arguments) {
 3:         int numViruses = Integer.parseInt(arguments[0]);
 4:         if (numViruses > 0) {
 5:             Virus[] virii = new Virus[numViruses];
 6:             for (int i = 0; i < numViruses; i++)
 7:                 virii[i] = new Virus();
 8:             System.out.println("There are " + Virus.getVirusCount()
 9:                 + " viruses.");
10:         }
11:     }
12: }
```

The VirusLook class is an application that takes one argument when you run it at the command line: the number of Virus objects to create. The following is an example of a command that can be used to run the application:

```
java VirusLook 200
```

Arguments are read into an application using a string array that's sent to the main() method. In the VirusLook class, this occurs in Line 2.

In order to work with an argument as an integer, it must be converted from a String object to an integer. This requires the use of the parseInt() class method of the Integer class. In Line 3, an int variable named numViruses is created from the first argument sent to the program on the command line.

If the numViruses variable is greater than 0, the following things take place in the VirusLook application:

- Line 5: An array of Virus objects is created with the numViruses variable determining the number of objects in the array.

- Lines 6–7: A for loop is used to call the constructor method for each Virus object in the array.
- Lines 8–9: After all of the Virus objects have been constructed, the getVirusCount() class method of the Virus class is used to count the number of its objects that have been created. This should match the argument that was set when the VirusLook application was run.

If the numViruses variable is not greater than 0, nothing happens in the VirusLook application.

After you compile the VirusLook.java file, test it with any command-line argument you'd like to try. The number of Virus objects that can be created depends on the memory that's available on your system when you run the VirusLook application. On the author's system, anything above 300,000 viruses causes the program to crash after displaying an OutOfMemoryError message.

If you don't specify more Virus objects than your system can handle, the output should be something like the following:

```
There are 125000 viruses.
```

Summary

You now have completed two of the three hours devoted to object-oriented concepts in this book. You've learned how to create an object, give behavior and attributes to the object and its class of objects, and convert objects and variables into other forms by using casting.

Thinking in terms of objects is one of the tougher challenges of the Java programming language. Once you start to understand it, however, you realize that the entire language makes use of objects and classes.

During the next hour, you'll learn how to give your objects parents and children.

Q&A

Q Can constructor methods send back a value like other methods?

A No, because there's no way to receive that value. Unlike other methods that can be used as part of an equation, the argument of a method, or other statements, constructors are only handled in response to a new statement. There's no way for that statement to receive a value that would be sent by the method.

Q Do you have to create an object to use class variables or methods?

A Because class variables and methods aren't associated with a specific object, you don't need to create an object solely for the purpose of using them. The use of the `Integer.parseInt()` method is an example of this because you don't have to create a new `Integer` object just to convert a string to an `int` value.

Q When I run the `VirusLook` application without an argument, the program crashes with an `ArrayIndexOutOfBoundsException` error. What can I do to correct this?

A This error occurs because of the effort to call the `Integer.parseInt()` method with a null string as the value of `arguments[0]`. One solution would be to test the value of `arguments[0]` with an `if` statement and call `Integer.parseInt()` only if `arguments[0]` is not `null`. This would require a default value for the `numViruses` variable. Arguments often require some kind of testing to make sure they have acceptable values before you use them.

Q What's the difference between the `Integer` object and the `int` variable type?

A The first is an object, and the second is a simple variable type. Each of the variable types, such as `char`, `int`, and `float`, has a corresponding object. The object is used when you want to make use of an object's methods or treat the variable like an object. Because an `Integer` object can do things in a program that the `int` variable type cannot, it is convenient to have both.

Quiz

The following questions will see if you have the attributes and behavior to understand object-oriented programming techniques.

Questions

1. What is a method an example of in a Java class?

   (a) `attributes`

   (b) `statements`

   (c) `behavior`

2. If you want to make a variable a class variable, what statement must you use when it is created?

   (a) `new`

   (b) `public`

   (c) `static`

3. What is the name for the part of a program in which a variable lives?

   (a) Its nest

   (b) The scope

   (c) Variable valley

Answers

1. c. A method is made up of statements, but it's an example of behavior.

2. c.

3. b.

Activities

If all this talk of viruses didn't make you sick, you can increase your knowledge of this hour's topics with the following activity:

- Add a `private` variable to the `Virus` class that stores an integer called `newSeconds`. Create methods to return the value of `newSeconds` and change the value of `newSeconds` only if the new value is between 60 and 100.

- Write a Java application that takes an argument as a string, converts it to a `float` variable, converts that to a `Float` object, and finally turns that into an `int` variable. Run it a few times with different arguments to see what results.

To see Java programs that implement these activities, visit the book's Web site at `http://www.prefect.com/java24`.

Hour **12**

Making the Most of Existing Objects

This might be a surprise to you, but your Java objects are ideally suited for childbearing. When you create a program as an object—a set of attributes and behavior—you have designed something that's ready to pass these qualities on to offspring. Like most offspring, these child objects will take on a lot of the attributes and behavior of their parents. They also can do some things differently than their parents do; some extra attributes and behavior can be added that Pop is incapable of.

This system is called *inheritance*, and it's something every superclass parent gives to its subclass children. Inheritance is one of the most useful aspects of object-oriented programming, and you'll be learning more about it during this hour.

Another useful aspect of object-oriented programming is the ability to create an object that can be used with different programs. Reusability speeds up the software development process and makes it easier to develop error-free, reliable programs. Using Java and special development tools, you'll be able to develop JavaBeans—completely reusable Java objects that are easily incorporated into programs.

The following topics will be covered:

- Superclasses and subclasses
- An inheritance hierarchy
- Overriding methods
- Creating a subclass
- Developing JavaBeans

The Power of Inheritance

Without knowing it, you have used inheritance every time you used one of the standard Java classes such as `String` or `Math`. Java classes are organized into a pyramid-shaped hierarchy of classes in which all classes descend from the `Object` class.

A class of objects inherits from all superclasses that are above it. To get a working idea of how this operates, you'll look at the `Applet` class. This class is a superclass of all applets, which are Java programs written to run on the World Wide Web. The `JApplet` class, which is used to create Java 2 applets, is a subclass of `Applet`.

A partial family tree of `Applet` is shown in Figure 12.1. Each of the boxes is a class, and the lines connect a superclass to any subclasses below it.

FIGURE 12.1

The family tree of the `Applet` *class.*

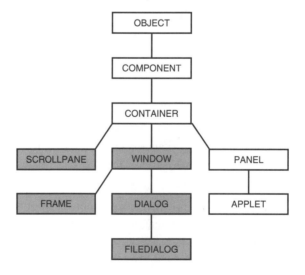

At the top is the Object class. Applet has four superclasses above it in the hierarchy: Panel, Container, Component, and Object. The Applet class inherits attributes and behavior from each of these classes because each is directly above it in the hierarchy of superclasses. Applet does not inherit anything from the five shaded classes in Figure 12.1, which include Dialog and Frame, because they are not above it in the hierarchy.

If this seems confusing, think of the hierarchy as a family tree. Applet will inherit from its parents, their parents, and on upward. It even might inherit some things from its great-great-grandparent, Object. The Applet class won't inherit from its siblings or its cousins, however.

Setting up a complicated hierarchy of classes is a difficult thing, but it makes it easier to create new programs later. The amount of work you need to do to write a new class of objects is reduced. Creating a new class boils down to the following task: You only have to define the ways in which it is different from an existing class. The rest of the work is done for you.

As an example, consider the popular video game Tetris. Since the game was invented by Soviet mathematician Alexey Pajitnov, it has been adapted for dozens of different operating systems, processors, and programming languages—including several different Java adaptations. In case you somehow avoided Tetris during the past decade by lapsing into a coma or falling into a deep meditative trance, the game works as follows: Blocks of different shapes fall from the top of the screen, and you must organize them into unbroken horizontal lines before they stack up too high.

The Java source file for several adaptations of Tetris is available for your use. If you wanted to create a new version of Tetris based on one of these existing classes, you could make your game a subclass of an existing Tetris game. All you would have to do is create the things that are new or different about your version, and you'd end up with a new game.

Inheriting Behavior and Attributes

The behavior and attributes of a class are a combination of two things: its own behavior and attributes and all behavior and attributes it inherited from its superclasses.

The following are some of the behavior and attributes of Applet:

- The equals() method determines whether an Applet object has the same value as another object.
- The setBackground() method sets the background color displayed on the applet window.

- The add() method adds user interface components such as buttons and text fields to the applet.

- The showStatus() method displays a line of text in a Web browser's status bar.

The Applet class can use all of these methods, even though showStatus() is the only one it didn't inherit from another class. The equals() method is defined in Object, setBackground() comes from Component, and add() comes from Container.

Overriding Methods

Some of the methods defined in the Applet class of objects also were defined in one of its superclasses. As an example, the resize() method is set up in both the Applet class and the Component class. This method is used to resize a component on a graphical user interface. When a method is defined in a subclass and its superclass, the subclass method is used. This enables a subclass to change, replace, or completely wipe out some of the behavior or attributes of its superclasses.

Creating a new method in a subclass to change behavior inherited from a superclass is called overriding the method. You need to override a method any time the inherited behavior will produce an undesired result.

Establishing Inheritance

You establish a class as the subclass of another class with the extends statement, as in the following:

```
class AnimatedLogo extends java.applet.JApplet {
    // behavior and attributes go here
}
```

The extends statement establishes the AnimatedLogo class of objects as a subclass of JApplet, using the full class name of java.awt.swing.JApplet. As you will see during the next hour, all Java 2 applets must be subclasses of JApplet because they need the functionality this class provides in order to run on a World Wide Web page.

One method that AnimatedLogo will have to override is the paint() method, which is used to draw all things that are shown on the program's display area. The paint() method is implemented by the Component class and is passed all the way down to AnimatedLogo. However, the paint() method does not do anything. It exists so that subclasses of Component have a method they can use when something must be displayed when that subclass is running.

To override a method, you must start the method in the same way it started in the super-class from which it was inherited. A `public` method must remain public, the value sent back by the method must be the same, and the number and type of arguments to the method must not change.

The `paint()` method of the `Component` class begins as follows:

```
public void paint(Graphics g) {
```

When `AnimatedLogo` overrides this method, it must begin with a statement like this:

```
public void paint(Graphics screen) {
```

The only difference is in the name of the `Graphics` object, which does not matter when determining if the methods are created in the same way. These two statements match because the following things match:

- Both `paint()` methods are `public`.
- Both methods return no value, as declared by the use of the `void` statement.
- Both have a `Graphics` object as their only argument.

Using this and super in a Subclass

Two keywords that are extremely useful in a subclass are `this` and `super`.

As you learned during the previous hour, the `this` keyword is used to refer to the current object. When you're creating a class and you need to refer to the specific object created from that class, `this` can be used, as in the following statement:

```
this.title = "Cagney";
```

This statement sets the object's `title` variable to the text `Cagney`.

The `super` keyword serves a similar purpose: It refers to the immediate superclass of the object. `super` can be used in several different ways:

- To refer to a constructor method of the superclass, as in `super("Adam", 12)`
- To refer to a variable of the superclass, as in `super.hawaii = 50`
- To refer to a method of the superclass, as in `super.dragNet()`

One of the ways you'll use the `super` keyword is in the constructor method of a subclass. Because a subclass inherits all of the behavior and attributes of its superclass, you have to associate each constructor method of that subclass with a constructor method of its superclass. Otherwise, some of the behavior and attributes might not be set up correctly, and the subclass won't be able to function properly.

To make sure that this happens, the first statement of a subclass constructor method must be a call to a constructor method of the superclass. This requires the super keyword, as in the following statements:

```
public ReadFiles(String name, int length) {
    super(name,length);
}
```

This example is the constructor method of a subclass, and it uses super(name,length) to call a comparable constructor in its superclass.

> If you don't use super to call a constructor method in the superclass, the program still might compile and run successfully. If no superclass constructor is called, Java automatically calls one with no arguments when the subclass constructor begins. If this superclass constructor doesn't exist or provides unexpected behavior, errors will result, so it's much better to call a super-class constructor yourself.

Working with Existing Objects

One of the things you have learned about object-oriented programming is how it encourages reuse. If you develop an excellent spellchecking object for use with one Java programming project, it should be possible to incorporate that object into another project without modification.

If a Java class is well-designed, it's possible to make that class available for use in other programs. As long as the class is documented thoroughly, a programmer should be able to work with that class as if it were part of the official Java language itself.

This is an idea that has great potential for software developers. The more objects that are available for use in your programs, the less work you have to do when creating your own software. If there's an excellent spellchecking object that suits your needs, you can use it instead of writing your own. Ideally, you can even give your boss a false impression about how long it took to add spellchecking functionality to your project, and use this extra time to make personal long-distance calls from the office.

> The author of this book, like many in his profession, is self-employed and works out of his home. Please keep this in mind when evaluating his advice on how to conduct yourself in the workplace.

When Java was first introduced, the system of sharing objects was largely an informal one. Programmers developed their objects to be as independent as possible and protected them against misuse through the use of private variables and public methods to read and write those variables.

Sharing objects becomes more powerful when there's a standard for developing reusable objects. The benefits of a standard include the following:

- There's less need to document how an object works, because anyone who knows the standard already knows a lot about how it functions.
- Development tools can be designed that follow the standard, making it possible to work more easily with these objects.
- Two objects that follow the standard will be able to interact with each other without special programming to make them compatible.

The standard for developing reusable objects in Java is called JavaBeans, and each individual object is called a Bean.

Developing JavaBeans

JavaBeans are Java classes that are designed specifically for the purpose of being reused. These reusable classes, which are called software components in many programming languages, are developed under a standard set of rules.

Developing Beans requires a programming tool in addition to the Java Development Kit. Sun Microsystems offers its own tool, the Beans Development Kit, at `http://java.sun.com/beans/software`.

There also are numerous commercial programs that make it possible to develop Beans and incorporate them into programs. These include Borland JBuilder, Symantec Visual Café, Lotus BeanMachine, and SunSoft Java WorkShop.

The Beans Development Kit, also called the BDK, includes the BeanBox, a visual tool that is used to add Beans to a Java program and make those Beans work with each other. The BeanBox, which is a Java program itself, is shown in Figure 12.2.

In Figure 12.2, the BeanBox is being used to link together three Beans: Two buttons and an animated Bean that displays the Java mascot, an anthropomorphic cuspid, named Duke, juggling some giant beans. A lot of JavaBeans programming can be accomplished by using a tool like the BeanBox—some projects can be accomplished entirely with the mouse and no coding of your own classes.

FIGURE 12.2

Using the BeanBox to create a Java program out of several Beans.

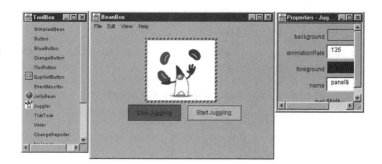

Bean programming is a specialized aspect of Java that's best learned after you have mastered the basics of the language. However, a beginning programmer can accomplish a lot by working with existing Beans, so you'll benefit by becoming more familiar with JavaBeans as you learn to program.

> If you're ready to percolate your own JavaBeans after completing this book, *Sams Teach Yourself JavaBeans in 21 Days* offers a hands-on tutorial that's similar to the approach taken here. The book uses the Beans Development Kit and version 1.1 of the Java Development Kit.

You'll be developing skills throughout this book that are directly applicable to JavaBeans programming. A prime example is encapsulation, which you learned about during the previous hour. Using methods to read and write the values of a variable is a fundamental part of JavaBeans development.

During the previous hour, you saw how `getSeconds()` and `setSeconds()` methods could be used in a class to read and write a variable called `newSeconds`:

```
public int getSeconds() {
    return newSeconds;
}

public void setSeconds(int newValue) {
    if (newValue > 60)
        newSeconds = newValue;
}
```

If the `newSeconds` variable is `private`, these methods are an example of encapsulation. One of the rules of JavaBeans programming is to limit access to object variables according to the following rules:

- The variable should be `private`.
- A `public` method to read the variable should begin with `get`, end with a name that describes the variable being read, and return the same type of data as the variable.
- A `public` method to write the variable should begin with `set`, end with a name that describes the variable being written, and return `void`.
- If there are both reading and writing methods, they should end with the same name to describe the variable.

The preceding example follows all of these rules with the `getSeconds` and `setSeconds` methods. Because of this, if these methods are part of a Bean, the `newSeconds` variable can be manipulated directly within a tool like the BeanBox.

In Figure 12.3, the Properties window shows a `seconds` property that can be changed from within the BeanBox. This shows up because a `setSeconds()` method exists in a Bean that's selected in the main BeanBox window.

FIGURE 12.3

Manipulating a Bean's variables with the BeanBox's Properties window.

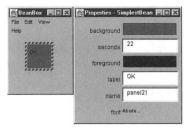

Much of the work that's done creating JavaBeans is for the benefit of programmers using a development environment such as the BeanBox. The more a Bean can be customized, the more useful it is.

Following the `set` and `get` rules for using an object variable is a first step towards making a class a Bean, and they demonstrate the kind of programming that JavaBeans requires.

These rules make sense for all object-oriented programming that you do, because they present a useful and safe interface between an object and the other classes that will use it. You'll learn more skills that are useful in Bean development during Hour 15, "Playing Sound in an Applet."

12

Workshop: Creating a Subclass

To see an example of inheritance at work, you will create a class called Point3D that represents a point in three-dimensional space. A two-dimensional point can be expressed with an (x,y) coordinate. Applets use an (x,y) coordinate system to determine where text and graphics should be displayed. Three-dimensional space adds a third coordinate, which can be called z.

The Point3D class of objects should do three things:

- Keep track of an object's (x,y,z) coordinate.
- Move an object to a new (x,y,z) coordinate when needed.
- Move an object by a certain amount of x, y, and z values as needed.

Java already has a standard class that represents two-dimensional points; it's called Point. It has two integer variables called x and y that store a Point object's (x,y) location. It also has a move() method to place a point at the specified location, and a translate() method to move an object by an amount of x and y values.

Run your word processor and create a new file called Point3D.java. Enter the text of Listing 12.1 into the file, and save it when you're done.

LISTING 12.1 THE FULL TEXT OF Point3D.java

```
 1: import java.awt.*;
 2:
 3: public class Point3D extends Point {
 4:     public int z;
 5:
 6:     public Point3D(int x, int y, int z) {
 7:         super(x,y);
 8:         this.z = z;
 9:     }
10:
11:     public void move(int x, int y, int z) {
12:         this.z = z;
13:         super.move(x, y);
14:     }
15:
16:     public void translate(int x, int y, int z) {
17:         this.z += z;
18:         super.translate(x, y);
19:     }
20: }
```

Compile this file with the javac compiler tool, and you will have a class you can use in programs. The Point3D class does not have a main() block statement, so you cannot run it with the java interpreter.

The Point3D class only has to do work that isn't being done by its superclass, Point. This primarily involves keeping track of the integer variable z, and receiving it as an argument to the move() method, translate() method, and Point3D() constructor method.

All of the methods use the keywords super and this. The this statement is used to refer to the current Point3D object, so this.z = z; line 8 sets the object variable z equal to the z value that was sent as an argument to the method in line 6.

The super statement refers to the superclass of the current object, Point. It is used to set variables and call methods that were inherited by Point3D. The statement super(x,y) in line 7 calls the Point(x,y) constructor in the superclass, which then sets the (x,y) coordinates of the Point3D object. Because Point already is equipped to handle the x and y axes, it would be redundant for the Point3D class of objects to do the same thing.

To test out the Point3D class you have compiled, create a program that uses Point and Point3D objects and moves them around. Create a new file in your word processor and enter Listing 12.2 into it. Save the file as TryPoints.java.

LISTING 12.2   THE FULL TEXT OF TryPoints.java

```
 1: import java.awt.*;
 2:
 3: class TryPoints {
 4:     public static void main(String[] arguments) {
 5:         Point object1 = new Point(11,22);
 6:         Point3D object2 = new Point3D(7,6,64);
 7:
 8:         System.out.println("The 2D point is located at (" + object1.x
 9:             + ", " + object1.y + ")");
10:         System.out.println("\tIt's being moved to (4, 13)");
11:         object1.move(4,13);
12:         System.out.println("The 2D point is now at (" + object1.x
13:             + ", " + object1.y + ")");
14:         System.out.println("\tIt's being moved -10 units on both the x
"
15:             + "and y axes");
16:         object1.translate(-10,-10);
17:         System.out.println("The 2D point ends up at (" + object1.x
18:             + ", " + object1.y + ")\n");
19:
```

continues

LISTING **12.2**   CONTINUED

```
20:          System.out.println("The 3D point is located at (" + object2.x
21:             + ", " + object2.y + ", " + object2.z +")");
22:          System.out.println("\tIt's being moved to (10, 22, 71)");
23:          object2.move(10,22,71);
24:          System.out.println("The 3D point is now at (" + object2.x
25:             + ", " + object2.y + ", " + object2.z +")");
26:          System.out.println("\tIt's being moved -20 units on the x, y "
27:             + "and z axes");
28:          object2.translate(-20,-20,-20);
29:          System.out.println("The 3D point ends up at (" + object2.x
30:             + ", " + object2.y + ", " + object2.z +")");
31:      }
32: }
```

After you compile this file and run it with the java interpreter, the following should be shown:

OUTPUT
```
The 2D point is located at (11, 22)
    It's being moved to (4, 13)
The 2D point is now at (4, 13)
    It's being moved -10 units on both the x and y axes
The 2D point ends up at (-6, 3)

The 3D point is located at (7, 6, 64)
    It's being moved to (10, 22, 71)
The 3D point is now at (10, 22, 71)
    It's being moved -20 units on the x, y and z axes
The 3D point ends up at (-10, 2, 51)
```

Summary

When people talk about the miracle of birth, they're probably not speaking of the way a superclass can give birth to subclasses or the way behavior and attributes are inherited in a hierarchy of classes.

However, if the real world worked the same way that object-oriented programming does, every grandchild of Mozart could choose to be a brilliant composer. All descendants of Mark Twain could wax poetic about Mississippi riverboat life. Everyone in Jim Thome's forthcoming bloodline would decide if hitting mammoth home runs in knee-high socks is his or her reason for being. Every skill your direct ancestors worked to achieve would be handed to you without an ounce of toil.

On the scale of miracles, inheritance isn't quite up to par with continuing the existence of a species and getting a good tax break. However, it's an effective way to design software with a minimum of redundant work.

Another timesaver you may come to rely on are JavaBeans, objects that are ready-made for use in other programs. Whether you're using Beans that were developed by other programmers or designing your own, you have one more way to achieve something with fewer ounces of actual toil.

Q&A

Q **Can a class have more than one superclass so that it inherits additional methods and behavior?**

A It is possible with some object-oriented programming languages but not Java. One of the goals when Java was developed was to provide a simpler language than an object-oriented language such as C++, and limiting inheritance to a single superclass was one way to achieve this. You can use a special type of class called an interface to inherit behavior that isn't received from superclasses.

Q **Most Java programs created up to this point have not used extends to inherit from a superclass. Does this mean they exist outside of the class hierarchy?**

A All classes you create in Java are part of the hierarchy because the default superclass for the programs you write is Object when the extends keyword is not used. The equals() and toString() methods of all classes are part of the behavior that automatically is inherited from Object.

Q **Are JavaBeans anything like ActiveX controls?**

A JavaBeans and Microsoft ActiveX are different answers to the question, "What's the best way to create reusable software components?" ActiveX is a simplified adaptation of the Component Object Model, a complex standard for software component programming that can be implemented in many different programming languages. ActiveX controls can be developed with several different languages, including Java. One of the things a JavaBeans programmer learns is how to turn a Bean into an ActiveX control.

Q **When is the full name of a class, such as java.applet.Applet, needed in an extends clause instead of a shorter name such as Applet?**

A You must use the full name whenever you don't use an import java.applet.Applet; or import.java.applet.*; statement at the beginning of your program. The import statement is used solely to make it easier to refer to class names in programs. Each class of objects in Java has a full name that identifies the group of classes to which it belongs. For instance, the Math class is part of the java.lang group of classes. A group of classes is also called a *package*.

Quiz

To determine what kind of knowledge you inherited from the past hour's work, answer the following questions.

Questions

1. If a superclass handles a method in a way you don't want to use in the subclass, what can you do?

    (a) Delete the method in the superclass.

    (b) Override the method in the subclass.

    (c) Write a nasty letter to the editor of the *San Jose Mercury News* hoping that Java's developers will read it.

2. Which of the following is not a benefit of JavaBeans?

    (a) Objects can be shared easily with other programmers.

    (b) A Bean can be used with any development tool that supports the standard.

    (c) They cause emissions that violate stringent air quality standards in most countries.

3. What statement can you use to refer to the methods and variables of a the current object?

    (a) `this`

    (b) `that`

    (c) `theOther`

Answers

1. b. Because you can override the method, you don't have to change any aspect of the superclass or the way it works.

2. c. You're thinking of an entirely different type of bean. This question is dedicated to my father, who is prohibited by local statute from eating Ranch Style Beans in a poorly ventilated environment.

3. a.

Activities

If a fertile imagination has birthed in you a desire to learn more, you can spawn more knowledge of inheritance with the following activities:

- Create a `Point4D` class that adds a `t` coordinate to the (x,y,z) coordinate system created by the `Point3D` class. The `t` coordinate stands for time, so you will need to ensure that it is never set to a negative value.

- Take the members of a football team's offense—lineman, wide receiver, tight end, running back, and quarterback. Design a hierarchy of classes that represent the skills of these players, putting common skills higher up in the hierarchy. For example, blocking is behavior that should probably be inherited by the linemen and tight end classes, and speed is something that should be inherited by wide receivers and running backs.

To see Java programs that implement these activities, visit the book's Web site at `http://www.prefect.com/java24`.

12

PART IV

Creating Applets for the World Wide Web

Hour

Hour **13**

Learning How Applets Work

Now that Java has made the transition from a child prodigy to an established language, it is being used for all kinds of large-scale business software and other applications. However, for many people, the core appeal of the language lies in a new type of program that Java made possible: the applet.

Applets are programs designed to run as part of a World Wide Web page. When a Java applet is encountered on a page, it is downloaded to the user's computer and begins running.

During this hour you'll be introduced to applet programming. Programming applets with Java is much different from creating applications with Java. Because applets must be downloaded off a page each time they are run, applets are smaller than most applications to reduce download time. Also, because applets run on the computer of the person using the applet, they have numerous security restrictions in place to prevent malicious or damaging code from being run.

The following topics will be covered:

- Setting up an applet
- Displaying information in an applet
- Stopping and starting an applet
- Putting an applet on a Web page
- Using applet HTML tags and attributes
- Running applets with the Java Plug-in

Standard Applet Methods

The first step in the creation of an applet is to make it a subclass of JApplet, a class that's part of the com.sun.java.swing package. This package is called Swing, and it provides a set of classes for the creation of a graphical user interface, graphics, and other visual elements of a computer program. An applet is treated as a visual window inside a Web page, so JApplet is part of Swing alongside clickable buttons, scrollbars, and other components of a program's user interface.

JApplet is a subclass of Applet, a class in the java.applet package. Being part of this hierarchy enables the applets you write to use all the behavior and attributes they need to be run as part of a World Wide Web page. Before you begin writing any other statements in your applets, they will be able to interact with a Web browser, load and unload themselves, redraw their window in response to changes in the browser window, and handle other necessary tasks.

In applications, programs begin running with the first statement inside the main() block statement and end with the last closing bracket (}) that closes out the block. There is no main() method in a Java applet, so there is no set starting place for the program. Instead, an applet has a group of standard methods that are handled in response to specific events as the applet runs.

The following are the events that could prompt one of the applet methods to be handled:

- The program is loaded for the first time
- Something happens that requires the applet window to be redisplayed
- The program is stopped by the browser
- The program restarts after a stop
- The program is unloaded as it finishes running

The following is an example of a bare-bones applet:

```
public class Skeleton extends com.sun.java.swing.JApplet {
    // program will go here
}
```

Unlike applications, applet class files must be `public` in order to work. (However, if your applet uses other class files of your own creation, they do not have to be declared `public`.) Your applet's class inherits all of the methods that are handled automatically when needed: `init()`, `paint()`, `start()`, `stop()`, and `destroy()`. However, none of these methods do anything. If you want something to happen in an applet, you have to override these methods with new versions in your applet program. The two methods you will override most often are `paint()` and `init()`.

The `paint()` Method

The `paint()`method should be a part of almost every applet you write because you can't display anything without it. Whenever something needs to be displayed or redisplayed on the applet window, the `paint()` method handles the task. You also can force `paint()` to be handled with the following statement:

```
repaint();
```

> The `repaint()` method can be used inside any method of the applet's class, but you should avoid calling it inside the `paint()` method. This causes a quick-running loop that makes the Java interpreter run inefficiently and might cause the Web browser running the applet to crash.

Aside from the use of `repaint()`, the main time the `paint()` method is handled is when something changes in the browser or the operating system running the browser. For example, if a Windows 95 user minimizes a Web page containing an applet, the `paint()` method will be called to redisplay everything that was onscreen in the applet when the applet is later restored to full size.

13

Unlike the other methods you will be learning about during this hour, `paint()` takes an argument. The following is an example of a simple `paint()` method:

```
public class paint(Graphics screen) {
    // display statements go here
}
```

The argument is a `Graphics` object. The `Graphics` class of objects represents an environment in which something can be displayed, such as an applet window. The methods of a related class, `Graphics2D`, are used to display text, graphics, and other information.

Later this hour, you'll learn about drawString(), a method for the display of text that's available in both the Graphics and Graphics2D classes.

If you are using a Graphics or Graphics2D object in your applet, you have to add the following import statements before the class statement at the beginning of the source file:

```
import java.awt.Graphics;
import java.awt.Graphics2D;
```

> If you are using several classes that are a part of the java.awt package of classes, use the statement import java.awt.*; instead. It makes all of these classes available for use in your program.

In a Java 2 applet, the first statement in the paint() method should be a call to the paint() method of its superclass. This ensures that the applet window is updated correctly. The following statement handles this task:

```
super.paint(screen);
```

This example sends a Graphics object called screen to the paint() method of the superclass. The object must be the same one that was sent to your applet's paint() method.

The init() Method

The init() method is handled once—and only once—when the applet is run. As a result, it's an ideal place to set up values for any objects and variables that are needed for the applet to run successfully. This method is also a good place to set up fonts, colors, and the screen's background color.

> Variables and objects should not be created inside an init() method because they will only exist within the scope of that method. For example, if you create an integer variable called displayRate inside the init() method and try to use it in the paint() method, you'll get an error when you attempt to compile the program. Create any variables you need to use throughout a class as object variables right after the class statement and before any methods.

The start() and stop() Methods

At any point when the applet program starts running, the start() method will be handled. When a program first begins, the init() method is followed by the start() method. After that, in many instances there will never be a cause for the start() method to be handled again. In order for start() to be handled a second time or more, the applet has to stop execution at some point.

The stop()method is called when an applet stops execution. This event can occur when a user leaves the Web page containing the applet and continues to another page. It also can occur when the stop() method is called directly in a program.

In the programs you'll write as you're starting out with the Java language, start() and stop() will have the most use in animation. You'll learn more about this use during Hour 18, "Creating Animation."

The destroy() Method

The destroy() method is an opposite of sorts to the init() method. It is handled just before an applet completely closes down and completes running. This method is used in rare instances when something has been changed during a program and it should be restored to its original state. It's another method you'll use more often with animation than with other types of programs.

Putting an Applet on a Web Page

Applets are placed on a Web page in the same way that anything unusual is put on a page: HTML commands are used to describe the applet, and the Web browser loads it along with the other parts of the page. If you have used HTML to create a Web page, you know that it's a way to combine formatted text, images, sound, and other elements together. HTML uses special commands called tags that are surrounded by < and > marks, including <IMG> for the display of images, <P> for the insertion of a paragraph mark, and <CENTER> to center the text that follows until a </CENTER> tag is reached.

The performance of some of these HTML tags can be affected by attributes that determine how they function. For example, SRC is an attribute of the <IMG> tag, and it provides the name of the image file that should be displayed. The following is an example of an <IMG> tag:

```
<IMG SRC="Graduation.jpg">
```

One way to place applets on a Web page is by using an <APPLET> tag and several attributes. The following is an example of the HTML required to put an applet on a page:

```
<APPLET CODE="StripYahtzee.class" CODEBASE="javadir" HEIGHT=300 WIDTH=400>
Sorry, no dice ... this requires a Java-enabled browser.
</APPLET>
```

The CODE attribute identifies the name of the applet's class file. If more than one class file is being used with an applet, CODE should refer to the main class file that is a subclass of the JApplet class.

If there is no CODEBASE attribute, all files associated with the applet should be in the same folder as the Web page that loads the program. CODEBASE should contain a reference to the folder or subfolder where the applet and any related files can be found. In the preceding example, CODEBASE indicates that the StripYahtzee applet can be found in the javadir subfolder.

The HEIGHT and WIDTH attributes designate the exact size of the applet window on the Web page. It must be big enough to handle the things you are displaying in your applet.

In between the opening <APPLET> tag and the closing </APPLET> tag, you can provide an alternate of some kind for Web users whose browser software cannot run Java programs. In the preceding example, a line of text is displayed indicating that Java is required to play the game.

Another attribute you can use with applets is ALIGN. It designates how the applet will be displayed in relation to the surrounding material on the page, including text and graphics. Values include ALIGN="Left", ALIGN="Right", and others.

A Sample Applet

The first program you wrote was a Java application that revealed a depressing fact about the U.S. financial condition—one minute's worth of the National Debt. If it isn't too painful a prospect, you'll take a look at how applets are structured by writing the same program as an applet.

Load your word processor and create a new file called BigDebtApplet.java. Enter the text of Listing 13.1 into the file and save it when you're done.

LISTING 13.1   THE FULL TEXT OF BigDebtApplet.java

```
 1: import java.awt.*;
 2:
 3: public class BigDebtApplet extends com.sun.java.swing.JApplet {
 4:     int debt;
 5:
 6:     public void init() {
 7:         debt = 446000000;
 8:         debt = debt / 1440;
 9:     }
10:
11:     public void paint(Graphics screen) {
12:         super.paint(screen);
13:         Graphics2D screen2D = (Graphics2D)screen;
14:         screen2D.drawString("A minute's worth of debt is $"
15:             + debt, 5, 50);
16:     }
17: }
```

This applet does not need to use the `start()`, `stop()`, or `destroy()` methods, so they are not included in the program. Compile the program with the `javac` compiler tool.

Using the `drawString()` Method

Text is displayed in an applet window by using the `drawString()` method of the `Graphics2D` class or the same method in the `Graphics` class. The `Graphics2D` class is used in `BigDebtApplet` because it provides better results for the display of text and graphics.

The `drawString()` method is similar in function to the `System.out.println()` method that displays information to the system's standard output device.

Before you can use the `drawString()` method of the `Graphics2D` class, you must have a `Graphics2D` object that represents the applet window.

The `paint()` method of all applets includes a `Graphics` object as its only argument. This object represents the applet window, so it can be used to create a `Graphics2D` object that also represents the window.

As you might suspect, you use casting to convert a `Graphics` object into a `Graphics2D` object. `Graphics2D` is a subclass of `Graphics`, which makes the following statement possible:

```
Graphics2D screen2D = (Graphics2D)screen;
```

This statement casts a `Graphics` object named `screen` into a `Graphics2D` object named `screen2D`. You'll see a statement like this often in the `paint()` method of applets.

When you have created a `Graphics2D` object like this, you can call its `drawString()` method to display text on the area represented by the object.

The following three arguments are sent to `drawString()`:

- The text to display, which can be several different strings and variables strung together with the + operator
- The x position (in an (x,y) coordinate system) where the string should be displayed
- The y position where the string should be displayed

The (x,y) coordinate system in an applet is used with several methods. It begins with the (0,0) point in the upper-left corner of the applet window. Figure 13.1 shows how the (x,y) coordinate system works in conjunction with the statement on line 14 of `BigDebtApplet.java`.

Testing the `BigDebtApplet` Program

Although you have compiled the `BigDebtApplet` program into a class file, you cannot run it using the `java` interpreter. If you do, you'll get an error message such as the following:

```
In class BigDebtApplet: void main(String argv[]) is not defined
```

Figure 13.1

Drawing a string to an (x,y) position.

The error occurs because the java interpreter runs Java applications beginning with the first statement of the main() block. To run an applet, you need to create a Web page that loads the applet. To create a Web page, open up a new file on your word processor and call it BigDebtApplet.html. Enter Listing 13.2 and then save the file.

LISTING 13.2 THE FULL TEXT OF BigDebtApplet.html

```
 1: <html>
 2: <head>
 3: <title>The Big Debt Applet</title>
 4: </head>
 5: <body bgcolor="#000000" text="#FF00FF">
 6: <center>
 7: This a Java applet:<br>
 8: <applet code="BigDebtApplet.class" height=150 width=300>
 9: You need a Java-enabled browser to see this.
10: </applet>
11: </body>
12: </html>
```

All applets you write can be tested with the appletviewer tool that comes with the Java Development Kit. You can see the output of the BigDebtApplet applet by typing the following:

appletviewer BigDebtApplet.html

One thing to note about appletviewer is that it only runs the applets that are included in a Web page and does not handle any of the other elements such as text and images. Figure 13.2 shows a screen capture of BigDebtApplet loaded into appletviewer.

FIGURE 13.2

The BigDebtApplet program displayed with the appletviewer tool.

> Some beta versions of the JDK 1.2 appletviewer experienced problems dis-
> playing fonts and colored text. You can correct this by using the command-
> line argument -J-Djava2d.font.usePlatformFont=true when using the
> appletviewer, as in the following statement:
>
> ```
> appletviewer -J-Djava2d.font.usePlatformFont=true WebPageName.html
> ```

Using the New <OBJECT> Tag

When Java was introduced, applets were the only kind of program that could be run on a Web page. Because of this, the <APPLET> tag was introduced into HTML specifically to handle these programs.

Today, there are all kinds of interactive programs on the Web, including Python programs, ActiveX controls, and NetRexx applets—executable Java bytecode created with the NetRexx language instead of Java. To deal with these Web-delivered programs while leaving room for others in the future, the <OBJECT> tag has been added to HTML.

The <OBJECT> tag is used for all interactive programs and other external elements that can be included on a page from a separate file. These are called objects just as individual software components are called objects, and they have reasonably similar meanings. The <OBJECT> tag is supported by versions 4.0 and higher of both Netscape Navigator and Microsoft Internet Explorer.

The <OBJECT> tag takes the following form:

```
'<OBJECT CLASSID="java:Face.class" CODEBASE="jdir" HEIGHT=50 WIDTH=450">
</OBJECT>
```

Switching from <APPLET> to <OBJECT> requires the following changes:

- The <OBJECT> tag should be used instead of <APPLET>.
- The CODE attribute should be replaced by CLASSID, and the text "java:" should be placed before the name of the applet's class file. For example, if the applet is in Face.class, the CLASSID attribute should be java:Face.class.

Otherwise, the attributes of the tags are the same, including ALIGN, CODEBASE, HEIGHT, and WIDTH. During the next hour, you'll see how both the <OBJECT> and <APPLET> tags can use optional <PARAM> tags to configure how an applet functions.

Although the <OBJECT> tag is supported by the current versions of the two major browsers, it is not supported in many previous versions. Until the audience using the newest browsers is large enough, you might decide to use <APPLET> to reach the widest number of people. The <OBJECT> tag isn't supported by appletviewer, so you can't use it with applets you want to test using that tool.

13

Listing 13.3 contains a Web page that loads the `BigDebtApplet` program using the `<OBJECT>` tag. Everything else is the same as the previous example in Listing 13.2.

LISTING 13.3   THE FULL TEXT OF `BigDebtApplet2.html`

```
 1: <html>
 2: <head>
 3: <title>The Big Debt Applet</title>
 4: </head>
 5: <body bgcolor="#000000" text="#FF00FF">
 6: <center>
 7: This a Java applet:<br>
 8: <object classid="java:BigDebtApplet.class" height=150 width=300>
 9: You need a Java-enabled browser to see this.
10: </object>
11: </body>
12: </html>
```

Getting Ready for the Java Plug-in

Because there are now three major versions of the Java language (1.0, 1.1, and now 2), one of the things you must concern yourself with as an applet programmer is the version your audience can handle.

At the time of this writing, Netscape Navigator and Microsoft Internet Explorer are both currently at version 4.0. Neither of these browsers supports Java 2—Navigator offers near-complete support for Java 1.1, and Microsoft does not currently plan for Internet Explorer ever to support 1.1 in full. An exception is Internet Explorer for the Macintosh, which can be configured to work with different Java interpreters. One of these is the Macintosh Runtime Java, which currently supports version 1.1 of the language.

Applet programmers who want their programs to run on Navigator and Internet Explorer can use Java 1.02—the version of the language supported fully on both of the leading browsers.

However, Java 1.02 is a much simpler language than Java 2, lacking many of the best features of the language, including Swing, better handling of mouse interaction, JavaBeans, and other changes that reflect three years of feedback from Java developers.

To make it possible for Java 2 applets to be written for current browsers, Sun Microsystems is developing the Java Plug-in for both Navigator and Internet Explorer.

A *plug-in* is a program that works in conjunction with a Web browser to expand its functionality. Plug-ins handle a type of data that the browser normally could not handle. For example, Apple offers a plug-in to display QuickTime movies and Macromedia has released a plug-in to run Flash animation files.

The Java Plug-in runs Java applets that could not otherwise be run by the Web browser. It works according to the following process:

- An applet programmer who wrote a Java 2 applet indicates on the applet's Web page that it should be run by a different interpreter: the Java Plug-in.
- When a Web user loads that page in either Navigator or Internet Explorer, if they don't have the plug-in, they will have a chance to download it.
- Once the Java Plug-in is installed, all future Java 2 applets will run automatically if they specify that the plug-in should be used to run them.

Figure 13.3 shows what Navigator users see when they first encounter an applet set up to use the Java Plug-in.

FIGURE 13.3

Choosing whether to install the Java Plug-in for Netscape Navigator.

If a user chooses to install the plug-in, he or she will be taken to a page at Sun's Java site where it can be downloaded and installed. The Java Plug-in must be installed once for each browser, so a user who has both Navigator and Internet Explorer must download and install it twice.

The Java Plug-in is available for Windows and Solaris users, and Apple has announced plans to develop a version of the plug-in for Macintosh users. The easiest way to install the plug-in on your own system is to wait until you visit a Web page that requires it. If you want to jump-start the process, you can find applets that use the Java Plug-in by visiting http://java.sun.com/products/plugin.

You also can visit this Web page to download the Java Plug-in directly and read documentation about the software.

The <APPLET> and <OBJECT> tags you have learned about up to this point do not specify that the Java Plug-in be used to run applets. Browsers that encounter standard tags like these will attempt to run the Java programs with their own built-in Java interpreters.

At the time this book goes to press, Sun has completed the Java Plug-in for version 1.1 of the language, and it can be specially configured to support Java 2 for your own system. Built-in plug-in support for Java 2 may be available at the time you're reading this. See Sun's Java Plug-in Web page for more details.

In order to make an applet run on the Java Plug-in, you must make some fairly complex changes to the Web page containing the applet. These changes are made more complex by the fact that Internet Explorer and Netscape Navigator require different HTML tags to support the plug-in.

Sun makes the process much easier with the Java Plug-in HTML Converter. The converter, a Java application that's available for all platforms that support Java, changes a standard Web page containing an applet into one that runs the applet with the Java Plug-in.

The converter can be downloaded from the same page as the plug-in itself. The best way to make use of the converter is with the following steps:

- Put the applet on a page using the <APPLET> tag (the converter does not support the <OBJECT> tag).
- Test the applet using the appletviewer tool.
- If the applet works, use the converter on the Web page containing the applet so that it supports the Java Plug-in.

The converter, shown in Figure 13.4, uses an existing <APPLET> tag on a Web page to determine how it can be modified to work with the Java Plug-in. The converter enables a backup copy of the page to be made, so you'll be able to return to the original if needed.

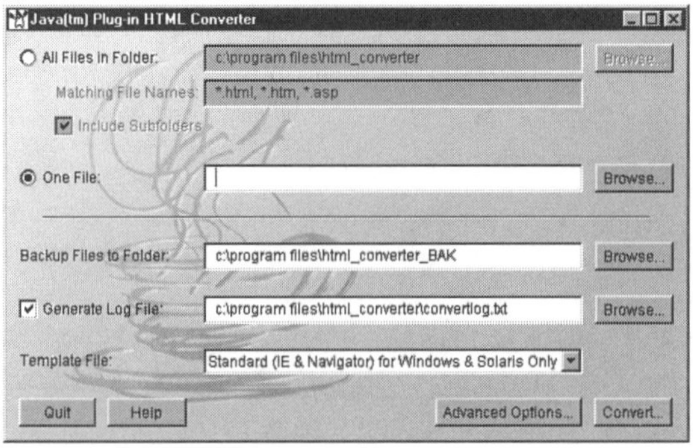

FIGURE 13.4

Using the Java Plug-in HTML Converter.

The Java Plug-in is still in an early stage of development relative to other aspects of Java. At the time of this writing, there are some browser compatibility issues being resolved by Sun.

When a full Java 2 version of the Plug-in is available from Sun, it should make it possible to reach a wide audience with version 2 applets instead of using version 1.02 of the language.

Workshop: Enhancing the `BigDebtApplet` Project

As a short exercise to close out the hour, you'll enhance the `BigDebtApplet` program by making it accumulate the debt over time, displaying how much the National Debt grows.

Open up a new file with your word processor and call it `Ouch.java`. Enter Listing 13.4 and save the file when you're done.

LISTING 13.4   THE FULL TEXT OF `Ouch.java`

```
 1: import java.awt.*;
 2:
 3: public class Ouch extends com.sun.java.swing.JApplet {
 4:     int debt = 683;
 5:     int totalTime = 1;
 6:
 7:     public void paint(Graphics screen) {
 8:         super.paint(screen);
 9:         Graphics2D screen2D = (Graphics2D)screen;
10:         screen2D.drawString(totalTime + " seconds worth of debt is $"
11:             + (debt * totalTime), 5, 30);
12:         totalTime++;
13:     }
14: }
```

The `Ouch` program increases the debt total each time the `paint()` method is called in the applet. As you learned earlier, this method is called when the applet's display area needs to be repainted. Some of the events that can cause this are when the window comes out from behind another window and when a user reloads the page containing the applet.

To try out the program, you need to compile it with the `javac` compiler tool and create a Web page that runs the applet. Create a new file on your word processor and enter Listing 13.5 into the file. Save it when you're done.

LISTING 13.5 THE FULL TEXT OF Ouch.html

```
1: <applet code="Ouch.class" height=300 width=300>
2: </applet>
```

This Web page only contains the HTML tags that are required to add an applet to a page. Load this Web page into the `appletviewer` tool by typing the following at a command line:

```
appletviewer Ouch.html
```

You will see an applet that begins with the calculation of a second's worth of debt. To see an update of the total, obscure the `appletviewer` window with another item from your system such as a different program or a file folder. The following is an example of the text that is displayed as the applet runs:

```
13 second's worth of debt is $67106
```

Summary

This hour was the first of several that will focus on the development of applets. You got a chance to become acquainted with the `init()` and `paint()` methods, which you will be using frequently when you're developing applets.

Writing applets is a good way for beginners to develop their skills as Java programmers for the following reasons:

- Applets are usually smaller in scope, making their creation a less daunting task.
- You can find thousands of sample applets on the World Wide Web, including many with the source file available from which to learn.
- You can make applets available to a global audience at low to no cost through the Web, exposing your work to more people who can offer comments and suggestions.

There's a "code war" of sorts afoot among the hundreds of Java programmers who are putting their work on the Web, and many new applets announced on sites like `http://www.jars.com` demonstrate new things that can be done with the language.

Q&A

Q Can arguments be sent to applets, as they can to applications?

A You can't use arguments, but parameters serve a similar function to arguments in applet programming. You can use the <PARAM> tag with its NAME and VALUE attributes to send parameters to Java programs. It's described fully in Hour 14, "Creating a Threaded Applet."

Q Is there a reason why the CODEBASE attribute should be used in an <APPLET> or <OBJECT> tag?

A If all Java programs are grouped into their own subfolder, as indicated by CODEBASE, this structure might improve the way a Web site is organized, but there's no other reason why using CODEBASE is better than omitting it. The choice is a matter of personal preference.

Q What happens if the height and width specified for an applet don't leave enough room for the information that is displayed in the paint() method?

A The information will be drawn offscreen, beyond the edges of the applet window, and won't be visible at any point while the applet runs. Choosing the right dimensions for an applet is largely a matter of trial-and-error until you find the right size for both the HEIGHT and WIDTH attributes of the <APPLET> tag. You can't resize an applet window from within a Java program, so the only way to control its size is by using the HEIGHT and WIDTH attributes. Fortunately, you can change the Web page's HTML without having to recompile the Java program.

Quiz

The following questions test your knowledge of applets.

Questions

1. What type of argument is used with the paint() method?

    (a) A Graphics object

    (b) A Graphics2 object

    (c) None

2. Which method is handled right before an applet finishes running?

    (a) decline()

    (b) destroy()

    (c) defenestrate()

13

3. Why can't all variables needed in an applet be created inside the init() method?

   (a) The scope of the variables would be limited to the method only.

   (b) Federal legislation prohibits it.

   (c) They can be created there without any problems.

Answers

1. a. The Graphics object keeps track of the behavior and attributes needed to display things onscreen in the applet window. You might create a Graphics2 object inside the method, but it isn't sent as an argument.

2. b.

3. a. Variables that are used in more than one method of a class should be created right after the class statement but before any methods begin.

Activities

You can apply your applet programming knowledge with the following activity:

- Write an applet in which the text that is displayed moves each time the applet window is repainted.

- Install the Java Plug-in with your preferred browser, if you're on a Windows or Solaris system, and try the sample applets provided from Sun's Java Plug-in page.

To see a Java program that implements the first activity, visit the book's Web site at http://www.prefect.com/java24.

HOUR 14

Creating a Threaded Applet

A computer term that is used often to describe the hectic pace of daily life is *multitasking*. (Another term is used more often around my house, but the editors asked that it be omitted.) Multitasking means to do more than one thing at once—such as surfing the Web at your desk while participating in a conference call and using the Buttmaster exercise device to achieve more shapely shanks. The term multitasking comes from the world of operating systems, where a multitasking computer is one that can handle more than one program at a time.

One of the most sophisticated features of the Java language is the ability to write programs that can multitask. Under Java, each of the simultaneous tasks the computer handles is called a thread and the overall process is called *multithreading*. Threading is useful in animation and many other programs.

During this hour, you'll learn how to make applets more sophisticated through the use of threads and another new feature: parameters. Parameters are the applet's answer to arguments, the information that can be sent to a program from the command-line as it is run. Parameters are placed on the Web page that runs an applet and read when the applet begins running.

The following topics will be covered:

- Using an interface with a program
- Creating threads
- Starting, stopping, and pausing threads
- Catching errors
- Sending parameters to Java applets
- Receiving parameters in an applet program
- Writing a program that uses parameters

Sending Parameters from a Web Page

Now that you have had some experience writing computer programs, you might be feeling one of the strongest emotions of the programmer: compiler angst. Even though it takes no more than 15 seconds to compile most programs, that time can seem interminable when you're debugging a program. Write, Save, Compile, Aargh—an error! Write, Save, Compile, Aargh! Write, Save, Compile, Aargh!... As this vicious cycle repeats itself, it's easy to become world-weary as a program is compiled and recompiled.

One of the driving forces behind parameter use in Java applets is the fear and loathing of compilation. Parameters enable you to change elements of an applet without editing or recompiling anything. They also make the program more useful.

Parameters are stored as part of the Web page that contains an applet. They are created using the HTML tag `<PARAM>` and its two attributes: `NAME` and `VALUE`. You can have more than one `<PARAM>` tag with an applet, but all of them must be between the opening `<APPLET>` tag and the closing `</APPLET>` tag (or the `<OBJECT>` and `</OBJECT>` tags, which also support parameters). The following is an `<APPLET>` tag that includes several parameters:

```
<APPLET CODE="ScrollingHeadline.class" HEIGHT=50 WIDTH=400>
<PARAM NAME="Headline1" VALUE="Dewey defeats Truman">
<PARAM NAME="Headline2" VALUE="Stix nix hix pix">
<PARAM NAME="Headline3" VALUE="Man bites dog">
</APPLET>
```

This example could be used to send news headlines to an applet that scrolls them across the screen. Because news changes all the time, the only way to create a program of this kind is with parameters. No other solution would work; just imagine how long it would take to recompile a Java program every time a National Basketball Association star player ran afoul of the law.

You use the NAME attribute to give the parameter a name. This attribute is comparable to giving a variable a name. The VALUE attribute gives the named parameter a value.

Receiving Parameters in the Applet

You have to do something in your Java program to retrieve the parameters on the Web page or they will be ignored. The getParameter() method of the JApplet class retrieves a parameter from a <PARAM> tag on a Web page. The parameter name, which is specified with the NAME attribute on the page, is used as an argument to getParameter(). The following is an example of getParameter() in action:

```
String display1 = getParameter("Headline1");
```

The getParameter() method returns all parameters as strings, so you have to convert them to other types as needed. If you want to use a parameter as an integer, you could use statements such as the following:

```
int speed;
String speedParam = getParameter("SPEED");
if (speedParam != null)
    speed = Integer.parseInt(speedParam);
```

This example sets the speed variable by using the speedParam string. You have to test for null strings before setting speed because the parseInt() method cannot work with a null string. When you try to retrieve a parameter with getParameter() that was not included on a Web page with the <PARAM> tag, it will be sent as null, which is the value of an empty string.

Handling Parameters in an Applet

The next project you'll undertake has little practical value, except perhaps as a taunting device. The ShowWeight applet takes a person's weight and displays it under several different units. The applet takes two parameters: a weight in pounds and the name of the person who weighs that amount. The weight is used to figure out the person's weight in ounces, kilograms, and metric tons, all of which are displayed.

Create a new file with your word processor and give it the name ShowWeight.java. Enter Listing 14.1 into the file. Then save and compile the file.

14

LISTING 14.1   THE FULL TEXT OF ShowWeight.java

```java
 1: import java.awt.*;
 2:
 3: public class ShowWeight extends com.sun.java.swing.JApplet {
 4:     float lbs = (float)0;
 5:     float ozs;
 6:     float kgs;
 7:     float metricTons;
 8:     String name = "somebody";
 9:
10:     public void init() {
11:         String lbsValue = getParameter("weight");
12:         if (lbsValue != null) {
13:             Float lbsTemp = Float.valueOf(lbsValue);
14:             lbs = lbsTemp.floatValue();
15:         }
16:         String personValue = getParameter("person");
17:         if (personValue != null)
18:             name = personValue;
19:
20:         ozs = (float)(lbs * 16);
21:         kgs = (float)(lbs / 2.204623);
22:         metricTons = (float)(lbs / 2204.623);
23:     }
24:
25:     public void paint(Graphics screen) {
26:         super.paint(screen);
27:         Graphics2D screen2D = (Graphics2D) screen;
28:         screen2D.drawString("Studying the weight of " + name, 5, 30);
29:         screen2D.drawString("In pounds: " + lbs, 55, 50);
30:         screen2D.drawString("In ounces: " + ozs, 55, 70);
31:         screen2D.drawString("In kilograms: " + kgs, 55, 90);
32:         screen2D.drawString("In metric tons: " + metricTons, 55, 110);
33:     }
34: }
```

The init() method is where the two parameters are loaded into the applet. Because they come from the Web page as strings, they must be converted into the form you need: a floating-point number for the lbs variable and a string for name. Converting a string to a floating-point number requires two steps: converting the string to a Float object and then converting that object to a variable of the type float.

As you learned with strings, objects and variables are treated differently in Java programs, and there are different things you can do with them. The reason there is a `Float` object and a `float` variable type is so you can use a floating-point number as either an object or a variable. The `Float` object class also has useful methods, such as `valueOf()` and `floatValue()`, that you can use to convert floating-point numbers into different types of variables.

Lines 20–22 are used to convert the `lbs` variable into different units of measure. Each of these statements has `(float)` in front of the conversion equation. This is used to cast the result of the equation into a floating-point number.

The `paint()` method of the applet uses the `drawString()` method of the `Graphics2D` class to display a line of text onscreen. The `paint()` method has three arguments: the text to display and the x and y positions where the text should be shown.

Before you can test the `ShowWeight` applet, you need to create a Web page that contains the applet. Open up a new file on your word processor and name it `ShowWeight.html`. Enter Listing 14.2 and save it when you're done.

LISTING 14.2 THE FULL TEXT OF `ShowWeight.html`

```
1: <applet code="ShowWeight.class" height=170 width=210>
2: <param name="person" value="Konishiki">
3: <param name="weight" value=605>
4: </applet>
```

Use the `appletviewer` tool to see the `ShowWeight` applet. This demonstration uses Konishiki as its example because the American-born sumo wrestling champion weighs in at more than 605 pounds, making him the largest of the immodest bikini-wearing behemoths. You can substitute anyone whose weight is either exemplary or well-known. Figure 14.1 shows an example of output from the applet. As you can see, Konishiki's workout regimen doesn't include a lot of fat-free SnackWell's Devil's Food Cakes.

To make the applet display a different name along with a different value for the `"weight"` parameter, all you have to change is the `ShowWeight.html` file. The applet itself will continue to work correctly.

FIGURE 14.1

The output of the
ShowWeight *applet.*

A Revolving-Link Applet

To provide more information on how applets are programmed, the remainder of this hour includes an extended project describing the design of a threaded applet. The program you'll be writing will rotate through a list of Web site titles and the addresses used to visit them.

The title of each page and the Web address will be displayed in a continuous cycle. Users will be able to visit the currently displayed site by clicking a button on the applet window. This program operates over a period of time; information on each Web site must be shown long enough to be read, and then the next site will be shown. Because of this time element, threads are the best way to control the program.

Instead of entering this program into your word processor first and learning about it afterward, you'll get a chance to enter the full text of the Revolve applet at the end of the hour. Before then, each section of the program will be described.

The `class` Declaration

The first thing you need to do in this applet is to use import to make some classes available.

The java.awt group of classes is needed because you'll be using one of them, Graphics2D, to display text onscreen. The java.net group will be used when you work with the Web addresses, and the java.applet group is needed when you tell the browser to load a new page. Finally, the java.awt.event group is needed to respond to mouse clicks so that a user can visit one of the addresses shown, and the com.sun.java.swing package is needed because it is used to create the applet window and other user interface elements.

Use the following import statements:

```
import java.applet.*;
import java.awt.*;
import java.awt.event.*;
```

```
import com.sun.java.swing.*;
import java.net.*;
```

> You might be wondering why the java.lang group of classes does not need to be imported. It automatically is available to all Java programs that you write and contains a lot of the classes you will use most often. The String, Integer, and Math classes are three examples of classes that belong to java.lang.

After you have used import to make some classes available, you're ready to begin the applet with the following statement:

```
public class Revolve extends JApplet
    implements Runnable, ActionListener {
```

This statement creates the Revolve class as a subclass of the JApplet class, as you do for all Java 2 applets. It also uses a new statement called implements.

The implements statement enables this class to inherit some extra methods beyond those that were inherited from the JApplet class. The Runnable and ActionListener classes are called *interfaces*.

An interface is a special type of class that is only useful in conjunction with the implements statement. An interface extends the capabilities of a class. In this case, Runnable provides the behavior an applet needs in order to become a thread. By implementing the Runnable class, you will be able to use a run() method in this applet to make a thread begin running. The ActionListener interface enables the applet to respond to actions the user takes with the mouse. Implementing it enables the actionPerformed() method to be called when a mouse button is clicked.

Setting Up Variables

The first thing to do in the Revolve class is to create the variables and objects needed throughout the program. Create two arrays with six elements—an array of String objects called pageTitle and an array of URL objects called pageLink:

```
String[] pageTitle = new String[6];
URL[] pageLink = new URL[6];
```

The pageTitle array will store the titles of the six Web sites that will be displayed. The URL class of objects stores the value of a Web site address. URL has all the behavior and attributes needed to keep track of a Web address and use it to load the page with a Web browser. Both of these arrays are set up without any values at this point, so you'll have to provide them later.

14

The last two things to be created are an integer variable called current and a Thread object called runner:

```
int current = 0;
Thread runner;
```

The current variable will be used to keep track of which site is being displayed so you can cycle through the sites. The Thread object runner represents the only thread this program runs. You will call methods of the runner object when you start, stop, and pause the operation of the applet.

Starting with init()

The init() method of an applet automatically is handled once when the applet first starts to run. In this example, this method is used to assign values to the two arrays created for this applet, pageTitle and pageLink. It also is used to create a clickable button that will appear on the applet. The method consists of the following statements:

```
public void init() {
    Color background = new Color(255, 255, 204);
    setBackground(background);
    pageTitle[0] = "Sun's Java site";
    pageLink[0] = getURL("http://java.sun.com");
    pageTitle[1] = "Java News";
    pageLink[1] = getURL("http://www.intelligence.com/java");
    pageTitle[2] = "JavaWorld";
    pageLink[2] = getURL("http://www.javaworld.com");
    pageTitle[3] = "Java 2 in 24 Hours";
    pageLink[3] = getURL("http://www.prefect.com/java24");
    pageTitle[4] = "Macmillan Computer Publishing";
    pageLink[4] = getURL("http://www.mcp.com");
    pageTitle[5] = "Java Applet Rating Service";
    pageLink[5] = getURL("http://www.jars.com");
    Button goButton = new Button("Go");
    goButton.addActionListener(this);
    FlowLayout flow = new FlowLayout();
    Container pane = getContentPane();
    pane.setLayout(flow);
    pane.add(goButton);
    setContentPane(pane);
}
```

The first two statements of this method set up a background color for the applet. You'll learn how to do this during Hour 16, "Using Fonts and Color in Applets."

Strings are assigned to the six elements of the pageTitle array, which stores the title of each Web page. The elements of the pageLink array are assigned a value returned by the getURL() method, which you will be creating for this program.

The last seven statements of the init() method are used to create a button and place it on the applet window. The button has the name goButton and is labeled with the text Go. Creating user interface components like buttons and using them in programs will be explained in detail during Hour 19, "Building a Simple User Interface with Swing," and Hour 20, "Responding to User Events with Swing."

Catching Errors as You Set Up URLs

When you set up a URL object, you must make sure that the text used to set up the address is in a valid format. http://java.sun.com and http://www.mcp.com are valid, but something such as http:www.javaworld.com would not be because of the missing // marks.

A special statement called try...catch is used to catch errors inside the program instead of letting them cause it to stop running, as many errors do. The try statement lets your program try to do something that might cause an error. If an error does occur, the catch statement is used to catch the error before it brings the program to a crashing halt.

> If you're having trouble with the concept of try and catch statements, think of what it would be like to be one of Superman's best pals. Jimmy Olsen and Lois Lane can try all kinds of dangerous stunts without worrying as much about the consequences if they make an error. No narrow ledge or runaway locomotive is too risky an endeavor for them to attempt to navigate. If they try and fail, Superman will be there to catch them. No matter what you try in a Java program, you can create a catch statement that will catch errors.

The getURL() method takes a string of text as an argument. The string is checked to see if it's a valid Web address, and, if it is, the method returns that valid address. If it's erroneous, the method sends back a null value. The following is the getURL() method:

```
URL getURL(String urlText) {
    URL pageURL = null;
    try {
        pageURL = new URL(getDocumentBase(), urlText);
    }
    catch (MalformedURLException m) { }
    return pageURL;
}
```

The first line of this method includes three things, in this order:

- The type of object or variable that is returned by the method—a URL object in this case. If this is void, no information is returned by the method.

14

- The name of the method—getURL.
- The argument or arguments, if any, that this method takes—only one in this example, a String variable called urlText.

The try statement is followed by { and } marks. The program handles any statements between these marks, and, if they generate any exception or error conditions, these will be sent to the catch statement.

The catch statement also has { and } marks as part of the statement. If catch is set up to catch an error from the try block statement, anything between the { and } marks will be handled. In this example, if a MalformedURLException error occurs during the try block of statements, any statements between the { and } marks after catch will be handled. Because there are no statements between { and } in this method, catch ignores any MalformedURLException errors that occur.

If the string variable sent to the method is a valid Web address, it will be sent back as a valid URL object. If not, null is returned. Because you were assigning values to six different URL objects in the pageURL array, the getURL() method makes this process easier to do.

Handling Screen Updates in the paint() Method

The paint() method of any applet is handled when the screen needs to be updated. This situation can be caused by the Web browser or operating system outside of the applet if they obscure part of an applet window or change its dimensions in some way. The paint() method also can be called manually within an applet when the screen needs to be updated.

If you put a repaint(); statement in an applet, it forces the paint() method to be handled. This statement is a way you can tell the program that you have done something that requires a screen update. For example, if you are writing an animation program and you move an image from one place to another, you need to use repaint(); so the image is shown in its new location.

The Revolve applet has a short paint() method:

```
public void paint(Graphics screen) {
    super.paint(screen);
    Graphics2D screen2D = (Graphics2D) screen;
    screen2D.drawString(pageTitle[current], 5, 60);
    screen2D.drawString("" + pageLink[current], 5, 80);
}
```

The two statements inside the method display lines of text on the screen at the (x,y) positions of (5,60) and (5,80). The first line that is displayed is an element of the pageTitle array. The second line displayed is the address of the URL object, which is stored in the pageLink array. The current variable is used to determine which elements of these arrays to display.

Starting the Thread

One of the objects created for this program is a Thread object called runner. In order for a thread to get started, a place is needed where the thread is given a value and told to begin running. In this applet, the runner thread will start whenever the start() method is handled and stop whenever stop() is handled.

The start() method of an applet is handled at two different times: right after the init() method and every time the program is restarted after being stopped. An applet is stopped any time a user switches from the applet page to another Web page. It starts again when a user returns to the original page. The following is the start() method of the Revolve applet:

```
public void start() {
    if (runner == null) {
        runner = new Thread(this);
        runner.start();
    }
}
```

This method does only one thing: If the runner thread is not already started, it creates a new runner thread and starts it. The runner object equals null when it has not been started yet, so you can test for this condition with the if statement.

The statement runner = new Thread(this); creates a new Thread object with one argument—the this statement. Using this makes the applet itself the program that will run in the runner thread.

The runner.start(); statement causes the thread to begin running. When a thread begins, the run() method of that thread is handled. Because the runner thread is the applet itself, the run() method of the applet is handled.

Running the Thread

The run() method is where the main work of a thread takes place. It is comparable to the main() block statement of a Java application. In the Revolve applet, the following represents the run() method:

```
public void run() {
    Thread thisThread = Thread.currentThread();
    while (runner == thisThread) {
        repaint();
        current++;
        if (current > 5)
            current = 0;
        try {
            Thread.sleep(10000);
        } catch (InterruptedException e) { }
    }
}
```

The first thing that takes place in the run() method is to create a Thread object called thisThread. A class method of the Thread class, currentThread(), is used to set up the value for the thisThread object. The currentThread() method keeps track of the thread that's currently running.

All of the statements in this method are part of a while loop that compares the runner object to the thisThread object. Both of these objects are threads, and as long as they have the same value, the while loop will continue looping. There's no statement inside this loop that causes the runner and thisThread objects to have different values, so it will loop indefinitely unless something outside of the loop changes one of the Thread objects.

The run() method first uses the repaint(); statement to cause the paint() method to be handled. Next, the value of the current variable increases by 1, and if current exceeds 5, it is set to 0 again. The current variable is used in the paint() method to determine which Web site information to display. Changing current causes a different site to be displayed the next time paint() is handled.

This method includes another try...catch statement that handles an error that might occur. The Thread.sleep(10000); statement causes a thread to pause for 10,000 milliseconds. This statement causes the thread to wait long enough for users to read the name of the Web site and its address. The catch statement takes care of any InterruptedException errors that might occur while the Thread.sleep() statement is being handled. These errors would occur if something interrupted the thread while it was trying to sleep().

Stopping the Thread

The stop() method is handled any time the applet is stopped because the applet's page is exited, and it is the best place to stop the running thread. The stop() method for the Revolve applet contains the following statements:

```
public void stop() {
    if (runner != null) {
        runner = null;
    }
}
```

The if statement tests to see whether the runner object is equal to null. If it is, there isn't an active thread that needs to be stopped. Otherwise, the statement sets runner equal to null.

Setting the runner object to a null value causes it to have a different value than the thisThread object. When this happens, the while loop inside the run() method will stop running.

Handling Mouse Clicks

Anything the user does with a mouse or keyboard in an applet is called an *event*, and the process of responding to events in a program is called *event-handling*. You'll learn all about events in Hour 20.

The last thing to take care of in the Revolve applet are mouse clicks. Whenever you click the Go button, the Web browser should open the Web site that is listed. This is done with a method called actionPerformed(). The actionPerformed() method is called whenever the button is clicked.

The following is the actionPerformed() method of the Revolve applet:

```
public void actionPerformed(ActionEvent evt) {
    if (runner != null) {
        runner = null;
    }
    AppletContext browser = getAppletContext();
    if (pageLink[current] != null)
        browser.showDocument(pageLink[current]);
}
```

The first thing that happens in this method is that the runner thread is stopped in the same way it was stopped in the applet's stop() method. The next statement creates a new AppletContext object called browser.

An AppletContext object represents the environment in which the applet is being presented—in other words, the page it's located on and the Web browser that loaded the page.

The showDocument() method of this object is called with a single argument: a URL object representing a World Wide Web address. If the page represented by pageLink[current] is a valid address, showDocument() is used to request that the browser load the page.

Workshop: Revolving Links

Now that all aspects of the Revolve applet have been described, you're ready to create the program and test it. Run your word processor and create a new file called Revolve.java. Enter the text of Listing 14.1 and save the file when you're done.

LISTING 14.1 THE FULL TEXT OF Revolve.java

```
 1: import java.applet.*;
 2: import java.awt.*;
 3: import java.awt.event.*;
 4: import javax.swing.*;
 5: import java.net.*;
 6:
 7: public class Revolve extends JApplet
 8:     implements Runnable, ActionListener {
 9:
10:     String[] pageTitle = new String[6];
11:     URL[] pageLink = new URL[6];
12:     int current = 0;
13:     Thread runner;
14:
15:     public void init() {
16:         Color background = new Color(255, 255, 204);
17:         setBackground(background);
18:         pageTitle[0] = "Sun's Java site";
19:         pageLink[0] = getURL("http://java.sun.com");
20:         pageTitle[1] = "Java News";
21:         pageLink[1] = getURL("http://www.intelligence.com/java/");
22:         pageTitle[2] = "JavaWorld";
23:         pageLink[2] = getURL("http://www.javaworld.com");
24:         pageTitle[3] = "Java 2 in 24 Hours";
25:         pageLink[3] = getURL("http://www.prefect.com/java24");
26:         pageTitle[4] = "Macmillan Computer Publishing";
27:         pageLink[4] = getURL("http://www.mcp.com");
28:         pageTitle[5] = "Java Applet Rating Service";
29:         pageLink[5] = getURL("http://www.jars.com");
30:         Button goButton = new Button("Go");
31:         goButton.addActionListener(this);
32:         FlowLayout flow = new FlowLayout();
33:         Container pane = getContentPane();
34:         pane.setLayout(flow);
35:         pane.add(goButton);
36:         setContentPane(pane);
37:     }
38:
39:     URL getURL(String urlText) {
40:         URL pageURL = null;
41:         try {
```

```
42:                      pageURL = new URL(getDocumentBase(), urlText);
43:                  } catch (MalformedURLException m) { }
44:                  return pageURL;
45:          }
46:
47:          public void paint(Graphics screen) {
48:              super.paint(screen);
49:              Graphics2D screen2D = (Graphics2D) screen;
50:              screen2D.drawString(pageTitle[current], 5, 60);
51:              screen2D.drawString("" + pageLink[current], 5, 80);
52:          }
53:          public void start() {
54:              if (runner == null) {
55:                  runner = new Thread(this);
56:                  runner.start();
57:              }
58:          }
59:
60:          public void run() {
61:              Thread thisThread = Thread.currentThread();
62:              while (runner == thisThread) {
63:                  repaint();
64:                  current++;
65:                  if (current > 5)
66:                      current = 0;
67:                  try {
68:                      Thread.sleep(10000);
69:                  } catch (InterruptedException e) { }
70:              }
71:          }
72:
73:          public void stop() {
74:              if (runner != null) {
75:                  runner = null;
76:              }
77:          }
78:
79:          public void actionPerformed(ActionEvent evt) {
80:              if (runner != null) {
81:                  runner = null;
82:              }
83:              AppletContext browser = getAppletContext();
84:              if (pageLink[current] != null)
85:                  browser.showDocument(pageLink[current]);
86:          }
87: }
```

After you compile this program with the `javac` compiler tool, you need to create a Web page on which to put the applet. Create a new file with your word processor and name it

Revolve.html. Enter Listing 14.2 and save the file. Note that some HTML tags have been included so you can see the applet in the way it might be presented on a real page.

LISTING 14.2   THE FULL TEXT OF Revolve.html

```
 1: <html>
 2: <head>
 3: <title>Homer's Home Page</title>
 4: </head>
 5: <body bgcolor="#C4C4C4">
 6: <font face="Arial" size=3>
 7: <table>
 8: <tr>
 9:
10: <td bgcolor="#FFCCFF" width=300 valign="TOP" align="CENTER">
11: <h2>Homer's Home Page</h2>
12: <p>Welcome to the cyberspace home of Homer! This page is under
13: construction.
14: </td>
15:
16: <td bgcolor="#FFFFCC" width=200 valign="TOP" align="RIGHT">
17: <i><b>Some of my favorite links:</b></i>
18: <applet code="Revolve.class" height=100 width=200>
19: </applet>
20: <center>
21: <i>Click to visit</i>
22: </center>
23: </td>
24:
25: </tr>
26: </table>
27: </font>
28: </body>
28: </html>
```

When you're done, load this file into appletviewer. You can test the applet itself from this program, but you will not see the surrounding HTML or be able to load a new Web page when the Go button is clicked. These features require the use of a Web browser that is equipped to handle Java 2 programs. Figure 14.2 shows the output of the Revolve applet in the appletviewer tool.

So that you can see how this applet would look on a Web browser, Figure 14.2 shows a modified version of Revolve using Netscape Navigator. This version uses Java 1.02, so it can be used on any browser that supports Java.

FIGURE 14.2

A screen capture of the Revolve *applet using* appletviewer.

FIGURE 14.3

A screen capture of a modified Revolve *applet using Netscape Navigator.*

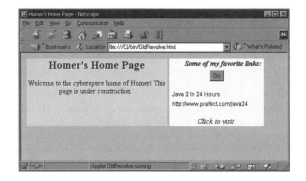

If you'd like to run this modified version using a Web browser, you can find it on the book's Web site at http://www.prefect.com/java24.

Summary

Now that you have programmed applets that make use of parameters and threads, you should be getting a better idea of the behind-the-scenes work that takes place in an applet. Many of the methods in these programs often are called automatically, such as paint().

With or without threads, writing applets requires an understanding of the methods that might be included in an applet and how they function. In the next several hours, you'll get more chances to see which methods are called automatically and how to use them in your own programs.

Even if you learned nothing else from this hour, you now have a new 90s term to describe your frenzied lifestyle. Use it in a few sentences to see if it grabs you:

- "Boy, I was really multithreading yesterday after Mom was indicted for mail fraud."

- "I multithreaded all through lunch, and it gave me gas."
- "Not tonight, dear, I'm multithreading."

Q&A

Q Why isn't `com.sun.java.swing.JApplet` needed in the `class` statement of the `Revolve` applet?

A It isn't needed because of the `import` statement that makes all of the `com.sun.java.swing` classes available to the program. The only purpose of `import` is to make it easier to refer to classes in a program. If you don't use it, you have to use full class references such as `com.sun.java.swing.JApplet` instead of simply `JApplet`. You could write all of your Java programs without using `import`, though it would make the source files more difficult to understand.

Q If the `Revolve` applet only has one thread, what's the point of using threads at all?

A Multithreading has benefits even it's really just one-threading. One of the main benefits is that you can start, stop, and pause a thread from within a program; you don't have the same kind of control without threads. Also, by making an applet a thread, even for a single-thread project, you make it easier to implement additional threads as needed later on.

Q Are there any reasons not to leave a pair of empty brackets after a `catch` statement, which causes errors to be disregarded?

A It depends on the type of error or exception that is being caught. In the `Revolve` applet, you know with both `catch` statements what the cause of an exception would be. Because of this knowledge, you can handle the error. In the `getURL()` method, the `MalformedURLException` would only be caused if the URL sent to the method were invalid.

Q Does the name of a parameter on a Web page have to be capitalized exactly as it is shown as an argument to the `getParameter()` method?

A Like all HTML tags and attributes, the `NAME` and `VALUE` attributes of the `<PARAM>` tag do not have to be capitalized a specific way to work. The text `"Speed"` and `"speed"` and `"SPEED"` all refer to the same parameter.

Quiz

Set aside your threads (in the Java sense, not the nudity sense), and answer the following questions about multithreading in Java.

Questions

1. What class must be implemented for an applet to use threads?

    (a) `Runnable`

    (b) `Thread`

    (c) `Applet`

2. When the `getParameter()` method is used to load a parameter value into a program, what type of information is loaded?

    (a) A `String` variable

    (b) A different type depending on the parameter

    (c) An array of characters

3. You're admiring the work of another programmer who has created an applet that handles four simultaneous tasks. What should you tell him?

    (a) "That's not half as exciting as the Debbie Matenopoulos screen saver I downloaded off the Web."

    (b) "You're the wind beneath my wings."

    (c) "Nice threads!"

Answers

1. a. `Runnable` must be used with the `implements` statement. `Thread` is used inside a multithreaded program, but it is not needed in the class statement that begins a program.

2. a. All parameters are received by an applet as `String` objects. They have to be converted to another type of variable or object if you want to use them differently.

3. c. This compliment could be confusing if the programmer is well-dressed, but let's be honest—what are the chances of that?

Activities

If this long workshop hasn't left you feeling threadbare, expand your skills with the following activities:

- If you are comfortable with HTML, create your own home page that includes the `Revolve` applet and six of your own favorite Web sites. Use the applet along with other graphics and text on the page.

- Add a parameter to the ShowWeight applet that specifies the ideal weight of the person. Display how many weeks of dieting it would take them to reach it, given five pounds of weight loss per week.

To see Java programs that implement these activities, visit the book's Web site at http://www.prefect.com/java24.

HOUR 15

Playing Sound in an Applet

If you're a science-fiction fan, the concept of talking computers should be one that is well-familiar to you. For years, television shows such as *Star Trek* have featured computers with the gift of gab. These machines could talk, listen, and comprehend the quirks of spoken language better than many professional baseball players.

After watching the movie *2001, A Space Odyssey* as a teenager, I was deeply disappointed when my brand new Commodore 64 computer resisted all efforts to learn the English language. (On the plus side, it never tried to kill me, so there are some benefits to owning a less capable system.)

Today, sound is becoming more sophisticated in computer software, which brings us closer to the day when computers talk to us as comfortably as the HAL 9000 spoke to the astronauts in *2001*. Java offers the ability to play audio files in numerous formats, and you'll get a chance to make your machine sound off as you learn the following topics during this hour:

- The sound capabilities of the `JApplet` class
- Sound file formats that you can use
- Loading a sound into an `AudioClip` for playback
- Starting and stopping playback of sounds
- Creating a looping sound
- Mixing different sounds together
- Packaging an applet's files into a Java archive

Retrieving and Using Sounds

All sound capabilities of the Java language are handled through the `JApplet` class, the superclass of all Java 2 applets. Although this might make you think that sounds are strictly for use in applets, you can load and play sound files in any of your Java programs.

Grouping sound capabilities with applets is a quirk of the Java language's original design. When Java had many fewer classes as of version 1.0, audio features were included in the `Applet` class, perhaps because they were used most often with applets. `JApplet` inherits from the `Applet` class.

There are two ways that sounds can be played in a program: as a one-time occurrence or in a repeating loop.

Sounds are loaded from a file that must have a format supported by the `JApplet` class. Although past versions of the Java language could handle only one sound file format, Java 2 has been extended to handle each of the following formats:

- AU files
- AIFF files
- WAV files

Each of these formats is a way to digitally represent actual sounds. To create a sound file in one of these formats, the actual sound is recorded by a computer and converted into a form that can be saved to a file.

The names of these sound formats are used as their filename extensions, so WAV files are saved with the `.WAV` extension, AU with `.AU`, and AIFF with `.AIFF`.

Java also can handle three different MIDI-based sound file formats: Type 0 MIDI, Type 1 MIDI, and RMF. These formats break down sound into the musical notes, instruments, and loudness used to create that sound. Each computer that can play MIDI files knows how to represent each of these things when they are encountered.

For example, if a MIDI file contains several musical notes played in a tuba-like sound, the software playing the file will encounter the notes and dutifully call upon its information on what a tuba sounds like and play the notes.

MIDI files are much smaller than their digital counterparts and are great for playing instrumental music and sound effects. What they can't do is represent more complex sounds such as the spoken voice.

Simple Sound Playback

The simplest way to retrieve and play a sound is through the play() method of the JApplet class.

In an applet, the play() method can be called with two arguments:

- A URL object representing the folder on the World Wide Web that contains the sound file
- A string indicating the name of the file

If the URL object is a specific Web folder such as http://www.prefect.com/java24, the sound file should be stored in this folder. However, if you move the applet to a new World Wide Web site later, you must change the source code of the program for it to continue working.

A more flexible solution is to use the applet's getCodeBase() method to provide a URL. This method returns the folder that contains the Java applet playing the sound file. As long as you store the applet and sound file in the same folder, the program will work without modification.

The following example retrieves and plays the sound kaboom.au, which is stored in the same place as the applet:

```
play(getCodeBase(), "kaboom.au");
```

The play() method retrieves and plays the given sound as soon as possible. You won't see an error message if the sound can't be found—silence is the only indicator that something might not be working as desired.

Loading Sounds into `AudioClip` Objects

If you want to do other things with a sound file, such as play it repeatedly or start and stop the sound, you must load the file into an `AudioClip` object. This is handled in an applet with the following two steps:

- Create an `AudioClip` object without calling a constructor method.
- Give this `AudioClip` object a value by calling the applet's `getAudioClip()` method.

The `getAudioClip()` method can be called with the same two arguments as the applet's `play()` method: a URL object (or `getCodeBase()`) and the name of the sound file.

The following statement loads a sound file into the `dance` object:

```
AudioClip dance = getAudioClip(getCodeBase(),
    "audio/chachacha.wav");
```

The filename includes a folder reference in this example, so the file `chachacha.wav` will be loaded from the subfolder `audio`.

The `getAudioClip()` method can be used only in an applet. If you want to load a sound file into an application, you must create an `AudioClip` object and give it a value by calling a class method of the `JApplet` class.

In an application, before you can create a new `AudioClip` object, you must create a URL object that identifies the name of the sound file.

The name should be preceded with the text `"file:"` to indicate that it is being loaded from a local file rather than a location on the Internet.

The following example can be used in an application to create an `AudioClip` object associated with the file `chachacha.wav` in a subfolder named `audio`:

```
URL dance = new URL("file"audio/chachacha.wav");
AudioClip danceClip = JApplet.newAudioClip(dance);
```

Playing and Looping `AudioClip` Objects

After you have created an `AudioClip` object and associated it with a sound file, you can use three of its methods to control how the sound is used.

- The `play()` method plays the sound once.
- The `loop()` method plays the sound repeatedly.
- The `stop()` method stops the sound from playing.

These methods are called without any arguments. Before you call them on an `AudioClip` object, you should make sure that the object does not have a value of `null`. This prevents

you from trying to use the sound if the getAudioClip() or newAudioClip() methods did not find the sound file. Calling the methods of a null object will result in an error.

If you play more than one sound at a time, Java will automatically mix the sounds together, which enables some interesting effects. An example would be a MIDI file playing as background music while WAV files are used for sound effects in the foreground.

The LaughTrack applet in Listing 15.1 uses Java to create a laugh track. If this term is new to you, you're probably one of the people responsible for the declining viewership of broadcast television. While you're off reading books, hiking, building ships-in-a-bottle, and engaging in other enriching pursuits, the rest of us are watching primetime television comedies. On these comedies, canned laughter often is played to make the shows seem more comic than they might appear otherwise. This laughter is called a laugh track.

To create a laugh track in a Java applet, four different WAV files containing the sound of laughing people will be loaded into AudioClip objects. Each object then will be played in a loop, creating an impromptu laugh track. You'll have to decide if the end result approximates the sound of a television audience in fits of uncontrolled hysterics.

Enter the text of Listing 15.1 using your preferred word processor, and save the file as LaughTrack.java when you're done.

LISTING 15.1   THE FULL SOURCE CODE OF LaughTrack.java

```
 1: import java.awt.*;
 2: import java.applet.AudioClip;
 3:
 4: public class LaughTrack extends com.sun.java.swing.JApplet
 5:     implements Runnable {
 6:
 7:     AudioClip[] laugh = new AudioClip[4];
 8:     Thread runner;
 9:
10:     public void start() {
11:         if (runner == null) {
12:             runner = new Thread(this);
13:             runner.start();
14:         }
15:     }
16:
17:     public void stop() {
18:         if (runner != null) {
19:             for (int i = 0; i < laugh.length; i++)
20:                 if (laugh[i] != null)
21:                     laugh[i].stop();
22:             runner = null;
```

continues

LISTING **15.1**   CONTINUED

```
23:            }
24:        }
25:
26:        public void init() {
27:            for (int i = 0; i < laugh.length; i++)
28:                laugh[i] = getAudioClip(getCodeBase(),
29:                    "laugh" + i + ".wav");
30:        }
31:
32:        public void run() {
33:            for (int i = 0; i < laugh.length; i++)
34:                if (laugh[i] != null)
35:                    laugh[i].loop();
36:            Thread thisThread = Thread.currentThread();
37:            while (runner == thisThread) {
38:                try {
39:                    Thread.sleep(5000);
40:                } catch (InterruptedException e) { }
41:            }
42:        }
43:
44:        public void paint(Graphics screen) {
45:            Graphics2D screen2D = (Graphics2D) screen;
46:            screen2D.drawString("Playing Sounds ...", 10, 50);
47:        }
48: }
```

After you have saved LaughTrack.java, you can compile it with the following command:

```
javac LaughTrack.java
```

The next step is to create a Web page that contains the applet. Enter the text of Listing 15.2 into your word processor and save the file as LaughTrack.html.

LISTING **15.2**   THE FULL TEXT OF LaughTrack.html

```
1: <applet code="LaughTrack.class" height=80 width=140>
2: </applet>
```

The final task that's required before you can test this applet is to download the audio files being used in this project. The LaughTrack applet requires four files: laugh0.wav, laugh1.wav, laugh2.wav, and laugh3.wav. These are available from this book's Web site at http://www.prefect.com/java24. Download these files and save them in the same folder as the LaughTrack applet's class file.

This hour's workshop also requires its own files from the book's Web site: the WAV files `plus.wav`, `equals.wav`, and 11 numbered files beginning with `number0.wav` and ending with `number10.wav`. You can save some time by downloading these now.

When you have downloaded all of the files used in the `LaughTrack` applet, load the Web page `LaughTrack.html` by using the `appletviewer` tool. The text "Playing Sounds ..." will appear in the applet window accompanied by four people laughing.

If the result sounds anything like a real audience watching a television show being taped, it may explain why the stars of *Seinfeld* were ready to stop working on such a lucrative TV show. Bret Butler's stress-related departure from *Grace Under Fire* and similar troubles experienced by other stars also seem more understandable.

The `LaughTrack` applet runs in a thread using techniques you learned about during the previous hour, "Creating a Threaded Applet." Sound files, like animation, require a lot of processing time, so it's more efficient to place them into one or more threads.

Java Archives

Applets that use sound or graphics often require several different files to be loaded before the program can run successfully. The `LaughTrack` applet is a good example of this, requiring five different files: `LaughTrack.class` and four `.WAV` audio files.

Because of the way the World Wide Web functions, each of these files requires its own connection between the Web server offering the applet and the user running the program during a Web surfing session. The same is true of World Wide Web pages—each graphic requires its own connection.

One way to reduce the time required to load an applet is to package all of its files into a single archive file.

The Java Development Kit includes a command-line tool called `jar` that enables Java archive files to be created, examined, and unpackaged.

Java archive files have the `.JAR` file extension. The `jar` tool is used to package a group of files into a single `.JAR` file. If you wanted to archive all five files associated with the `LaughTrack` applet into a single `.JAR` file, the following command could be entered at a command-line:

```
jar cf LaughTrack.jar LaughTrack.class laugh*.wav
```

No file folders are included with the filenames in this example, so it must be used in the same folder that contains LaughTrack.class and the four .wav files used by the applet.

The jar tool takes the following arguments when it is run:

- Options determining what jar should do (cf in the previous example)
- The name of the archive (LaughTrack.jar)
- The file (or files) to be archived, with each filename separated by a space (LaughTrack.class and laugh*.wav)

Wildcards can be used when specifying filenames, so laugh*.wav refers to any file with a name that begins with laugh and ends with .wav. You also can list each file separately.

> The jar tool includes its own built-in help feature. To see a brief rundown of the ways it can be used, enter jar at the command-line without any arguments.

After you have created a Java archive containing all files used in an applet, the ARCHIVE attribute of the <APPLET> tag is used to associate this archive with the applet.

Listing 15.3 contains an example—a Web page loading the LaughTrack applet and all of its files from the LaughTrack.jar archive.

LISTING 15.3 THE FULL TEXT OF LaughTrack2.html.

```
1: <applet code="LaughTrack.class" archive="LaughTrack.jar"
2: height=80 width=140>
3: </applet>
```

When the ARCHIVE attribute is used with an applet, the applet's main class file should be included in the specified archive file. The CODE attribute must still be used, because the name of the main class file must still be identified, whether it's loaded directly or from an archive.

Java archives are a way to speed up the presentation of applets and to organize other multifile projects. All JavaBeans components are packaged into .jar files, making them more self-contained and keeping them in a single file that's easier to make available for use in other Java programs.

Workshop: Making Your Computer Talk to You

At this point, you've seen how Java's audio capabilities can be used to either simulate hysterics or to promote them. Your workshop project this hour puts Java's aural features to more productive use by creating a simple math tutor.

The MathMan applet uses 12 sound files that are available from the book's Web site: plus.wav, equals.wav, and 10 numbered files from number0.wav to number10.wav. If you haven't retrieved these files yet, visit http://www.prefect.com/java24. All 12 files should be saved in the same folder you're going to use for this workshop's .java, .class, and .html files.

Each of these files contains a computer-synthesized voice speaking a specific word. See if you can guess what these words are as you enter the text of Listing 15.4 into your word processor.

LISTING 15.4 THE FULL SOURCE CODE OF MathMan.java

```
 1: import java.awt.*;
 2: import java.applet.AudioClip;
 3:
 4: public class MathMan extends com.sun.java.swing.JApplet
 5:     implements Runnable {
 6:
 7:     AudioClip[] number = new AudioClip[11];
 8:     AudioClip plus;
 9:     AudioClip equals;
10:     int sum, num1, num2;
11:     Thread runner;
12:
13:     public void start() {
14:         if (runner == null) {
15:             runner = new Thread(this);
16:             runner.start();
17:         }
18:     }
19:
20:     public void stop() {
21:         if (runner != null)
22:             runner = null;
23:     }
24:
25:     public void init() {
26:         equals = getAudioClip(getCodeBase(), "equals.wav");
```

continues

LISTING **15.4**   CONTINUED

```
27:          plus = getAudioClip(getCodeBase(), "plus.wav");
28:          for (int i = 0; i < number.length; i++)
29:              number[i] = getAudioClip(getCodeBase(),
30:                  "number" + i + ".wav");
31:      }
32:
33:    public void run() {
34:        Thread thisThread = Thread.currentThread();
35:        while (runner == thisThread) {
36:            sum = (int) Math.floor(Math.random() * 10 + 1);
37:            num2 = (int) Math.floor(Math.random() * sum);
38:            num1 = sum - num2;
39:            repaint();
40:            number[num1].play();
41:            pause(600);
42:            plus.play();
43:            pause(600);
44:            number[num2].play();
45:            pause(600);
46:            equals.play();
47:            pause(600);
48:            number[sum].play();
49:            pause(5000);
50:        }
51:    }
52:
53:    public void paint(Graphics screen) {
54:        super.paint(screen);
55:        Graphics2D screen2D = (Graphics2D) screen;
56:        screen2D.drawString(num1 + " + " + num2 + " = " + sum, 40,
                40);
57:    }
58:
59:    private void pause(int duration) {
60:        try {
61:            Thread.sleep(duration);
62:        } catch (InterruptedException e) { }
63:    }
64: }
```

When you're done, save the file as MathMan.java and create a new file. Enter the text of Listing 15.5 and save it as MathMan.html.

LISTING **15.5**   THE FULL TEXT OF MathMan.html

```
1: <applet code="MathMan.class" height=50 width=80>
2: </applet>
```

Compile this applet with the following command:

```
javac MathMan.java
```

This applet will display a simple mathematical expression using addition, as shown in Figure 15.1.

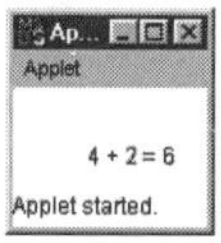

FIGURE 15.1

The MathMan *applet.*

Each of the 12 WAV files required by this applet is loaded into its own `AudioClip` object. These files will be played with calls to the `play()` method so that the mathematical expression is read aloud by the program.

Although this math tutor is a little basic for most people outside of the legislative branch of government, it's a good demonstration of how sound can enhance an educational presentation.

Summary

Now that you've had a chance to work with audio in your Java programs, you have a better perspective of the ever-present talking computers in science-fiction movies, TV shows, and novels.

When a computer talks on TV, it's just an example of a writer imagining how smart computers are supposed to be in the future. Making your own computer smart enough to talk requires more effort on your part.

Your Java programs now can do something my Commodore 64 was either unwilling or unable to do back in the early 80s: speak. Applets and applications also can play music, sound effects, and other noises.

Using audio files in an applet is a way to bring some attention to a World Wide Web page, because pages you can hear are still a rarity. However, when choosing your own files, it's important to use sound judgment: The `LaughTrack` applet is not likely to encourage repeat visits to a Web site.

Q&A

Q **Why is the `Thread.sleep()` method needed in the `MathMan` applet?**

A The call to `sleep()` causes the thread controlling the program to pause for a set amount of time. The integer argument to the method indicates the number of milliseconds to delay before continuing the thread. This prevents the running together of different sounds when the mathematical expression is being read aloud. Experiment with different durations for the pause to see how it affects playback of the audio.

Q **Is there a reason that `JApplet` should be used instead of the `Applet` class for audio playback?**

A The `JApplet` class inherits all of its sound capabilities from the `Applet` class, so it doesn't matter which class you use when working with sound. However, all Java 2 applets use the `JApplet` class, so there's no reason to use a different class when working with applet-related features.

Quiz

Test your knowledge of parameters with the following questions.

Questions

1. Which of the following is not an audio format supported by Java?

    (a) WAV

    (b) AU

    (c) DISCO

2. What's the benefit of using the `getCodeBase()` method to specify the location of a sound file in your applets?

    (a) The sound file loads more quickly.

    (b) You can move the applet to a new location on the World Wide Web without changing the program in any way.

    (c) All of your friends in the Java community already are doing it, so you won't be ostracized and ridiculed for being different.

3. What does URL stand for?

    (a) Universal Resource Locator

    (b) Uniform Resource Locator

    (c) Unexpected Radio Link

Answers

1. c. DISCO is not a valid audio format in Java. Some people might argue that it isn't a valid audio format in life, either, but you won't hear that from this author. I'm still saving clothes for the day when gold chains, Gloria Gaynor, and wide collars open to the navel make their triumphant comeback.

2. b.

3. b. Actually, a. isn't too off the mark, because URLs are sometimes referred to as Universal Resource Locators.

Activities

If your ears aren't ringing from all the sound advice you've received, consider the following activities:

- Create a new version of the MathMan applet that uses subtraction instead of addition, making sure that the mathematical expression does not include any numbers higher than 10 or lower than 0.

- Modify the LaughTrack applet so that it's an application instead of an applet.

To see Java programs that implement these activities, visit the book's Web site at http://www.prefect.com/java24.

HOUR 16

Using Fonts and Color in Applets

A famous catch phrase from the television show *Saturday Night Live* during the 1980s was, "It's not how you feel, but how you look…and darling, you look MAH-ve-lous." The quote epitomized the philosophy of Fernando, comedian Billy Crystal's eternally tan and impeccably groomed celebrity. Regardless of what was going on in his life, as long as his hair was styled properly and he was dressed for the occasion, everything was copacetic. After all, though Fernando hadn't been in a hit movie since *Won Ton Ton, the Dog Who Saved Hollywood*, he still looked good. Correction: He looked MAH-ve-lous.

If you're interested in making your Java applets look MAH-ve-lous, you should know about the `Font` and `Color` classes. No self-respecting applet would be seen in public without them. With these classes, you can present text in several different fonts and sizes and change the colors of text, graphics, and other elements.

One of the principles of object-oriented programming is to make an object work for itself, and the Font and Color objects follow this rule. They store all the information that's needed to display a font or change a color, and they can handle other related tasks that are required. The following topics will be covered during this hour:

- Using fonts in your applets
- Setting a font's style and size
- Displaying colors in applets
- Using the color constants
- Setting up the background color
- Using sRGB values to choose colors
- Using HSB values to choose colors
- Creating special text effects using colors

Using the Font Class

There are three things you need to know about a font in order to display it:

- The typeface of the font: Either a descriptive name (serif, sanserif, or monospaced) or an actual font name (Courier, Dialog, DialogInput, Helvetica, or TimesRoman)
- The style of the font: bold, italic, or plain
- The size of the font, in points

Before you can display text in a certain typeface, style, and point size, you need to create a Font object that holds this information. The following statement creates a 12 point serif italic Font object:

```
Font currentFont = new Font("serif", Font.ITALIC, 12);
```

When selecting a typeface, it's better to choose one of the descriptive names: serif, sanserif, and monospaced. This enables the system running the program to designate one of its own fonts that fits the description.

You choose the style of the font by using one or more constant variables. Specifying the style as Font.PLAIN makes it non-bold and non-italic, Font.BOLD makes it bold, and Font.ITALIC makes it italic. To combine bold and italic, use Font.BOLD+Font.ITALIC, as in the following code:

```
Font headlineFont = new Font("Courier", Font.BOLD+Font.ITALIC, 72);
```

The last argument specifies the point size of the font. To see a simple example of using fonts in an applet, open your word processor and create a new file called Fonts.java. Enter the text of Listing 16.1 and save the file.

LISTING 16.1   THE FULL TEXT OF Fonts.java

```
 1: import java.awt.*;
 2:
 3: public class Fonts extends com.sun.java.swing.JApplet {
 4:
 5:     public void paint(Graphics screen) {
 6:         Graphics2D screen2D = (Graphics2D) screen;
 7:         Font currentFont = new Font("TimesRoman", Font.PLAIN, 20);
 8:         screen2D.setFont(currentFont);
 9:         screen2D.drawString("If I've said it once, I've said it a "
10:             + "thousand times, darling,", 5, 50);
11:         currentFont = new Font("TimesRoman", Font.ITALIC, 40);
12:         screen2D.setFont(currentFont);
13:         screen2D.drawString("you look MAH-VE-LOUS", 5, 80);
14:     }
15: }
```

After you compile the file with the javac compiler tool, you need to create a Web page that contains the applet. Create a new file in your word processor called Fonts.html and enter the text of Listing 16.2.

LISTING 16.2   THE FULL TEXT OF Fonts.html

```
1: <applet code="Fonts.class" height=125 width=450>
2: </applet>
```

Save this file and then load this page into the appletviewer tool by using the following command:

```
appletviewer Fonts.html
```

The output should resemble Figure 16.1.

Using the Color Class

The simplest way to use a color in a Java program is to use one of the constant variables from the Color class. You can use the following constants: black, blue, cyan, darkGray, gray, green, lightGray, magenta, orange, pink, red, white, and yellow.

FIGURE 16.1

The output of the
Fonts *applet.*

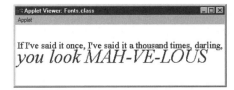

In an applet, you can set the background color of the applet window using these constants. The following is an example:

```
setBackground(Color.orange);
```

When you want to display text of a certain color or draw other graphics in different colors, you have to use a method that sets up the current color. You can do this from within the paint() method of an applet by using a setColor() method, as in the following:

```
public void paint(Graphics screen) {
    super.paint(screen);
    Graphics2D screen2D = (Graphics2D) screen;
    screen2D.setColor(Color.orange);
    screen2D.drawString("Go, Buccaneers!", 5, 50);
}
```

Unlike the setBackground() method, which is inherited directly from the JApplet class, the setColor() method must be used on an object that can handle a color change. The preceding example shows the setColor() method of the screen2D object being used to change the current color of the applet window.

Other Ways to Choose Colors

To use a color not included in the 13 constant variables, you must specify the color's sRGB or HSB values. sRGB, which stands for Standard Red Green Blue, defines a color by the amount of red, green, and blue that is present in the color. Each value ranges from 0, which means there is none of that color, to 255, which means the maximum amount of that color is present. Most graphics editing and drawing programs will identify a color's sRGB values.

If you know a color's sRGB values, you can use it to create a Color object. For example, an sRGB value for dark red is 235 red, 50 green, and 50 blue, and an sRGB value for light orange is 230 red, 220 green, and 0 blue. The following is an example of an applet that displays dark red text on a light orange background:

```
import java.awt.*;

public class GoBucs extends com.sun.java.swing.JApplet {
```

```
public void init() {
    Color lightOrange = new Color(230, 220, 0);
    setBackground(lightOrange);
}

public void paint(Graphics screen) {
    super.paint(screen);
    Graphics2D screen2D = (Graphics2D) screen;
    Color darkRed = new Color(235, 50, 50);
    screen2D.setColor(darkRed);
    screen2D.drawString("Go, Buccaneers!", 5, 50);
}
}
```

Dark red on a light orange background isn't much more attractive on a Java applet than it used to be on the National Football League's Tampa Bay Buccaneers, which might be the reason they switched to brass-and-pewter uniforms this past season. Using sRGB values enables you to select from more than 16.5 million possible combinations, although most computer monitors can only offer a close approximation for most of them. For guidance on whether light-light-light-semidark-midnight-blue goes well with medium-light-semidark-baby-green, purchase a copy of the upcoming *Sams Teach Yourself Color Sense While Waiting in Line at This Bookstore*.

Another way to select a color in a Java program is the HSB system, which stands for Hue Saturation Brightness. Each of these values is represented by a floating-point number that ranges from 0.0 to 1.0. The HSB system isn't as commonly supported in graphics software, so you won't be using it as often in your programs as you use RGB values. However, one thing HSB values are convenient for is changing a color's brightness without changing anything else about the color. You'll see an example of this use and an example of using HSB values to choose a color in this hour's workshop.

Workshop: Displaying a Danger Message

You can use Java applets to present news headlines and other information in different ways. One special effect you might see on a Web page is text that fades to black. You also might see the reverse—text that brightens from black to white. This hour's workshop uses the Font and Color classes to create text that cycles in brightness from dark to bright. The text looks like an alert about impending danger, so the applet will be called Danger.

To make the applet more useful, the text of the warning will be set from a parameter on a Web page. The text that will be used in this example warns of a "Core breach in Sector 12," but you can substitute other threatening text of similar length.

If you're at a secure place in your life right now and can't think of anything suitably menacing, feel free to choose one of the following:

- "Mother-in-law wants to visit"
- "Boss approaching"
- "Dallas Cowboys scheduled to play here"
- "We have no bananas today"
- "No hamburger—cheeseburger"

Create a new file in your word processor called Danger.java. Each section of the applet will be described as you enter it. Begin with the following statements:

```
import java.awt.*;

public class Danger extends com.sun.java.swing.JApplet
    implements Runnable {

    String text = "No text has been specified";
    float hue = (float) 0.5;
    float saturation = (float) 0.8;
    float brightness = (float) 0.0;
    Font textFont = new Font("Dialog", Font.BOLD, 20);
    int textX;
    Thread runner;
```

The program begins like most applets you will create. The java.awt classes, such as Font, Color, and FontMetrics, are made available for use in this program with the import statement. The class statement defines Danger as a subclass of the JApplet class. It also uses the implements keyword to indicate that Danger implements the Runnable interface, which is required for all classes that are threads.

The next several lines define variables and objects that will be used during the program. The string variable text is created with a default value, and it will be used to store the text that should be displayed onscreen. Three floating-point variables are used to store values for a color using its Hue Saturation Brightness ratings. The (float) portion of each line converts the value that follows it into a floating-point number. This conversion must be done because the hue, saturation, and brightness variables must be of type float.

The text of the applet will be displayed in 20 point Dialog bold. In order to do this, you need to create a Font object to store that font's values. The Font object, called textFont, is created for this purpose. Finally, the integer variable textX will be used when you're centering text from left-to-right on the screen, and a Thread object called runner is created to hold the thread that will run the Danger class.

After inserting a blank line, continue entering the Danger program by entering the init() method of the applet:

```
public void init() {
    setBackground(Color.black);
    String paramName = getParameter("TEXT");
    if (paramName != null)
        text = paramName;
    FontMetrics fm = getFontMetrics(textFont);
    textX = getSize().width / 2 - fm.stringWidth(text) / 2;
}
```

The init() method is handled once when the applet is first run, and then it is never handled again. It's a good place to set up some things that weren't set up when variables and objects were created. The first thing that happens in this method is the background of the applet is set to black by using the setBackground() method inherited by Danger from the JApplet class.

Next, the parameter called TEXT is retrieved from the Web page that contains this applet. If no parameter is found, the default text stored in text will be displayed. Otherwise, the text specified by the parameter will be stored in text.

The FontMetrics class measures how wide a line of text will appear when it is displayed. Using the stringWidth() method of FontMetrics and the applet's size() method, you can center text onscreen. The textX variable stores the horizontal position where the text should be displayed.

Now continue by entering the paint() method of your class, which is called whenever the display onscreen needs to be updated. After leaving a blank line after the init() method, enter the following:

```
public void paint(Graphics screen) {
    Graphics2D screen2D = (Graphics2D) screen;
    Color textColor = Color.getHSBColor(hue, saturation,
        brightness);
    screen2D.setColor(textColor);
    screen2D.setFont(textFont);
    screen2D.drawString(text, textX, 30);
}
```

The paint() method takes a Graphics object called screen as an argument, and then uses this object to cast a Graphics2D object called screen2D. The screen2D object holds all the information you need to display something onscreen, and it has several methods you'll use.

The Color object called textColor is created using the HSB variables to select the color. The textColor object then becomes the current display color using the setColor() method of screen.

Using the drawString() method of screen2D, the variable text is displayed at the (x,y) position of textX and 30. The color of the text is the current display color.

The paint() method handles most of the display work that takes place during the Danger applet. All you have left to add are two short methods called update() and pause(). Enter a blank line at the end of your program, and then continue with the following statements:

```
public void update(Graphics screen) {
    paint(screen);
}

void pause(int duration) {
    try {
        Thread.sleep(duration);
    } catch (InterruptedException e) { }
}
```

The update()method is one of the methods that normally works behind the scenes as an applet runs. It is handled any time the screen needs to be repainted or the repaint() statement is used. The update() method clears the screen and calls on paint() to do its work.

However, clearing the screen when you're changing graphics or text often causes things to flicker badly in a Java program. In this code, you're overriding the update() method so it does not clear the screen at all, which will improve the quality of your applet's display. You'll learn more about this during Hour 18, "Creating Animation."

The next thing in your applet is the pause() method, which takes an argument called duration. The method pauses the thread by using the Thread.sleep() method with an argument specifying the number of milliseconds to pause. When you are displaying changing graphics or text, you might need pauses of some kind to prevent things from changing too quickly. This pause() method shows one way to create these pauses.

To finish off the Danger applet, you need to add start(), stop(), and run() methods that control the threaded animation of the text. Add the following statements:

```
public void start() {
    if (runner == null) {
        runner = new Thread(this);
        runner.start();
    }
}

public void stop() {
    if (runner != null) {
        runner = null;
    }
}

public void run() {
    Thread thisThread = Thread.currentThread();
    while (runner == thisThread) {
        pause(75);
        brightness += 0.05;
        if (brightness > 1) {
            brightness = (float) 0.0;
            pause(75);
        }
        repaint();
    }
}
}
```

The stop() and start() methods are identical to those used previously during Hour 14, "Creating a Threaded Applet."

The run() method begins with the same two statements used in other threaded programs. A Thread object is created that holds the currently running thread, and it is compared to the runner object in a while loop.

This while loop is what causes the animation of the text to take place. The pause(75) statement causes the animation to pause 75 milliseconds between each update of the applet window. Without a pause of some kind, the text would flash different colors as quickly as a Java interpreter could handle it.

You have to change the value of the brightness variable for the text to change in brightness. The program increases the variable .05 (a 5 percent change), and, if the variable has reached the maximum brightness of 1.0, it is reset to 0.0. Whenever brightness must be reset to 0.0, the program calls the pause() method.

The last thing that takes place in the run() method's while loop is a call to the repaint() statement. You use this statement any time you need to redraw the screen because something has changed. Because the brightness variable changes each time through the while loop, you know there's a need to redisplay the text after every pause. The repaint() statement causes the paint() method to begin again.

Save the Danger.java file, which should resemble Listing 16.3. The only difference might be in the way you have indented methods and other statements. That does not have to be changed for the program to run, but indentation and other spacing can make a program easier to understand.

LISTING 16.3 THE FULL TEXT OF Danger.java

```
 1: import java.awt.*;
 2:
 3: public class Danger extends com.sun.java.swing.JApplet
 4:     implements Runnable {
 5:
 6:     String text = "No text has been specified";
 7:     float hue = (float) 0.5;
 8:     float saturation = (float) 0.8;
 9:     float brightness = (float) 0.0;
10:     Font textFont = new Font("Dialog", Font.BOLD, 20);
11:     int textX;
12:     Thread runner;
13:
14:     public void init() {
15:         setBackground(Color.black);
16:         String paramName = getParameter("TEXT");
17:         if (paramName != null)
18:             text = paramName;
19:         FontMetrics fm = getFontMetrics(textFont);
20:         textX = getSize().width / 2 - fm.stringWidth(text) / 2;
21:     }
22:
23:     public void paint(Graphics screen) {
24:         Graphics2D screen2D = (Graphics2D) screen;
25:         Color textColor = Color.getHSBColor(hue, saturation,
26:             brightness);
27:         screen2D.setColor(textColor);
28:         screen2D.setFont(textFont);
29:         screen2D.drawString(text, textX, 30);
30:     }
31:
32:     public void update(Graphics screen) {
33:         paint(screen);
34:     }
35:
36:     void pause(int duration) {
37:         try {
38:             Thread.sleep(duration);
39:         } catch (InterruptedException e) { }
```

```
40:     }
41:
42:     public void start() {
43:         if (runner == null) {
44:             runner = new Thread(this);
45:             runner.start();
46:         }
47:     }
48:
49:     public void stop() {
50:         if (runner != null) {
51:             runner = null;
52:         }
53:     }
54:
55:     public void run() {
56:         Thread thisThread = Thread.currentThread();
57:         while (runner == thisThread) {
58:             pause(75);
59:             brightness += 0.05;
60:             if (brightness > 1) {
61:                 brightness = (float) 0.0;
62:                 pause(75);
63:             }
64:             repaint();
65:         }
66:     }
67: }
```

After compiling the file with the javac compiler tool, you need to create a Web page that contains the Danger applet. Create a new file with your word processor called Danger.html, and enter the text of Listing 16.4 into the file.

LISTING 16.4 THE FULL TEXT OF Danger.html

```
1: <applet code="Danger.class" height=60 width=400>
2: <param name="TEXT" value="Core breach in Sector 12">
3: </applet>
```

You can change the value in line 2 to any other menacing sounding text, as long as it is similar in size to Core breach in Sector 12. Use the appletviewer tool to view the Web page with the following command:

```
appletviewer Danger.html
```

Figure 16.2 shows the output of the Danger applet.

FIGURE 16.2

A screen capture of the
Danger *applet as it*
runs with the
appletviewer *tool.*

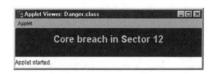

Summary

Now that you can use Font and Color objects in your programs to change the color scheme, you can no longer feign ignorance when it comes to designing an attractive applet. By using fonts and color instead of sticking to the familiar black text on a light gray background, you can draw more attention to elements of your programs and make them more compelling for users.

By combining these features, you're now one step closer to writing programs that look MAH-ve-lous. It's what Fernando would want you to do.

Q&A

Q Is there a limit to the point size that can be used for text?

A The limiting factor is the height and width of your applet window or the part of an applet in which the text is supposed to be displayed. Point sizes typically range from 9 point text for small lines that are readable to 48 point text for large headlines. Choosing the right size depends on the font typeface as well as the size, so it's largely a matter of trial and error.

Q What happens if a color defined in a Java program can't be displayed on the monitor of someone displaying the program? For example, if my monitor is set to display only 256 colors, what will occur if I choose one of the 16.5 million colors that isn't in those 256?

A When a monitor can't display a color selected with a setColor() or setBackground() method, it shows the closest existing color as a substitute. An example of this kind of substitution is the Danger applet, which runs differently depending on the number of colors that can be shown as the text cycles from black to light blue to white.

Quiz

Test whether your font and color skills are MAH-ve-lous by answering the following questions.

Questions

1. Which one of the following is *not* a constant used to select a color?

    (a) `Color.cyan`

    (b) `Color.teal`

    (c) `Color.magenta`

2. When you change the color of something and redraw it on an applet window, what must you do to make it visible?

    (a) Use the `drawColor()` method.

    (b) Use the `repaint()` statement.

    (c) Do nothing.

3. What do the initials HSB stand for?

    (a) Hue Saturation Brightness

    (b) Hue Shadows Balance

    (c) Lucy in the Sky with Diamonds

16

Answers

1. b.

2. b. The call to `repaint()` causes the `paint()` method to be manually called.

3. a. If c were the right answer, you could use colors that would only be visible years later during flashbacks.

Activities

To further explore the spectrum of possibilities when using fonts and color in your programs, do the following activities:

- Remove the `update()` method from the `Danger` applet to see what effect it has on the quality of the display.

- Add a way to specify the background of the `Danger` applet by sending parameters for the sRGB values of the desired background color.

To see Java programs that implement these activities, visit the book's Web site at `http://www.prefect.com/java24`.

Part V

Improving the Look of Your Programs

Hour

HOUR 17

Working with 2D Graphics

During the previous hour you had a chance to experience the joy of text by displaying strings in a variety of fonts and colors. Using these Java classes makes the programming language an enjoyable text aid, but at some point you probably were expecting more. There's more to life than text, and this hour is evidence of that. You'll get a chance to draw shapes of different colors in a program—everything from rectangles to ovals to lines.

The following subjects will be covered:

- The drawing methods of the Graphics2D class
- Drawing lines
- Drawing rectangles and rounded rectangles
- Drawing polygons
- Drawing ellipses
- Drawing with different colors
- Drawing filled and unfilled shapes

Using Graphics in an Applet

This isn't meant as a knock to those of us who enjoy displaying arrays, incrementing variables, or using a constructor method, but let's face it—many subjects in a programming language such as Java tend to be dry. It's hard to impress your non-programming acquaintances with the way your do...while loop determines which method to use in a mathematical application. Dates don't get nearly as excited as you do when a switch...case block statement handles a variety of different circumstances correctly. Nobody ever attracted a mate because they use the conditional operator (using conditioner, on the other hand...).

Graphics programming is the exception to this general rule. When you write a program that does something interesting with graphics, it's a way to have fun with a programming language and impress relatives, friends, strangers, and prospective employers.

Drawing things such as lines and polygons is as easy in a Java applet as displaying text. All you need are Graphics and Graphics2D objects to define the drawing surface and objects that represent the things to draw.

The Graphics class stores information required to display something onscreen. The most common use of the class is as an object that represents the applet window. One of these objects is sent to the paint() method of an applet as an argument, which the following simple paint() method illustrates:

```
public void paint(Graphics screen) {
    // ...
}
```

Inside the paint() method, the Graphics object argument is used to create a Graphics2D object, as in the following statement:

```
Graphics2D screen2D = (Graphics2D) screen;
```

Once you have a Graphics2D object, you draw by calling its methods. This Graphics2D object is called screen2D throughout this book, and its methods are used to draw text with a command such as the following:

```
screen2D.drawString("Draw, pardner!", 15, 40);
```

This statement causes the text Draw, pardner! to be displayed at the (x,y) coordinates of (15,40).

All of the shape- and line-drawing methods work using the same (x,y) coordinate system as text. The (0,0) coordinate is at the upper-left corner of the applet window. x values go up as you head to the right, and y values go up as you head downward. You can determine the maximum (x,y) value you can use in an applet with the following statements:

```
int maxXValue = getSize().width;
int maxYValue = getSize().height;
```

Drawing Lines and Shapes

Figure 17.1 shows JavaMan, an illustration composed of all the different things you'll be learning to draw during this hour:

- Lines: JavaMan's arm and fingers are lines.
- Rounded rectangles: The border of the illustration is a rectangle with rounded corners.
- Rectangles: JavaMan's torso is composed of a filled gray rectangle covered with 100 unfilled rectangles. His mouth is another rectangle.
- Ellipses: JavaMan's eyes are ovals.
- Polygons: JavaMan's hat is a polygon.

FIGURE 17.1

JavaMan, a figure composed of Java polygons and lines.

With the exception of lines, all of the shapes you can draw can be filled or unfilled. A filled shape is drawn with the current color completely filling the space taken up by the shape. Unfilled shapes just draw a border with the current color. The rounded rectangle around Figure 17.1 is an example of an unfilled shape. Only the border of the rectangle is drawn. JavaMan's hat is a filled shape because the entire hat is filled in with the same color.

Before you create an applet to draw JavaMan, each of the drawing methods will be described. The screen2D object will be used as the Graphics2D object throughout this section.

Drawing Lines

A 2D drawing operation in Java requires two steps:

- An object is created that represents the shape that is being drawn.
- A method of a Graphics2D object is called to actually draw that shape.

The objects that define shapes all are part of the java.awt.geom package of classes. There are two classes that can be used to create lines: Line2D.Float and Line2D.Double. These classes differ only in the way they are created: One is created using floating-point numbers to specify the beginning (x,y) point and ending (x,y) point of the line, and the other uses double values.

The following statement creates a line from the point (40,200) to the point (70,130):

```
Line2D.Float ln = new Line2D.Float(40F, 200F, 70F, 130F);
```

Each of the arguments to the Line2D.Float constructor is a number followed by an F, which indicates that the number is a floating-point value. This is necessary when creating a Line2D.Float object.

> Line2D.Float may look unusual because it includes a . character as part of the name. Normally, you'd expect this to mean that Line2D.Float refers to a variable called Float in the Line2D class. Float actually refers to an inner class that is defined inside the Line2D class. The capital letter that begins the name Float is an indicator that it's something other than a variable, because class and object variable names are either all lowercase or all uppercase. Line2D.Float is treated like any other class. The only difference is the . in the name.

After you create a drawing object of any kind, whether it's a line, ellipse, rectangle, or another shape, it is drawn by calling a method of the Graphics2D class. The draw() method draws the shape as an outline and the fill() method draws it as a filled shape.

The following statement will draw the ln object created in the previous example:

```
screen2D.draw(ln);
```

Drawing Rectangles

Rectangles can be filled or unfilled, and they can have rounded corners or square ones. They can be created using the Rectangle2D.Float class and specifying the following four arguments:

- The x coordinate at the upper left of the rectangle
- The y coordinate at upper left
- The width of the rectangle
- The height

The following statement draws an unfilled rectangle with square corners:

```
Rectangle2D.Float rr = new
    Rectangle2D.Float(245F, 65F, 20F, 10F);
```

This statement creates a rectangle with its upper-left corner at the (x,y) coordinate of (245,65). The width of the rectangle is 20 and the height is 10. These dimensions are expressed in pixels, the same unit of measure used for coordinates. To draw this rectangle as an outline, the following statement could be used:

```
screen2D.draw(rr);
```

If you want to make the rectangle filled in, use the `fill()` method instead of `draw()`, as in this statement:

```
screen.fill(rr);
```

You can create rectangles with rounded corners instead of square ones by using the `RoundRectangle2D.Float` class. The constructor to this class starts with the same four arguments as the `Rectangle2D.Float` class, and adds the following two arguments:

- A number of pixels in the x direction away from the corner of the rectangle
- A number of pixels in the y direction away from the corner

These distances are used to determine where the rounding of the rectangle's corner should begin.

The following statement creates a rounded rectangle:

```
RoundRectangle2D.Float ro = new RoundRectangle.Float(
    10F, 10F,
    100F, 80F,
    15F, 15F);
```

This rectangle has its upper-left corner at the (10,10) coordinate. The last two arguments to `drawRoundRect()` specify that the corner should begin rounding 15 pixels away from the corner at (10,10) and the other three corners also.

As with other rectangle methods, the third and fourth arguments specify how wide and tall the rectangle should be. In this case, it should be 100 pixels wide and 80 pixels tall.

After the rounded rectangle is created, it is drawn using the `draw()` and `fill()` methods of a `Graphics2D` object.

Drawing Ellipses and Circles

Ellipses and circles both can be created with the same class: `Ellipse2D.Float`. This class takes four arguments: the (x,y) coordinates of the ellipse and its width and height.

The (x,y) coordinates do not indicate a point at the center of the ellipse or circle, as you might expect. Instead, the (x,y) coordinates, width, and height describe an invisible rectangle that the ellipse fits into. The (x,y) coordinate is the upper-left corner of this rectangle. If it has the same width and height, the ellipse is a circle.

The following statement creates a circle at (245,45) with a height and width of 5 each:

```
Ellipse2D.Float cir = new Ellipse2D.Float(
    245F, 45F, 5F, 5F);
```

Drawing this object requires a call to draw(cir) or fill(cir).

Drawing Polygons

Polygons are the most complicated shape to create because they have a varying number of points. The first step in creating a polygon is to create a GeneralPath object that will hold it. This object starts off without any points in the polygon being defined:

```
GeneralPath polly = new GeneralPath();
```

Once this object is created, its moveTo() method is used to define the first point in the polygon. For a closed polygon, such as an octagon, this can be any of the points. You also can define open polygons, and, in this case, your first point should be one of the end points of the polygon.

The moveTo() method takes two arguments: an x and a y coordinate. This (x,y) coordinate defines the point on the polygon. The following statement is an example:

```
polly.moveTo(100,20);
```

After you have established the initial point in this manner, each successive point is added with the lineTo() method. This method also takes an x coordinate and y coordinate as arguments, as in the following statement:

```
polly.lineTo(80,45);
```

You can call lineTo() as often as needed to create the sides of the polygon. When you have added the last point, you can close off the polygon by calling the closePath() method with no arguments:

```
polly.closePath();
```

If you don't call closePath(), the polygon will be open.

When you have finished creating the shape, it can be drawn with the draw() and fill() methods like any other drawn object.

Creating JavaMan

To put all of these shapes together, load your word processor and create a new file called JavaMan.java. Enter Listing 17.1 into the file and save it when you're done.

LISTING 17.1   THE FULL TEXT OF JavaMan.java

```
 1: import java.awt.*;
 2: import javax.swing.*;
 3: import java.awt.geom.*;
 4:
 5: public class JavaMan extends JApplet {
 6:     float height;
 7:     float width;
 8:
 9:     public void init() {
10:         setBackground(Color.yellow);
11:     }
12:
13:     public void paint(Graphics screen) {
14:         Graphics2D screen2D = (Graphics2D) screen;
15:         height = (float) getSize().height;
16:         width = (float) getSize().width;
17:         screen2D.setColor(Color.black);
18:         RoundRectangle2D.Float border = new RoundRectangle2D.Float(
19:             10F, 10F, width-20, height-20, 15F, 15F);
20:         screen2D.draw(border);
21:
22:         screen2D.setColor(Color.gray);
23:         Rectangle2D.Float box = new Rectangle2D.Float(
24:             200F, 90F, 100F, 100F);
25:         screen2D.fill(box);
26:
27:         screen2D.setColor(Color.blue);
28:         for (int x = 200; x < 300; x += 5)
29:             for (int y = 90; y < 190; y += 5) {
30:                 Rectangle2D.Float r =
31:                     new Rectangle2D.Float(
32:                         x, y, 5, 5);
33:                 screen2D.draw(r);
34:             }
35:
36:         screen2D.setColor(Color.black);
37:         Line2D.Float ln1 = new Line2D.Float(200F, 110F, 170F, 115F);
38:         Line2D.Float ln2 = new Line2D.Float(170F, 115F, 160F, 90F);
39:         Line2D.Float ln3 = new Line2D.Float(160F, 90F, 150F, 94F);
40:         Line2D.Float ln4 = new Line2D.Float(160F, 90F, 153F, 85F);
41:         Line2D.Float ln5 = new Line2D.Float(160F, 90F, 158F, 83F);
42:         Line2D.Float ln6 = new Line2D.Float(160F, 90F, 163F, 84F);
```

17

continues

LISTING 17.1   CONTINUED

```
43:            screen2D.draw(ln1);
44:            screen2D.draw(ln2);
45:            screen2D.draw(ln3);
46:            screen2D.draw(ln4);
47:            screen2D.draw(ln5);
48:            screen2D.draw(ln6);
49:
50:            screen2D.setColor(Color.white);
51:            Ellipse2D.Float head = new Ellipse2D.Float(220F, 30F, 60F,
               60F);
52:            screen2D.fill(head);
53:
54:            screen2D.setColor(Color.green);
55:            Ellipse2D.Float leftEye = new Ellipse2D.Float(245F, 45F,
56:                5F, 5F);
57:            Ellipse2D.Float rightEye = new Ellipse2D.Float(255F, 45F,
58:                5F, 5F);
59:            screen2D.fill(leftEye);
60:            screen2D.fill(rightEye);
61:
62:            screen2D.setColor(Color.black);
63:            Rectangle2D.Float mouth = new Rectangle2D.Float(245F,
64:                65F, 15F, 15F);
65:            screen2D.fill(mouth);
66:
67:            screen2D.setColor(Color.magenta);
68:            GeneralPath chapeau = new GeneralPath();
69:            chapeau.moveTo(205F, 43F);
70:            chapeau.lineTo(305F, 40F);
71:            chapeau.lineTo(240F, 15F);
72:            chapeau.lineTo(205F, 43F);
73:            chapeau.closePath();
74:            screen2D.fill(chapeau);
75:        }
76: }
```

After compiling the program successfully, create a new file in your word processor called JavaMan.html. Enter Listing 17.2 into the file.

LISTING 17.2   THE FULL TEXT OF JavaMan.html

```
1: <applet code="JavaMan.class" height=220 width=340>
2: </applet>
```

When you use `appletviewer` or a Java-capable Web browser to view this applet, you will discover why I chose computer book writing as a profession over illustration. If you're using `appletviewer`, resize the window a few times to see how the rounded black border changes.

Workshop: Drawing Attention to Something

To draw this hour to a close, you'll create an applet that uses a closed polygon, several open polygons, a rounded rectangle, and three ellipses. The finished product ought to be a familiar face.

Load your word processor and create a new file called `Drawing.java`. Enter the full text of Listing 17.3, and then save and compile the file when you're done.

LISTING 17.3 THE FULL TEXT OF `Drawing.java`

```
 1: import java.awt.*;
 2: import java.awt.geom.*;
 3: import javax.swing.*;
 4:
 5: public class Drawing extends JApplet {
 6:     GeneralPath hair;
 7:
 8:     public void init() {
 9:         hair = new GeneralPath();
10:         hair.moveTo(125F, 314F);
11:         hair.lineTo(131F, 122F);
12:         hair.lineTo(156F, 75F);
13:         hair.lineTo(217F, 57F);
14:         hair.lineTo(270F, 96F);
15:         hair.lineTo(314F, 287F);
16:         hair.lineTo(244F, 319F);
17:         hair.lineTo(233F, 118F);
18:         hair.lineTo(196F, 87F);
19:         hair.lineTo(162F, 92F);
20:         hair.lineTo(147F, 133F);
21:         hair.lineTo(153F, 203F);
22:         hair.lineTo(180F, 231F);
23:         hair.lineTo(189F, 258F);
24:         hair.lineTo(125F, 314F);
25:         hair.closePath();
26:         setBackground(Color.lightGray);
27:     }
28:
29:     public void paint(Graphics screen) {
30:         Graphics2D screen2D = (Graphics2D) screen;
```

continues

LISTING 17.3 CONTINUED

```
31:          screen2D.setColor(Color.white);
32:          RoundRectangle2D.Float face1 = new RoundRectangle2D.Float(
33:              147F, 84F, 103F, 74F, 23F, 23F);
34:          screen2D.fill(face1);
35:          Ellipse2D.Float face2 = new Ellipse2D.Float(
36:              147F, 94F, 103F, 132F);
37:          screen2D.fill(face2);
38:
39:          screen2D.setColor(Color.black);
40:          screen2D.fill(hair);
41:
42:          GeneralPath eyebrow1 = new GeneralPath();
43:          eyebrow1.moveTo(151F, 145F);
44:          eyebrow1.lineTo(168F, 140F);
45:          eyebrow1.lineTo(174F, 148F);
46:          eyebrow1.lineTo(171F, 184F);
47:          eyebrow1.lineTo(178F, 191F);
48:          eyebrow1.lineTo(193F, 188F);
49:          screen2D.draw(eyebrow1);
50:
51:          GeneralPath eyebrow2 = new GeneralPath();
52:          eyebrow2.moveTo(188F, 146F);
53:          eyebrow2.lineTo(197F, 141F);
54:          eyebrow2.lineTo(213F, 142F);
55:          eyebrow2.lineTo(223F, 146F);
56:          screen2D.draw(eyebrow2);
57:
58:          GeneralPath mouth = new GeneralPath();
59:          mouth.moveTo(166F, 199F);
60:          mouth.lineTo(185F, 200F);
61:          mouth.lineTo(200F, 197F);
62:          screen2D.draw(mouth);
63:
64:          Ellipse2D.Float eye1 = new Ellipse2D.Float(
65:              161F, 148F, 12F, 5F);
66:          screen2D.fill(eye1);
67:          Ellipse2D.Float eye2 = new Ellipse2D.Float(
68:              202F, 145F, 12F, 5F);
69:          screen2D.fill(eye2);
70:      }
71: }
```

The Drawing applet includes two methods, init() and paint(), and a single
GeneralPath object called hair. The GeneralPath object is used to store all the information that's needed to draw a polygon.

The polygon is created with a call to the hair object's moveTo() method followed by several lineTo() methods. Each method contains an (x,y) coordinate of a point on the polygon specified as a float value.

After all of the points have been added to the polygon, the closePath() method is called to close the polygon. The polygon can't be drawn yet because the applet's init() method does not have a Graphics object representing its drawing area.

The color of each drawing operation must be designated before the object is drawn. This requires the setColor() method of the Graphics2D class. Constants from the Color class such as Color.red and Color.green are used as arguments to the setColor() method. The following statement in the paint() method sets the current color to black:

```
screen2D.setColor(Color.black);
```

In addition to polygons, three ellipses are drawn in the Drawing applet. The following is one of the statements used to create an ellipse:

```
Ellipse2D.Float face2 = new Ellipse2D.Float(
    147F, 94F, 103F, 132F);
```

The first two arguments to the constructor are the (x,y) coordinates where the ellipse should be drawn. The last two arguments are the width and height of the ellipse.

After you have compiled Drawing.java successfully, open a new file in your word processor to create a Web page on which to put the applet. Create a new file called Drawing.html and enter Listing 17.4 into the file.

LISTING 17.4   THE FULL TEXT OF Drawing.html

```
1: <applet code="Drawing.class" height=340 width=340>
2: </applet>
```

After saving the file, view the applet with the appletviewer tool or a Web browser. Figure 17.2 shows what the finished product should look like.

If the long black hair, moony expression, and stoned smile aren't enough of a visual clue, this applet attempts to draw the Mona Lisa using a few polygons and lines. Leonardo da Vinci didn't have the chance to use Java 2D drawing commands when he created the real Mona Lisa in 1503–1506, so he used paint instead. His results were pretty impressive too, but it took him considerably longer than an hour to finish his version.

FIGURE 17.2

The output of the
Drawing *applet.*

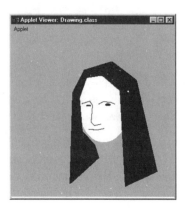

The Louvre, the home of the *Mona Lisa*, has an extensive Web site at
`http://mistral.culture.fr/louvre/`.

A picture of the Mona Lisa is displayed under the title *La Joconde (Monna Lisa)* at `http://mistral.culture.fr/louvre/anglais/musee/collec/monna.htm`.

Summary

Drawing something using the polygons and other shapes available with Java might seem like more trouble than it's worth, especially when you can load image files such as `.GIF` files and `.JPG` files, as you'll see in the next hour. However, graphics depicted with polygons have two advantages over graphics that are loaded from image files:

- Speed: Even a small graphic, such as an icon, would take longer to load and display than a series of polygons.

- Scaling: You can change the size of an entire image that uses polygons simply by changing the values to create it. For example, you could add a function to the Drawing class that doubles the values for every (x,y) point in a polygon before calling the `moveTo()` or `lineTo()` methods, and it would result in an image twice as large. Polygon images scale much more quickly than image files do and produce better results.

There are many instances where it makes more sense to use graphics files in your programs, but polygons can be a useful option.

Q&A

Q **Why does the JavaMan image flicker when I resize the applet window?**

A The reason for this flicker is that the screen is automatically cleared each time the screen must be repainted. This happens in a method called update() that normally works behind the scenes. You can override this method in your programs to prevent the flickering problem, as you will see during the next hour.

Q **Ellipses and circles don't have corners. What are the (x,y) coordinates specified with the `Ellipses.Float` constructor method?**

A The (x,y) coordinates represent the smallest x value and smallest y value of the oval or circle. If you drew an invisible rectangle around it, the upper-left corner of the rectangle would be the x and y coordinates used as arguments to the method.

17

Quiz

Test whether your Java graphics skills are taking shape by answering the following questions.

Questions

1. What method is used to change the current color before you draw something in a program?

    (a) `shiftColor()`

    (b) `setColor()`

    (c) Could you repeat the question?

2. If you want to use the height and width of an applet window to determine how big something should be drawn, what can you use?

    (a) A ruler and a friend who's good at math.

    (b) `getHeight()` and `getWidth()`

    (c) `getSize().height` and `getSize().width`

3. What personal failing did this book's author admit to during this hour?

    (a) Poor grooming

    (b) Poor drawing ability

    (c) Codependency

Answers

1. b. You can use the `setBackground()` method to set the background color of an applet, and you can use the `setColor()` method of the `Graphics` class to select the current color.

2. c.

3. b. JavaMan represents one of the high points of my illustrative career.

Activities

To draw upon your vast storehouse of graphical skills, do the following activities:

- Create a method that can multiply every integer in an array by some kind of common factor. You can use this method in the `Drawing` applet to change the points in a polygon to make it bigger or smaller before it is created.

- Add parameters to the `JavaMan` applet to control the colors used on the background, body, and hat.

To see Java programs that implement these activities, visit the book's Web site at `http://www.prefect.com/java24`.

Hour 18

Creating Animation

Like the final voyage of the S.S. *Minnow*, the trip through the visual side of Java programming is a three-hour tour. At this point, you have learned how to use text, fonts, color, lines, and polygons in your Java applets. Any adversity you have experienced should have been minor, at least in comparison to the castaways of *Gilligan's Island*. At this point in their tour, passengers were asking the Skipper if hurricane-force winds were a scheduled part of the itinerary.

This third hour shows how to display image files in the .GIF and .JPG formats in your applets and some tricks to use when presenting these images in an animation. The following topics will be covered:

- Using Image objects to hold image files
- Putting a series of images into an array
- Cycling through an image array to produce animation
- Using the update() method to reduce flickering problems
- Using the drawImage() command
- Drawing to an offscreen workspace
- Why double-buffering improves animation results
- Establishing rules for the movement of an image

Creating an Animated Applet

Computer animation at its most basic consists of drawing an image at a specific place, moving the location of the image, and telling the computer to redraw the image at its new location. Many animations on Web pages are a series of image files, usually .GIF or .JPG files, that are displayed in the same place in a certain order. You can do this to simulate motion or to create some other effect.

The first program you will be writing today uses a series of image files to create an animated picture of the lighthouse in St. Augustine, Florida. Several details about the animation will be customizable with parameters, so you can replace any images of your own for those provided for this example. Create a new file in your word processor called Animate.java. Enter Listing 18.1 into the file, and remember to save the file when you're done entering the text.

LISTING 18.1   THE FULL TEXT OF Animate.java

```
 1: import java.awt.*;
 2:
 3: public class Animate extends javax.swing.JApplet
 4:     implements Runnable {
 5:
 6:     Image[] picture = new Image[6];
 7:     int totalPictures = 0;
 8:     int current = 0;
 9:     Thread runner;
10:     int pause = 500;
11:
12:     public void init() {
13:         for (int i = 0; i < 6; i++) {
14:             String imageText = null;
15:             imageText = getParameter("image"+i);
16:             if (imageText != null) {
17:                 totalPictures++;
18:                 picture[i] = getImage(getCodeBase(), imageText);
19:             } else
20:                 break;
21:         }
22:         String pauseText = null;
23:         pauseText = getParameter("pause");
24:         if (pauseText != null) {
25:             pause = Integer.parseInt(pauseText);
26:         }
27:     }
28:
29:     public void paint(Graphics screen) {
30:         Graphics2D screen2D = (Graphics2D) screen;
```

```
31:            if (picture[current] != null)
32:                screen2D.drawImage(picture[current],0,0,this);
33:        }
34:
35:        public void start() {
36:            if (runner == null) {
37:                runner = new Thread(this);
38:                runner.start();
39:            }
40:        }
41:
42:        public void run() {
43:            Thread thisThread = Thread.currentThread();
44:            while (runner == thisThread) {
45:                repaint();
46:                current++;
47:                if (current >= totalPictures)
48:                    current = 0;
49:                try {
50:                    Thread.sleep(pause);
51:                } catch (InterruptedException e) { }
52:            }
53:        }
54:
55:        public void stop() {
56:            if (runner != null) {
57:                runner = null;
58:            }
59:        }
60:
61:        public void update(Graphics screen) {
62:            paint(screen);
63:        }
64: }
```

This program uses the same threaded applet structure that you used during Hour 14, "Creating a Threaded Applet." Threads are often used during animation programming because they give you the ability to control the timing of the animation. The Thread.sleep() method is an effective way to determine how long each image should be displayed before the next image is shown.

The Animate applet retrieves images as parameters on a Web page. The parameters should have names starting at "image0" and ending at the last image of the animation, such as "image3" in this hour's example. The maximum number of images that can be displayed by this applet is 6, but you could raise this number by making changes to lines 6 and 13.

The totalPicture integer variable determines how many different images will be displayed in an animation. If fewer than 6 image files have been specified by parameters, the Animate applet will determine this during the init() method when imageText equals null after line 15.

The speed of the animation is specified by a "pause" parameter. Because all parameters from a Web page are received as strings, the Integer.parseInt() method is needed to convert the text into an integer. The pause variable keeps track of the number of milliseconds to pause after displaying each image in an animation.

Preventing Flickering Animation

As with most threaded programs, the run() method contains the main part of the program. A while (runner == thisThread) statement in line 44 causes lines 45–51 to loop until something causes these two Thread objects to have different values.

The first thing that happens in the run() method is a repaint(); statement. This statement causes the update() method and paint() method to be handled, in that order, so that the screen can be updated. Use repaint() any time you know something has changed and the display needs to be changed to bring it up to date. In this case, every time the Animate loop goes around once, a different image should be shown.

The update() method contains only one statement, paint(screen);. The reason to use this method is that it overrides the behavior that update() normally performs. If you did not override update() in the Animate program, it would clear the screen before calling on the paint() method. This action causes flickering animation problems that have been mentioned in previous hours.

Loading and Displaying Images

The paint() method in lines 29–33 contains the following three statements:

```
Graphics2D screen2D = (Graphics2D) screen;
if (picture[current] != null)
    screen2D.drawImage(picture[current],0,0,this);
```

First, a Graphics2D object is cast so that it can be used when drawing to the applet window. Next, an if statement determines whether the Image object stored in picture [current] has a null value. When it does not equal null, this indicates that an image is ready to be displayed. The drawImage() method of the screen2D object displays the current Image object at the (x,y) position specified.

The this statement sent as the fourth argument to drawImage() enables the program to use a class called ImageObserver. This class tracks when an image is being loaded and when it is finished. The JApplet class contains behavior that works behind the scenes to take care of this process, so all you have to do is specify this as an argument to drawImage() and some other methods related to image display. The rest is taken care of for you.

An Image object must be created and loaded with a valid image before you can use the drawImage() method. The way to load an image in an applet is to use the getImage() method. This method takes two arguments: the Web address or folder that contains the image file and the file name of the image.

The first argument is taken care of with the getCodeBase() method, which is part of the JApplet class. This method returns the location of the applet itself, so if you put your images in the same folder as the applet's class file, you can use getCodeBase(). The second argument should be a .GIF file or .JPG file to load. In the following example, a turtlePicture object is created and an image file called Mertle.gif is loaded into it:

```
Image turtlePicture = getImage(getCodeBase(), "Mertle.gif");
```

As you look over the source code to the Animate applet, you might wonder why the test for a null value in line 31 is necessary. This check is required because the paint() method may be called before an image file has been fully loaded into a picture[] element. Calling getImage() begins the process of loading an image. To prevent a slowdown, the Java interpreter continues to run the rest of the program while images are being loaded.

18

Storing a Group of Related Images

In the Animate applet, images are loaded into an array of Image objects called pictures. The pictures array is set up to handle six elements in line 6 of the program, so you can have Image objects ranging from picture[0] to picture[5]. The following statement in the applet's paint() method displays the current image:

```
screen.drawImage(picture[current],0,0,this);
```

The current variable is used in the applet to keep track of which image to display in the paint() method. It has an initial value of 0, so the first image to be displayed is the one stored in picture[0]. After each call to the repaint() statement in line 45 of the run() method, the current variable is incremented by one in line 46.

The totalPictures variable is an integer that keeps track of how many images should be displayed. It is set when images are loaded from parameters off the Web page. When current equals totalPictures, it is set back to 0. As a result, current cycles through each image of the animation and then begins again at the first image.

Sending Parameters to the Applet

Because the `Animate` applet relies on parameters to specify the image files it should display, you need to create a Web page containing these filenames before you can test the program. After saving and compiling the `Animate.java` file, open up a new file in your word processor and call it `Animate.html`. Enter Listing 18.2 into that file and save it when you're done.

LISTING **18.2**　THE FULL TEXT OF `Animate.html`

```
1: <applet code="Animate.class" width=215 height=298>
2: <param name="image0" value="lh0.gif">
3: <param name="image1" value="lh1.gif">
4: <param name="image2" value="lh2.gif">
5: <param name="image3" value="lh3.gif">
6: <param name="pause" value="800">
7: </applet>
```

This file specifies four image files: `lh0.gif`, `lh1.gif`, `lh2.gif`, and `lh3.gif`. These files are listed as the values for the parameters `image0` through `image3`. You can find the files used in this example on this book's Web site at `http://www.prefect.com/java24`.

If you get the files from the Web site, look for the `Hour 18's graphics` link that's available on the main page of the site. You also can specify any of your own `.GIF` or `.JPG` files if desired. Whichever files you choose should be placed in the same folder as the `Animate.class` and `Animate.html` files. With the `"pause"` parameter, you can specify how long the program should pause after each image is displayed.

> You might be wondering why the files and the parameters are given names that start numbering with 0 instead of 1. This is done because the first element of an array in a Java program is numbered 0. Putting an `image0` called `lh0.gif` into `pictures[0]` makes it easier to know where these images are being stored.

Once the files have been put in the right place, you're ready to try out the `Animate` applet. Type the following command to use the `appletviewer` to view the page:

```
appletviewer Animate.html
```

Figure 18.1 shows one of the four images being displayed as the applet runs.

FIGURE 18.1

An image of the Animate *applet as it runs.*

Although this is a simple animation program, hundreds of applets on the Web use similar functionality to present a series of image files as an animation. Presenting a sequence of image files through Java is similar to the animated .GIF files that are becoming more commonplace on Web pages. Although Java applets are often slower to load than these .GIF files, they can provide more control of the animation and allow for more complicated effects.

Workshop: Follow the Bouncing Ball

This hour's workshop is an animation that definitely couldn't be replicated with an animated .GIF file or any other non-programming alternative. You'll write a program that bounces a tennis ball around the screen in lazy arcs, caroming off the sides of the applet window. Though a few laws of physics will be broken along the way, you'll learn one way to move an image file around the screen.

Create a new file in your word processor called Bounce.java, and enter the text of Listing 18.3 into it. Save and compile the file when you're done.

LISTING 18.3   THE FULL TEXT OF Bounce.java

```
 1: import java.awt.*;
 2:
 3: public class Bounce extends javax.swing.JApplet
 4:     implements Runnable {
 5:
 6:     Image ball;
 7:     float current = (float) 0;
 8:     Thread runner;
 9:     int xPosition = 10;
10:     int xMove = 1;
```

continues

LISTING 18.3   CONTINUED

```
11:      int yPosition = -1;
12:      int ballHeight = 102;
13:      int ballWidth = 111;
14:      int height;
15:      Image workspace;
16:      Graphics offscreen;
17:
18:      public void init() {
19:          workspace = createImage(getSize().width, getSize().height);
20:          offscreen = workspace.getGraphics();
21:          setBackground(Color.white);
22:          ball = getImage(getCodeBase(), "tennis.jpg");
23:      }
24:
25:      public void paint(Graphics screen) {
26:          Graphics2D screen2D = (Graphics2D) screen;
27:          height = getSize().height - ballHeight;
28:          if (yPosition == -1)
29:              yPosition = height;
30:          offscreen.setColor(Color.white);
31:          offscreen.fillRect(0,0,getSize().width,getSize().height);
32:          offscreen.drawImage(ball,
33:              (int) xPosition,
34:              (int) yPosition,
35:              this);
36:          screen2D.drawImage(workspace, 0, 0, this);
37:      }
38:
39:      public void start() {
40:          if (runner == null) {
41:              runner = new Thread(this);
42:              runner.start();
43:          }
44:      }
45:
46:      public void run() {
47:          Thread thisThread = Thread.currentThread();
48:          while (runner == thisThread) {
49:              repaint();
50:              current += (float) 0.1;
51:              if (current > 3)
52:                  current = (float) 0;
53:              xPosition += xMove;
54:              if (xPosition > (getSize().width - 111))
55:                  xMove *= -1;
56:              if (xPosition < 1)
57:                  xMove *= -1;
58:              double bounce = Math.sin(current) * height;
59:              yPosition = (int) (height - bounce);
```

```
60:                try {
61:                    Thread.sleep(200);
62:                } catch (InterruptedException e) { }
63:            }
64:        }
65:
66:        public void stop() {
67:            if (runner != null) {
68:                runner = null;
69:            }
70:        }
71:
72:        public void update(Graphics screen) {
73:            paint(screen);
74:        }
75: }
```

Before you dive into the discussion of what's taking place in this applet, you should see what it does. Create a new file in your word processor called `Bounce.html` and enter Listing 18.4 into it.

LISTING 18.4   THE FULL TEXT OF `Bounce.html`

```
1: <applet code="Bounce.class" width=500 height=300>
2: </applet>
```

After saving this file, you need to get a copy of the `tennis.jpg` file and put it in the same folder as `Bounce.class` and `Bounce.html`. This file is available from the same place as the lighthouse image files: the book's Web site at `http://www.prefect.com/java24`. Once you have copied `tennis.jpg` into the right place, use `appletviewer` or a Java-enabled Web browser to display this program. Figure 18.2 shows the `Bounce` applet running on `appletviewer`.

FIGURE 18.2

The Bounce *applet running on a Web page loaded by* appletviewer.

This applet displays a .JPG file of a tennis ball bouncing back and forth. It hits a point at the bottom edge of the applet window and rebounds upward close to the top edge of the window. When the ball hits the right or left edge of the window, it bounces in the opposite direction. If you're using appletviewer to try the applet out, resize the window by making the right and left edges smaller. The Bounce applet can keep track of your actions.

The Bounce applet is a relatively simple example of how to animate an image file using Java. It consists of the following steps:

- Draw the ball at its current location.
- Move the ball according to the rules that have been established for how the ball should move.
- Check whether the rules need to be changed based on the ball's new location.
- Repeat.

Drawing the Image

The Bounce applet has the same basic structure as the Animate applet. It's a threaded program with start(), stop(), and run() methods to control the operation of the thread. There's also an update() and a paint() method to display information on-screen.

The Image object called ball is loaded with the tennis.jpg image in the init() method. Several variables are used in the applet to keep track of the ball's location and its current rate of movement:

- xPosition   This variable is the x coordinate where the ball should be drawn. This coordinate begins as 10.
- xMove   This variable is the amount the ball should move along the x axis after every screen update. This amount starts out as 1, but it will change to -1 when the ball hits the right edge of the applet window. It changes back and forth from -1 to 1 every time it hits an edge, and this change is handled by lines 53–57.
- yPosition   This variable is the y coordinate where the ball should be drawn. This coordinate is initially set to -1, which is a signal to the paint() method that the yPosition needs to be set up before the ball can be drawn for the first time. The yPosition value varies from a point near the bottom of the applet window to the top edge.
- current   This floating-point number starts at 0 and increases by 0.1 each time the ball is redrawn. When it reaches 3, it is set back to 0 again. The current variable is used with a mathematical sine function to determine how high the ball bounces.

Sine waves are a good way to approximate the movements of a bouncing ball, and the `Math.sin()` method enables a sine value to be used in conjunction with animation. The tennis ball is traveling half a sine wave each time it goes from the ground to the top of the window and back.

The movement rules that you establish for an animation applet will vary depending on what you're trying to show. The `Bounce` applet uses the `Math.sin()` method to create the slow arcs traveled by the ball.

Drawing to a Hidden Screen

The `paint()` method uses a technique called *double-buffering* to make the animation display more smoothly. Double-buffering is drawing everything offscreen to a storage place that's the same size as the program's display area and copying it to the display only when all drawing is done. The advantage to using double-buffering is that it reduces flickering and other things that might be seen while the `paint()` method is drawing things onscreen.

All drawing in a Java 2 applet is done to a `Graphics2D` object that represents the applet window. The offscreen area is represented by an additional `Graphics` object. You also must create an `Image` object to hold everything that's being drawn to the hidden area. Lines 15–16 create an `Image` object called `workspace` and a `Graphics` object called `offscreen`. These objects are set up in the `init()` method. Line 19 uses the `createImage()` method to set up `workspace` as an empty image the size and width of the applet window. Line 20 associates the `offscreen` object with the `workspace` image, using the `getGraphics()` method of the `Image` class.

The key to double-buffering is to draw everything to the offscreen area in the `paint()` method. To do this, use the `offscreen` object for all display methods instead of the `screen2D` object. Each of these methods will update the `workspace` image with the things that are being displayed.

When all drawing has been done and you know the offscreen area looks the way the screen should look, draw that entire offscreen image to the applet window by using a statement such as the one on line 36:

```
screen2D.drawImage(workspace, 0, 0, this);
```

Because `workspace` is an `Image` object with the same dimensions as the applet window, you can use (0,0) as its coordinates, and it will fill the display area.

When you are drawing only one image to the screen during each update, as you did in the `Animate` applet, there's no reason to use double-buffering. However, if the animation involves more than one thing to draw, you will get better results by drawing to an offscreen area and then copying the whole thing to the screen at one time.

18

The Bounce applet requires an offscreen area because it clears the screen right before drawing the tennis ball during each update. The screen is cleared by drawing a filled white rectangle the size of the applet window. This rectangle is needed to remove the image of the ball in its last position before the new position is drawn.

Summary

Using the classes that come with the Java language, you can produce some interesting animated graphics and games. A lot of graphics functionality is built in and can be used in short programs like those written during this hour.

Because Java is an interpreted language, its programs run at speeds slower than compiled languages, such as C, can achieve. This makes it more of a challenge to produce animated graphics at acceptable speeds. However, many applets on display on World Wide Web pages showcase Java's graphics capabilities.

What you have learned about graphics and animation should keep you from running adrift if you venture into uncharted waters like Java game programming and other visually inventive projects. Java animation programming is quite a challenge, but it could be worse. The professor on *Gilligan's Island* had nothing to work with but coconuts and palm fronds, and he produced a washing machine.

Q&A

Q **Does a threaded animation program have to use `Thread.sleep()` to pause, or can you omit it to produce the fastest possible animation?**

A You have to put some kind of pause in place in an animation program, or the program will crash or behave erratically. Your applet is running as a part of a bigger program, the Web browser or `appletviewer`, and that program won't be able to keep up with constant `repaint()` requests without the pause. Part of the process of animation design in Java is finding the right display speed that all applet-running environments can handle.

Q **What happens if you draw something such as an image to coordinates that aren't within the applet window?**

A Methods that draw something to a coordinate will continue to draw it even if none of it is visible within the area shown by the applet window. To see this in action, reduce the height of the Bounce applet as it runs in the `appletviewer` tool. The tennis ball will drop below the window and bounce back upwards into the window.

Quiz

Animate yourself as much as you can muster and answer the following questions to test your skills.

Questions

1. Where is the (0,0) coordinate on an applet window?

    (a) In the offscreen double-buffering area

    (b) The exact center of the window

    (c) The upper-left corner of the applet window

2. What thing did you *not* learn during this hour?

    (a) How to use `Graphics` and `Image` objects to create an offscreen workspace

    (b) How to override the `update()` method to reduce animation flickering

    (c) Why Thurston Howell III and his wife Lovey packed so much clothing for a three-hour tour

3. In a threaded animation applet, where should you handle most of the movement of an image?

    (a) The `run()` method

    (b) The `init()` method

    (c) The `update()` method

Answers

1. c. The x value increases as you head to the right, and the y value increases as you head downward.

2. c. If the tiny ship had not been so weighted down with smoking jackets and evening gowns, the Skipper and Gilligan might have been able to outrun the storm.

3. a. Some movement might be handled by statements in the `paint()` method, but most of it will take place in `run()` or a method called from within `run()`.

Activities

Before you're stranded and the subject of graphics is abandoned, picture yourself doing the following activities:

- Change the `Bounce` applet so that the ball loses 10 percent of its bouncing strength each time it hits the ground. You can do this by creating a new variable called `strength` and using it as a multiplier at a specific point in the program.

Hour **19**

Building a Simple User Interface with Swing

Because of the popularity of Microsoft Windows and Apple Macintosh systems, computer users have come to expect certain things from their software. It should use a graphical user interface, be controllable with a mouse, and work like a lot of their other programs do. These expectations are a far cry from the heyday of MS-DOS and other command-line systems, when the user interface varied greatly with each program you used, and point-and-click was something photographers did.

Today's programs that use a graphical user interface and mouse control are called *windowing software*. Although you've been using a command-line interface to write Java programs, you can create windowing programs using a group of classes called Swing. You'll learn how to create a windowing program during this hour.

The following topics will be covered:

- Using user interface components such as buttons
- Putting components onscreen

- Putting components onto other components
- Using layout managers to organize an interface
- Organizing components into a grid
- Using labels, text fields, and other components
- Testing an interface

Swing and the Abstract Windowing Toolkit

Because Java is a cross-platform language that enables you to write programs for many different operating systems, its windowing software must be flexible. Instead of catering only to the Microsoft Windows style of windowing or the Apple Macintosh version, it must handle both along with other platforms.

With Java, the development of a program's user interface is based on a set of classes called the Abstract Windowing Toolkit, or AWT. The toolkit gets its name from the way it approaches interface design in as abstract a manner as possible, which enables Java programs to run on different platforms. This approach was needed so that programmers can offer their applets on the World Wide Web, which is used by people on dozens of different types of computers, operating systems, and Web browsers.

Recent versions of the Java language have offered an enhancement to the Abstract Windowing Toolkit called Swing. Swing, a set of classes, offers a number of different improvements affecting how a user interface looks, functions, and can be controlled by a user.

Swing includes everything you need to write programs that use a GUI (pronounced *gooey*). If you think GUI's the fourth nephew of Huey, Louie, and Dewey, you're quackers: The acronym stands for graphical user interface. With Java's windowing toolkit, you can create a GUI that includes all of the following:

- Buttons, check boxes, labels, and other simple components
- Text fields and other more complex components
- Dialog boxes and other windows
- Pull-down menus
- Applets that offer these interface components

Swing also includes classes that you have been using up to this point to offer fonts, color, and graphics in your programs. Another element of Swing and the Abstract Windowing Toolkit you'll be learning about, during Hour 20, "Responding to User Events with Swing," is how they can be used to receive mouse clicks and other user input.

Using Components

A Java program's graphical user interface is a user-friendly feature that's created by using techniques that might seem programmer-unfriendly at first. Once you step through the process a few times, you'll become comfortable with it quickly.

In general, to use components such as buttons and text fields in a Java program, you create a component object and use the add() method to add it to an existing component. This existing component is called a container because it can hold other components. An applet is an example of a container. You can add other components to the applet window.

One simple component you can add to a container is a JButton object. JButton, like many other components you'll be working with during this hour, is part of the javax.swing package. A JButton object is a clickable button with a label that describes what clicking the button will do. This label can be text, graphics, or both. The following statement creates a JButton called okButton and gives it the text label OK:

```
JButton okButton = new JButton("OK");
```

After a component such as JButton is created, it should be added to a container. To display a component on an applet, you must add components to a part of the applet window called the *content pane*.

The content pane represents the main area in which components are displayed in the window. This pane is an object of the Container class in the java.awt package. An applet's content pane is returned by the getContentPane() method of the applet.

The following statement creates a Container object called pane and sets it up with the value of an applet's content pane:

```
Container pane = getContentPane();
```

Because the pane object represents a content pane for a container, components can be added to this object by calling its add() method. The component to add should be the only argument to this method. For example, the previously created okButton object could be added to the pane container with the following statement:

```
pane.add(okButton);
```

When you add components to a container, you do not specify the place in the container where the component should be displayed. The arrangement of components is decided by a special type of object called a layout manager. The simplest of these managers is the FlowLayout class, which is part of the java.awt package.

To make a container use a specific layout manager, you must first create an object of that layout manager's class. A FlowLayout object is created with a statement such as the following:

```
FlowLayout fff = new FlowLayout();
```

Once a layout manager has been created, the container's setLayoutManager() method is called to associate the manager with the container. The only argument to this method should be the layout manager object, as in the following example:

```
pane.setLayoutManager(fff);
```

This statement designates the fff object as the layout manager for the pane container.

One of the most basic ways to use a component such as a button is to add it to an applet. The following Java applet creates a JButton object and a content pane, sets the layout manager for the pane, and adds the JButton object to it:

```
import java.awt.*;
import javax.swing.*;

public class ShowButton extends JApplet {
    JButton panicButton = new JButton("Panic");

    public void init() {
        FlowLayout flo = new FlowLayout();
        Container pane = getContentPane();
        pane.setLayout(flo);
        pane.add(panicButton);
        setContentPane(pane);
    }
}
```

The panicButton object is created as an object variable so you can use it in all methods of the applet program. The argument used with new JButton specifies the label of the button. The pane.add(panicButton); statement adds the JButton component to pane, the content pane of the ShowButton applet. Figure 19.1 shows what the output of this program would be.

FIGURE 19.1

A JButton component.

Many of the user components available as part of Swing can be added to an applet in this manner.

Because so many different user interface components must be introduced during this hour, the full source code used to create each figure is not listed here. You can find full versions of each program on the book's Web site at http://www.prefect.com/java24. Choose the Hour 19's programs link from the front page.

Labels and Text Fields

A JLabel component displays information that cannot be modified by the user. This information can be text, a graphic, or both. These components are named for their usefulness as a way to label other components in an interface. They often are used to identify text fields.

A JTextField component is an area where a user can enter a single line of text. You can set up the width of the box when you create the text field.

The following statements create a JLabel component and JTextField object and add them to an applet:

```
JLabel pageLabel = new JLabel("Web page address: ", JLabel.RIGHT);
JTextField pageAddress = new JTextField(20);
FlowLayout flo = new FlowLayout();
Container pane = getContentPane();
pane.setLayout(flo);
pane.add(pageLabel);
pane.add(pageAddress);
setContentPane(pane);
```

Figure 19.2 shows this label and text field side-by-side. Both of the statements in this example use an argument to configure how the component should look. The pageLabel label is set up with the text Web page address: and a JLabel.RIGHT argument. This last value indicates that the label should appear flush right. JLabel.LEFT aligns the label text flush left, and JLabel.CENTER centers it. The argument used with JTextField indicates that the text field should be approximately 20 characters wide. You also can specify default text that will appear in the text field with a statement such as the following:

```
JTextField state = new JTextField("TX", 2);
```

This statement would create a JTextField object that is two characters wide and has the text TX in the field.

FIGURE **19.2**

JLabel *and*
JTextField
components.

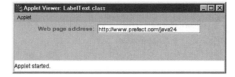

Check Boxes

A JCheckBox component is a box next to a line of text that can be checked or unchecked by the user. The following statements create a JCheckBox object and add it to an applet:

```
JCheckBox jumboSize = new JCheckBox("Jumbo Size");
FlowLayout flo = new FlowLayout();
Container pane = getContentPane();
pane.setLayout(flo);
pane.add(jumboSize);
setContentPane(pane);
```

The argument to the JCheckBox() constructor method indicates the text to be displayed alongside the box. If you wanted the box to be checked, you could use the following statement instead:

```
JCheckBox jumboSize = new JCheckBox("Jumbo Size", true);
```

A JCheckBox can be presented singly or as part of a group. In a group of check boxes, only one can be checked at a time. To make a JCheckBox object part of a group, you have to create a ButtonGroup object. Consider the following:

```
JCheckBox frogLegs = new JCheckBox("Frog Leg Grande", true);
JCheckBox fishTacos = new JCheckBox("Fish Taco Platter", false);
JCheckBox emuNuggets = new JCheckBox("Emu Nuggets", false);
FlowLayout flo = new FlowLayout();
Container pane = getContentPane();
ButtonGroup meals = new ButtonGroup();
meals.add(frogLegs);
meals.add(fishTacos);
meals.add(emuNuggets);
pane.setLayout(flo);
pane.add(jumboSize);
pane.add(frogLegs);
pane.add(fishTacos);
pane.add(emuNuggets);
setContentPane(pane);
```

This creates three check boxes that are all grouped under the ButtonGroup object called meals. The Frog Leg Grande box is checked initially, but if the user checked one of the other meal boxes, the check next to Frog Leg Grande would disappear automatically. Figure 19.3 shows the different check boxes from this section.

FIGURE 19.3

JCheckBox
components.

Combo Boxes

A JComboBox component is a pop-up list of choices that also can be set up to receive text input. When both options are enabled, you can select an item with your mouse or use the keyboard to enter text instead. The combo box serves a similar purpose to a group of check boxes, except that only one of the choices is visible unless the pop-up list is being displayed.

To create a JComboBox object, you have to add each of the choices after creating the object, as in the following example:

```
JComboBox profession = new JComboBox();
FlowLayout flo = new FlowLayout();
Container pane = getContentPane();
profession.addItem("Butcher");
profession.addItem("Baker");
profession.addItem("Candlestick maker");
profession.addItem("Fletcher");
profession.addItem("Fighter");
profession.addItem("Technical writer");
pane.setLayout(flo);
pane.add(profession);
setContentPane(pane);
```

This example creates a single JComboBox component that provides six choices from which the user can select. When one is selected, it appears in the display of the component. Figure 19.4 shows this example while the pop-up list of choices is being displayed.

FIGURE 19.4

*A JComboBox
component.*

To enable a JComboBox component to receive text input, its setEditable() method must be called with an argument of true, as in the following statement:

```
profession.setEditable(true);
```

This method must be called before the component is added to a container.

Text Areas

A JTextArea component is a text field that enables the user to enter more than one line of text. You can specify the width and height of the component. For example, the following statements create a JTextArea component with an approximate width of 50 characters and a height of 10 lines, and then add the component to an applet:

```
JTextArea comments = new JTextArea(10, 50);
FlowLayout flo = new FlowLayout();
Container pane = getContentPane();
pane.setLayout(flo);
pane.add(comments);
setContentPane(pane);
```

You can specify a string in the TextArea() constructor method to be displayed in the text area. You can use the newline character \n to send text to the next line, as in the following:

```
'TextArea desire = new TextArea("I should have been a pair\n"
    + "of ragged claws.", 10, 25);
```

If the user enters text that extends beyond the component's area, scrollbars will become active on the sides of the component, as shown in Figure 19.5. This JTextArea is 10 lines tall and approximately 50 characters wide.

FIGURE 19.5

A JTextArea component.

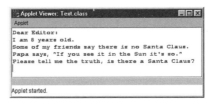

Panels

The last of the components you'll learn to create during this hour are panels, which are created in Swing using the JPanel class. JPanel objects are part of a broader category of objects known as *containers*. JPanel objects don't display anything. Instead, they are used to contain other components. The purpose of JPanel objects is to subdivide a display area into different groups of components. When the display is divided into sections, you can use different rules for how each section is displayed onscreen.

You can create a JPanel object and add it to an applet with the following statements:

```
JPanel topRow = new JPanel();
FlowLayout flo = new FlowLayout();
Container pane = getContentPane();
pane.setLayout(flo);
pane.add(topRow);
```

Panels are often used when arranging the components in an interface, as you'll see in the next section.

Another convenient use of JPanel is to create your own components that can be added to other classes. This is demonstrated in the NewShowButton project.

Listing 19.1 contains two classes: an applet called NewShowButton and a helper class called PanicPanel. This project displays a "Panic" button in the same manner as the ShowButton class earlier this hour.

LISTING 19.1   THE FULL TEXT OF NewShowButton.java

```
 1: import java.awt.*;
 2: import javax.swing.*;
 3:
 4: public class NewShowButton extends JApplet {
 5:     PanicPanel comp = new PanicPanel();
 6:
 7:     public void init() {
 8:         FlowLayout flo = new FlowLayout();
 9:         Container pane = getContentPane();
10:         pane.setLayout(flo);
11:         pane.add(comp);
12:         setContentPane(pane);
13:     }
14: }
15:
16: class PanicPanel extends JPanel {
17:     JButton panicButton = new JButton("Panic");
18:
19:     public PanicPanel() {
20:         FlowLayout flo = new FlowLayout();
21:         setLayout(flo);
22:         add(panicButton);
23:     }
24: }
```

This applet can be tested with the Web page in Listing 19.2.

LISTING 19.2   THE FULL TEXT OF NewShowButton.html

```
1: <applet code="NewShowButton.class" height=150 width=180>
2: </applet>
```

Because it's implemented as a separate class, you could add the PanicPanel class to the interface of any applet or application. In this way, you can add components of your own creation to a user interface.

Using Layout Managers

When you place components onto an applet or some other kind of container, the way they are organized onscreen is highly variable. The layout of buttons, text fields, and other components can be affected by the following things:

- The size of the applet window
- The size of other components and containers
- The layout manager that is being used

There are several layout managers you can use to affect how components are shown. The default manager is the FlowLayout class, which is what has been used for all of the examples shown up to this point. Under FlowLayout, components are dropped onto an area in the same way words are organized on a printed page—from left to right, and on to the next line when there's no more space.

To set up an applet to work under FlowLayout, create a FlowLayout object and then call the setLayout() method of the applet's content pane. The argument to setLayout() should be the layout manager to associate with the pane, which is shown in the following example:

```
Container pane = getContentPane();
FlowLayout topLayout = new FlowLayout();
pane.setLayout(topLayout);
```

You also can set up a layout manager to work within a specific container, such as a JPanel object. You can do this by using the setLayout() method of that container object. The following statements create a JPanel object called inputArea and set it up to use FlowLayout as its layout manager:

```
JPanel inputArea = new JPanel();
FlowLayout inputLayout = new FlowLayout();
inputArea.setLayout(inputLayout);
```

To give you an idea of how the different layout managers work, a simple applet will be shown under each of the classes. The Crisis applet has a graphical user interface with five buttons. Load your word processor and open up a new file called Crisis.java. Enter Listing 19.3 and save the file when you're done.

LISTING 19.3 THE FULL TEXT OF Crisis.java

```
 1: import java.awt.*;
 2: import javax.swing.*;
 3:
 4: public class Crisis extends JApplet {
 5:     JButton panicButton = new JButton("Panic");
 6:     JButton dontPanicButton = new JButton("Don't Panic");
 7:     JButton blameButton = new JButton("Blame Others");
 8:     JButton mediaButton = new JButton("Notify the Media");
 9:     JButton saveButton = new JButton("Save Yourself");
10:
11:     public void init() {
12:         Container pane = getContentPane();
13:         FlowLayout flo = new FlowLayout();
14:         pane.setLayout(flo);
15:         pane.add(panicButton);
16:         pane.add(dontPanicButton);
17:         pane.add(blameButton);
18:         pane.add(mediaButton);
19:         pane.add(saveButton);
20:     }
21: }
```

After saving the source file Crisis.java, you need to create a simple Web page that will display this applet. Create a new file called Crisis.html and enter Listing 19.4.

LISTING 19.4 THE FULL TEXT OF Crisis.html

```
1: <applet code="Crisis.class" height=228 width=308>
2: </applet>
```

Save the Web page, and then compile the Crisis.java file with the javac compiler tool. This applet does not specify a layout manager to use, so the rules default to FlowLayout. Use appletviewer to load the Web page, and you should see something resembling Figure 19.6.

FIGURE 19.6

The Crisis *applet with all of its components laid out under the* FlowLayout *class.*

The FlowLayout class uses the dimensions of its container as the only guideline for how to lay out components. Resize the window of appletviewer as it is showing the Crisis applet. Make the window twice as wide, and you'll see all of the Button components now are shown on the same line. Java programs often will behave differently when their display area is resized.

The GridLayout Manager

The GridLayout class organizes all components in a container into a specific number of rows and columns. All components are allocated the same amount of size in the display area. To see the Crisis applet with a grid layout, load the file Crisis.java back into your word processor and edit the init() method. Delete the first three statements immediately following the public void init() { statement and replace them with the following statements:

```
Container pane = getContentPane();
GridLayout crisisLayout = new GridLayout(2, 3);
pane.setLayout(crisisLayout);
```

Save and compile the new version of Crisis.java and load the Crisis.html Web page back into appletviewer. The output should resemble Figure 19.7.

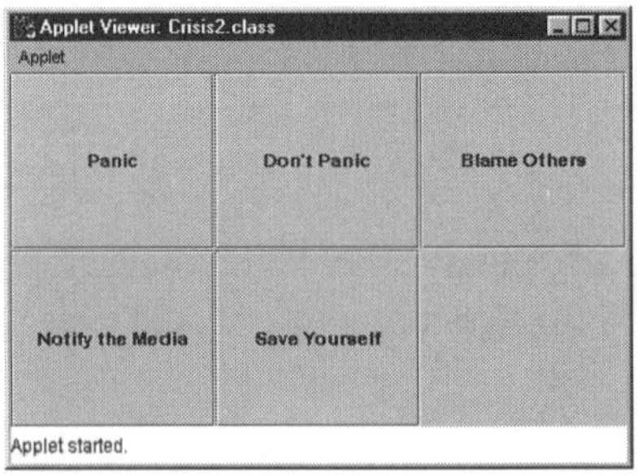

FIGURE 19.7

The Crisis *applet with all of its components laid out under the* GridLayout *class.*

GridLayout places all components as they are added into a place on a grid. Components are added from left to right until a row is full, and then the left-most column of the next grid is filled.

The BorderLayout Manager

The last layout manager left to experiment with is the BorderLayout class. Return to the Crisis.java file in your word processor, and replace the init() method with the following statements:

```
public void init() {
    Container pane = getContentPane();
    BorderLayout crisisLayout = new BorderLayout();
    pane.setLayout(crisisLayout);
    pane.add(panicButton, BorderLayout.NORTH);
    pane.add(dontPanicButton, BorderLayout.SOUTH);
    pane.add(blameButton, BorderLayout.EAST);
    pane.add(mediaButton, BorderLayout.WEST);
    pane.add(saveButton, BorderLayout.CENTER);
}
```

After you save the change and recompile the Crisis applet, the page you load with the appletviewer should resemble Figure 19.8.

FIGURE 19.8

The Crisis *applet with all of its components laid out under the* BorderLayout *class.*

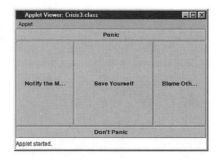

The BorderLayout manager arranges components into five areas: four denoted by compass directions and one for the center area. When you add a component under this layout, the add() method includes a second argument to specify where the component should be placed. This argument should be one of five class variables of the BorderLayout class: NORTH, SOUTH, EAST, WEST, and CENTER are used for this argument.

Like the GridLayout class, BorderLayout devotes all available space to the components. The component placed in the center is given all space that isn't needed for the four border components, so it usually is the largest.

Workshop: Laying Out an Applet

The layout managers you have seen thus far were applied to an applet's entire content pane; the setLayout() method of the pane was used, and all components followed the same rules. This setup can be suitable for some programs, but, as you try to develop a graphical user interface with Swing and the Abstract Windowing Toolkit, you often will find that none of the layout managers fit.

One way around this problem is to use a group of JPanel objects as containers to hold different parts of the applet window. You can set up different layout rules for each of these parts by using the setLayout() methods of each JPanel. Once these panels contain all of the components they need to contain, the panels can be added directly to the content pane.

This hour's workshop will be to develop a full interface for the program you will write during the next hour, "Responding to User Events with Swing." The program is a Lotto number cruncher that will assess a user's chance of winning one of the multimillion-dollar Lotto contests in the span of a lifetime. This chance will be determined by running random six-number Lotto drawings again and again until the user's numbers turn up as a big winner. Figure 19.9 shows the GUI you will be developing for the applet.

FIGURE 19.9

The LottoGUI applet.

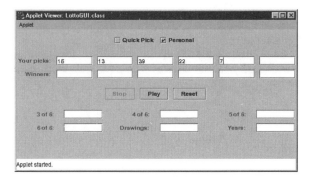

Create a new file in your word processor called LottoGUI.java. Enter Listing 19.5 and save the file when you're done.

LISTING 19.5 THE FULL TEXT OF LottoGUI.java

```
1: import java.awt.*;
2: import javax.swing.*;
3:
4: public class LottoGUI extends JApplet {
5:     // set up row 1
```

```
 6:        JPanel row1 = new JPanel();
 7:        ButtonGroup option = new ButtonGroup();
 8:        JCheckBox quickpick = new JCheckBox("Quick Pick", true);
 9:        JCheckBox personal = new JCheckBox("Personal", false);
10:        // set up row 2
11:        JPanel row2 = new JPanel();
12:        JLabel numbersLabel = new JLabel("Your picks: ", JLabel.RIGHT);
13:        JTextField[] numbers = new JTextField[6];
14:        JLabel winnersLabel = new JLabel("Winners: ", JLabel.RIGHT);
15:        JTextField[] winners = new JTextField[6];
16:        // set up row 3
17:        JPanel row3 = new JPanel();
18:        JButton stop = new JButton("Stop");
19:        JButton play = new JButton("Play");
20:        JButton reset = new JButton("Reset");
21:        // set up row 4
22:        JPanel row4 = new JPanel();
23:        JLabel got3Label = new JLabel("3 of 6: ", JLabel.RIGHT);
24:        JTextField got3 = new JTextField();
25:        JLabel got4Label = new JLabel("4 of 6: ", JLabel.RIGHT);
26:        JTextField got4 = new JTextField();
27:        JLabel got5Label = new JLabel("5 of 6: ", JLabel.RIGHT);
28:        JTextField got5 = new JTextField();
29:        JLabel got6Label = new JLabel("6 of 6: ", JLabel.RIGHT);
30:        JTextField got6 = new JTextField(10);
31:        JLabel drawingsLabel = new JLabel("Drawings: ", JLabel.RIGHT);
32:        JTextField drawings = new JTextField();
33:        JLabel yearsLabel = new JLabel("Years: ", JLabel.RIGHT);
34:        JTextField years = new JTextField();
35:
36:        public void init() {
37:            GridLayout appletLayout = new GridLayout(5, 1, 10, 10);
38:            Container pane = getContentPane();
39:            pane.setLayout(appletLayout);
40:
41:            FlowLayout layout1 = new FlowLayout(FlowLayout.CENTER,
42:                10, 10);
43:            option.add(quickpick);
44:            option.add(personal);
45:            row1.setLayout(layout1);
46:            row1.add(quickpick);
47:            row1.add(personal);
48:            pane.add(row1);
49:
50:            GridLayout layout2 = new GridLayout(2, 7, 10, 10);
51:            row2.setLayout(layout2);
52:            row2.setLayout(layout2);
53:            row2.add(numbersLabel);
54:            for (int i = 0; i < 6; i++) {
55:                numbers[i] = new JTextField();
```

continues

LISTING 19.5 CONTINUED

```
56:                    row2.add(numbers[i]);
57:             }
58:             row2.add(winnersLabel);
59:             for (int i = 0; i < 6; i++) {
60:                 winners[i] = new JTextField();
61:                 winners[i].setEditable(false);
62:                 row2.add(winners[i]);
63:             }
64:             pane.add(row2);
65:
66:             FlowLayout layout3 = new FlowLayout(FlowLayout.CENTER,
67:                 10, 10);
68:             row3.setLayout(layout3);
69:             stop.setEnabled(false);
70:             row3.add(stop);
71:             row3.add(play);
72:             row3.add(reset);
73:             pane.add(row3);
74:
75:             GridLayout layout4 = new GridLayout(2, 6, 20, 10);
76:             row4.setLayout(layout4);
77:             row4.add(got3Label);
78:             got3.setEditable(false);
79:             row4.add(got3);
80:             row4.add(got4Label);
81:             got4.setEditable(false);
82:             row4.add(got4);
83:             row4.add(got5Label);
84:             got5.setEditable(false);
85:             row4.add(got5);
86:             row4.add(got6Label);
87:             got6.setEditable(false);
88:             row4.add(got6);
89:             row4.add(drawingsLabel);
90:             drawings.setEditable(false);
91:             row4.add(drawings);
92:             row4.add(yearsLabel);
93:             years.setEditable(false);
94:             row4.add(years);
95:             pane.add(row4);
96:             setContentPane(pane);
97:         }
98: }
```

Compile this file with the `javac` compiler tool, and return to your word processor to create a Web page for this applet. Create a new file called `LottoGUI.html` and enter Listing 19.6. Save the file when you're done.

LISTING 19.6   THE FULL TEXT OF LottoGUI.html

```
1: <html>
2: <head>
3: <title>Lotto Madness</title>
4: </head>
5: <body bgcolor="#4b4b4b">
6: <applet code="LottoGUI.class" width=550 height=270>
7: </applet>
8: </body>
9: </html>
```

Try this Web page with the appletviewer tool, and you'll get a chance to see how the LottoGUI applet will work. Even though you haven't added any statements that make the program do anything yet, you can make sure that the graphical interface does what you need it to do.

This applet uses several different layout managers. If you look carefully at each of the components, you might be able to determine which manager is in use in the different areas of the program. To get a clearer picture of how the applet is laid out, take a look at Figure 19.10. The interface is divided into five horizontal rows which are separated by horizontal black lines in Figure 19.10. Each of these rows is a JPanel object, and the overall layout manager of the applet organizes these rows into a GridLayout of five rows and one column.

FIGURE 19.10

The way the LottoGUI class is organized.

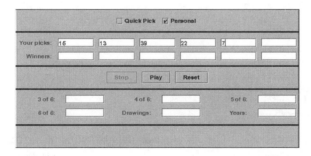

Within the rows, different layout managers are used to determine how the components should appear. Rows 1 and 3 use FlowLayout objects. Lines 41–42 of the program show how these are created:

```
FlowLayout layout1 = new FlowLayout(FlowLayout.CENTER,
    10, 10);
```

Three arguments are used with the FlowLayout() constructor method. The first argument, FlowLayout.CENTER, indicates that the components should be centered within their container—the horizontal Panel on which they are placed. The last two components specify the width and height that each component should be moved away from other components. Using a width of 10 pixels and a height of 10 pixels puts a small amount of extra distance between the components.

Row 2 of the applet is laid out into a grid that is two rows tall and seven columns wide. The GridLayout() constructor also specifies that components should be set apart from other components by 10 pixels in each direction. Lines 50 and 51 set up this grid:

```
GridLayout layout2 = new GridLayout(2, 7, 10, 10);
row2.setLayout(layout2);
```

Row 4 uses GridLayout to arrange components into a grid that is two rows tall and six columns wide.

The LottoGUI applet uses several of the components described during this hour. Lines 5–34 are used to set up objects for all of the components that make up the interface. The statements are organized by row. First, a JPanel object for the row is created, and then each component that will go on the row is set up. This code creates all of the components and containers, but they will not be displayed unless an add() method is used to put them onto the applet's content pane.

In lines 41–96, the components are added. Lines 41–48 are indicative of the entire init() method:

```
FlowLayout layout1 = new FlowLayout(FlowLayout.CENTER,
    10, 10);
option.add(quickpick);
option.add(personal);
row1.setLayout(layout1);
row1.add(quickpick);
row1.add(personal);
pane.add(row1);
```

After a layout manager object is created, it is used with the setLayout() method of the row's JPanel object—row1 in this case. Once the layout has been specified, components are added to the JPanel by using its add() method. Once all of the components have been placed, the entire row1 object is added to the applet's content pane by calling its own add() method.

Summary

Users have come to expect a point-and-click, visual environment for the programs they run. This expectation makes creating software more of a challenge, but Java puts these capabilities into your hands with the windowing toolkit. Swing and the Abstract Windowing Toolkit provide all the classes you will need to provide a working, useful GUI in the tradition of Windows and Macintosh software—regardless of what kind of setup on which you're running Java programs.

During the next hour, you'll learn more about the function of a graphical user interface. You'll get a chance to see the LottoGUI interface in use as it churns through lottery drawings and tallies up winners.

Q&A

Q Why are some of the text fields in the LottoGUI applet shaded in gray while others are white?

A The setEditable() method has been used on the gray fields to make them impossible to edit. The default behavior of a text field is to enable users to change the value of the text field by clicking within its borders and typing any desired changes. However, some fields are intended to display information rather than take input from the user. The setEditable() method prevents users from changing a field they should not modify.

Q Can more than one line of text be displayed on a Label?

A No, labels are limited to a single line of text. You cannot use newline characters (\n) as you might with a TextArea object to create default text that is more than one line long.

Quiz

If your brain hasn't been turned into a GUI mush with this hour's toil, test your skills by answering the following questions.

Questions

1. Which user component is used as a container to hold other components?

   (a) TupperWare

   (b) Panel

   (c) Choice

2. Which of the following must be done first within a container?

    (a) Establish a layout manager

    (b) Add components

    (c) Doesn't matter

3. Where does the BorderLayout class get its name from?

    (a) The border of each component

    (b) The way components are organized along the borders of a container

    (c) Sheer capriciousness on the part of Java's developers

Answers

1. b.

2. a. You must specify the layout manager before the components so you can add them in the correct way.

3. b. The border position of components must be specified as they are added to a container with the use of directional variables such as BorderLayout.WEST and BorderLayout.EAST.

Activities

To interface further with the subject of GUI design, undertake the following activity:

- Create a modified version of the Crisis applet with the panic and dontPanic objects organized under one layout manager and the remaining three buttons under another.

- Make a copy of the LottoGUI.java file that you can rename to NewGUI.java. Make changes to this program so the quick pick or personal choice is a combo box and the start, stop, and reset buttons are check boxes.

To see Java programs that implement these activities, visit the book's Web site at http://www.prefect.com/java24.

Hour **20**

Responding to User Events with Swing

The graphical user interface you developed during the past hour can run on its own without any changes. Buttons can be clicked, text fields filled with text, and the applet window can be resized with wild abandon. Sooner or later, however, even the least discriminating user is going to be left wanting more. The graphical user interface that a program offers has to cause things to happen when a mouse-click or keyboard entry occurs. Text areas and other components must be updated to show what's happening as the program runs.

These things are possible when your Java program can respond to user events. An *event* is something that happens when a program runs, and user events are things a user causes to happen by using the mouse, keyboard, or another input device. Responding to user events often is called *event handling*, and it's the activity you'll be learning about during this hour.

The following topics will be covered:

- Making your programs aware of events
- Setting up a component so it can cause events
- Components that can be ignored
- Where events end up in a program
- Storing information in the interface
- Using numeric variables with text fields

Getting Your Programs to Listen

Responding to user events in a Java program requires the use of one or more EventListener interfaces. As you might recall from using the Runnable interface for multithreaded programs, interfaces are special classes that enable a class of objects to inherit behavior it would not be able to use otherwise. Adding an EventListener interface involves two things right away. First, because the listening classes are part of the java.awt.event group of classes, you must make them available with the following statement:

```
import java.awt.event.*;
```

Secondly, the class must use the implements statement to declare that it will be using one or more listening interfaces. The following statement creates a class that uses ActionListener, an interface used with buttons and other components:

```
public class Graph extends javax.swing.JApplet implements ActionListener {
```

The EventListener interfaces enable a component of a graphical user interface to generate user events. A component cannot do anything that can be heard by other parts of a program without one of the listeners in place. A program must include a listener interface for each type of component to which it wants to listen. You must include the ActionListener interface to have the program respond to a mouse click on a button or the Enter key being pressed in a text field. To respond to the use of a choice list or check boxes, the ItemListener interface is needed. When you require more than one interface, separate their names with commas after the implements statement. The following is an example:

```
public class Graph3D extends javax.swing.JApplet
    implements ActionListener, MouseListener {
```

Setting Up Components to Be Heard

Once you have implemented the interface that is needed for a particular component, you have to set that component up so that it generates user events. A good example to consider is the use of JButton objects as components. When you use a button in an interface, something has to happen in response to the click of the button. Otherwise, the button's not needed for the interface at all.

The program that needs to respond to the button click should use the ActionListener interface. The name of the interface comes from calling a button click or the press of the Enter key an action event, because it signifies that some kind of action should be taken. To make a JButton object generate an event, use the addActionListener() method, as in the following:

```
JButton fireTorpedos = new JButton("Fire torpedos");
fireTorpedos.addActionListener(this);
```

This code creates the fireTorpedos object and then calls that object's addActionListener() method. The this statement indicates that the current class of objects will receive the user event and handle it as needed.

Handling User Events

When a user event is generated by a component that has a listener, a method will be called automatically. The method must be found in the class that was specified when the listener was attached to the component. For instance, in the example of the fireTorpedos object, the method must be located in the same program because the this statement was used.

Each listener has different methods that are called to receive their events. The ActionListener interface sends events to a class called actionPerformed(). The following is a short example of an actionPerformed() method:

```
void public actionPerformed(ActionEvent evt) {
    // method goes here
}
```

All action events sent in the program will go to this method. If only one component in a program can possibly send action events, you can put statements in this method to handle the event. If more than one component can send these events, you need to use the object that is sent to the method.

In this case, an ActionEvent object is sent to the actionPerformed() method. There are several different classes of objects that represent the user events that can be sent in a program. These classes have methods you can use to determine which component caused the

20

event to happen. In the `actionPerformed()` method, if the `ActionEvent` object is named evt, you can identify the component with the following statement:

```
String cmd = evt.getActionCommand();
```

The `getActionCommand()` method sends back a string. If the component is a button, the string will be the label that is on the button. If it's a text field, the string will be the text entered in the field. The `getSource()` method sends back the object that caused the event.

You could use the following `actionPerformed()` method to receive events from three components: a `JButton` object called start, a `JTextField` called speed, and another `JTextField` called viscosity:

```
public void actionPerformed(ActionEvent evt) {
    Object source = evt.getSource();
    if (source == speed) {
        // speed field caused event
    } else if (source == viscosity) {
        // viscosity caused event
    } else
        // start caused event
```

You can use the `getSource()` method with all types of user events to identify the specific object that caused the event.

Check Box and Combo Box Events

Combo boxes and check boxes require the `ItemListener` interface. Use the `addItemListener()` method to make one of these components generate events. For example, the following statements create a check box called superSize and cause it to send out user events when selected or deselected:

```
Checkbox superSize = new Checkbox("Super Size", true);
superSize.addItemListener(this);
```

These events are received by the `itemStateChanged()` method, which takes an `ItemEvent` object as an argument. To see which object caused the event, you can use the `getItem()` method.

To determine whether a check box is selected or deselected, use the `getStateChange()` method with the constants `ItemEvent.SELECTED` and `ItemEvent.DESELECTED`. The following is an example for an `ItemEvent` object called item:

```
int status = item.getStateChange();
if (status == ItemEvent.SELECTED)
    // item was selected
```

To determine the value that has been selected in a JComboBox object, use getItem() and convert that value to a string, as in the following:

```
Object which = item.getItem();
String answer = which.toString();
```

Enabling and Disabling Components

You may have seen a component in a program that appears shaded instead of its normal appearance. This shading indicates that users cannot do anything to the component because it is disabled. Disabling and enabling components as a program runs is done with the setEnabled() method of the component. A Boolean value is sent as an argument to the method, so setEnabled(true) enables a component for use, and setEnabled(false) disables a component.

This method is an effective way to prevent a component from sending a user event when it shouldn't. For example, if you're writing a Java applet that takes a user's address in text fields, you might want to disable a Continue button until all of the fields have some kind of value.

Workshop: A Little Lotto Madness

For more examples of how event handling works in the context of a Java program, you will finish the Lotto applet you began during Hour 19, "Building a Simple User Interface with Swing." The name of the applet will be changed from LottoGUI to LottoMadness to reflect its status as a program. The purpose of this applet is to assess the user's chances of winning a six-number Lotto drawing in a lifetime. Figure 20.1 shows a screen capture of the program as it continues to run.

FIGURE 20.1

The LottoMadness applet continues to run.

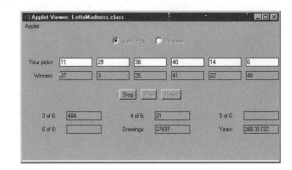

Instead of using probability to figure this problem out, the computer will take a more anecdotal approach: It will conduct drawing after drawing after drawing until you win. Because the 6-out-of-6 win is extremely unlikely, the program also will report on any combination of three, four, or five winning numbers.

The interface you created includes 12 text fields for Lotto numbers and two check boxes labeled Quick Pick and Personal. Six of the text fields are disabled from input, and they will be used to display the winning numbers of each drawing. The other six text fields are for the user's choice of numbers. If the user wants to select six numbers manually, he should select the Personal check box. If he selects the Quick Pick box instead, six random numbers will appear in the text fields.

Three buttons control the activity of the program: Stop, Play, and Reset. When the Play button is pressed, the program starts a thread called `playing` and generates Lotto drawings as fast as it can. Pressing the Stop button stops the thread, and pressing Reset clears all fields so the user can start all the number-crunching over again.

The `LottoMadness` applet implements three interfaces: `ActionListener`, `ItemListener`, and `Runnable`. The first two are needed to listen to user events generated by the buttons and check boxes on the applet. The program does not need to listen to any events related to the text fields because they will be used strictly to store the user's choice of numbers. The user interface handles this function automatically.

Listing 20.1 shows the full text of the `LottoMadness` applet. The shaded lines in the listing were unchanged from `LottoGUI.java`. The unshaded statements are what must be added to respond to user events and run the Lotto drawings.

Making this program aware of user events for some components requires only a few additions. The `class` statement in lines 5–7 is changed to use the interfaces. Lines 47–52 add the listeners needed for the two check boxes and three button components. One line is added to the program in the `init()` method where components are placed on the user interface.

The following methods are used in the program to accomplish specific tasks:

- Lines 152–163: The clearAllFields() method causes all text fields in the applet to be emptied out. This method is handled when the Reset button is pressed.
- Lines 165–169: The addOneToField() method converts a text field to an integer, increments it by one, and converts it back into a text field. Because all text fields are stored as strings, you have to take special steps to use some of them as numbers.
- Lines 171–176: The numberGone() method takes three arguments—a single number from a Lotto drawing, an array that holds several TextField objects, and a count integer. This method makes sure that each number in a drawing hasn't been selected already in the same drawing.
- Lines 178–185: The matchedOne() method takes two arguments—a TextField object and an array of six TextField objects. This method checks to see whether one of the user's numbers is a winner.

The actionPerformed() method of the applet receives the action events caused when the user presses Stop, Play, or Reset. The getActionCommand() method retrieves the label of the button that is used to determine which component was pressed. Pressing the Play button causes four components to be disabled so they do not interfere with the drawings as they are taking place. Pressing Stop reverses this by enabling every component except for the Stop button.

The itemStateChanged() method receives the user events caused when one of the check boxes is selected. The getItem() method sends back an Object, which is converted to a string to determine the label of the check box.

The LottoMadness applet uses numbers from 1 to 50 for each ball in the lottery. This is established in line 140, which multiplies the Math.random() method by 50, adds 1 to the total, and uses this as an argument to the Math.floor() method. The end result is a random integer from 1 to 50. If you replaced 50 with a different number, you could use LottoMadness for lottery contests that generate a wider or smaller range of values.

20

One last thing to note about the LottoMadness applet is the lack of variables used to keep track of things like the number of drawings, winning counts, and Lotto number text fields. This element of user interface programming differs from other types of programs. You can use the interface to store values and display them automatically.

Load the original LottoGUI.java program into your word processor and save the file under the new name LottoMadness.java. After changing the class statement to reflect the new name of the program and the interfaces it will use, insert all of the non-shaded lines from Listing 20.1 and save the file.

LISTING 20.1   THE FULL TEXT OF LottoMadness.java

```
 1: import java.awt.*;
 2: import javax.swing.*;
 3: import java.awt.event.*;
 4:
 5: public class LottoMadness extends JApplet
 6:     implements ItemListener, ActionListener,
 7:     Runnable {
 8:
 9:     Thread playing;
10:
11:     // set up row 1
12:     JPanel row1 = new JPanel();
13:     ButtonGroup option = new ButtonGroup();
14:     JCheckBox quickpick = new JCheckBox("Quick Pick", true);
15:     JCheckBox personal = new JCheckBox("Personal", false);
16:     // set up row 2
17:     JPanel row2 = new JPanel();
18:     JLabel numbersLabel = new JLabel("Your picks: ", JLabel.RIGHT);
19:     JTextField[] numbers = new JTextField[6];
20:     JLabel winnersLabel = new JLabel("Winners: ", JLabel.RIGHT);
21:     JTextField[] winners = new JTextField[6];
22:     // set up row 3
23:     JPanel row3 = new JPanel();
24:     JButton stop = new JButton("Stop");
25:     JButton play = new JButton("Play");
26:     JButton reset = new JButton("Reset");
27:     // set up row 4
28:     JPanel row4 = new JPanel();
29:     JLabel got3Label = new JLabel("3 of 6: ", JLabel.RIGHT);
30:     JTextField got3 = new JTextField();
31:     JLabel got4Label = new JLabel("4 of 6: ", JLabel.RIGHT);
32:     JTextField got4 = new JTextField();
33:     JLabel got5Label = new JLabel("5 of 6: ", JLabel.RIGHT);
34:     JTextField got5 = new JTextField();
35:     JLabel got6Label = new JLabel("6 of 6: ", JLabel.RIGHT);
36:     JTextField got6 = new JTextField(10);
37:     JLabel drawingsLabel = new JLabel("Drawings: ", JLabel.RIGHT);
38:     JTextField drawings = new JTextField();
39:     JLabel yearsLabel = new JLabel("Years: ", JLabel.RIGHT);
40:     JTextField years = new JTextField();
41:
42:     public void init() {
```

```
43:        GridLayout appletLayout = new GridLayout(5, 1, 10, 10);
44:        Container pane = getContentPane();
45:        pane.setLayout(appletLayout);
46:
47:        // Add listeners
48:        quickpick.addItemListener(this);
49:        personal.addItemListener(this);
50:        stop.addActionListener(this);
51:        play.addActionListener(this);
52:        reset.addActionListener(this);
53:
54:        FlowLayout layout1 = new FlowLayout(FlowLayout.CENTER,
55:            10, 10);
56:        option.add(quickpick);
57:        option.add(personal);
58:        row1.setLayout(layout1);
59:        row1.add(quickpick);
60:        row1.add(personal);
61:        pane.add(row1);
62:
63:        GridLayout layout2 = new GridLayout(2, 7, 10, 10);
64:        row2.setLayout(layout2);
65:        row2.setLayout(layout2);
66:        row2.add(numbersLabel);
67:        for (int i = 0; i < 6; i++) {
68:            numbers[i] = new JTextField();
69:            row2.add(numbers[i]);
70:        }
71:        row2.add(winnersLabel);
72:        for (int i = 0; i < 6; i++) {
73:            winners[i] = new JTextField();
74:            winners[i].setEditable(false);
75:            row2.add(winners[i]);
76:        }
77:        pane.add(row2);
78:
79:        FlowLayout layout3 = new FlowLayout(FlowLayout.CENTER,
80:            10, 10);
81:        row3.setLayout(layout3);
82:        stop.setEnabled(false);
83:        row3.add(stop);
84:        row3.add(play);
85:        row3.add(reset);
86:        pane.add(row3);
87:
88:        GridLayout layout4 = new GridLayout(2, 3, 20, 10);
89:        row4.setLayout(layout4);
90:        row4.add(got3Label);
91:        got3.setEditable(false);
92:        row4.add(got3);
```

continues

LISTING 20.1 CONTINUED

```
 93:            row4.add(got4Label);
 94:            got4.setEditable(false);
 95:            row4.add(got4);
 96:            row4.add(got5Label);
 97:            got5.setEditable(false);
 98:            row4.add(got5);
 99:            row4.add(got6Label);
100:            got6.setEditable(false);
101:            row4.add(got6);
102:            row4.add(drawingsLabel);
103:            drawings.setEditable(false);
104:            row4.add(drawings);
105:            row4.add(yearsLabel);
106:            years.setEditable(false);
107:            row4.add(years);
108:            pane.add(row4);
109:            setContentPane(pane);
110:        }
111:
112:        public void actionPerformed(ActionEvent event) {
113:            String command = event.getActionCommand();
114:            if (command == "Reset")
115:                clearAllFields();
116:            if (command == "Play") {
117:                playing = new Thread(this);
118:                playing.start();
119:                play.setEnabled(false);
120:                stop.setEnabled(true);
121:                reset.setEnabled(false);
122:                quickpick.setEnabled(false);
123:                personal.setEnabled(false);
124:            }
125:            if (command == "Stop") {
126:                stop.setEnabled(false);
127:                play.setEnabled(true);
128:                reset.setEnabled(true);
129:                quickpick.setEnabled(true);
130:                personal.setEnabled(true);
131:                playing = null;
132:            }
133:
134:        }
135:
136:        public void itemStateChanged(ItemEvent event) {
137:            Object command = event.getItem();
138:            if (item == quickpick)
139:                for (int i = 0; i < 6; i++) {
140:                    int pick;
141:                    do {
```

```
142:                          pick = (int) Math.floor(Math.random() * 50 + 1);
143:                      } while (numberGone(pick, numbers, i));
144:                      numbers[i].setText("" + pick);
145:                  }
146:          } else {
147:              for (int i = 0; i < 6; i++)
148:                  numbers[i].setText(null);
149:          }
150:      }
151:
152:      void clearAllFields() {
153:          for (int i = 0; i < 6; i++) {
154:              numbers[i].setText(null);
155:              winners[i].setText(null);
156:          }
157:          got3.setText(null);
158:          got4.setText(null);
159:          got5.setText(null);
160:          got6.setText(null);
161:          drawings.setText(null);
162:          years.setText(null);
163:      }
164:
165:      void addOneToField(JTextField field) {
166:          int num = Integer.parseInt("0" + field.getText());
167:          num++;
168:          field.setText("" + num);
169:      }
170:
171:      boolean numberGone(int num, JTextField[] pastNums, int count) {
172:          for (int i = 0; i < count; i++)
173:              if (Integer.parseInt(pastNums[i].getText()) == num)
174:                  return true;
175:          return false;
176:      }
177:
178:      boolean matchedOne(JTextField win, JTextField[] allPicks) {
179:          for (int i = 0; i < 6; i++) {
180:              String winText = win.getText();
181:              if ( winText.equals( allPicks[i].getText() ) )
182:                  return true;
183:          }
184:          return false;
185:      }
186:
187:      public void run() {
188:          Thread thisThread = Thread.currentThread();
189:          while (playing == thisThread) {
190:              addOneToField(drawings);
191:              int draw = Integer.parseInt(drawings.getText());
```

continues

LISTING 20.1   CONTINUED

```
192:                float numYears = (float)draw / 104;
193:                years.setText("" + numYears);
194:
195:                int matches = 0;
196:                for (int i = 0; i < 6; i++) {
197:                    int ball;
198:                    do {
199:                        ball = (int)Math.floor(Math.random() * 50 + 1);
200:                    } while (numberGone(ball, winners, i));
201:                    winners[i].setText("" + ball);
202:                    if (matchedOne(winners[i], numbers))
203:                        matches++;
204:                }
205:                switch (matches) {
206:                    case 3:
207:                        addOneToField(got3);
208:                        break;
209:                    case 4:
210:                        addOneToField(got4);
211:                        break;
212:                    case 5:
213:                        addOneToField(got5);
214:                        break;
215:                    case 6:
216:                        addOneToField(got6);
217:                        stop.setEnabled(false);
218:                        play.setEnabled(true);
219:                        playing = null;
220:                }
221:            }
222:        }
223: }
```

After saving the LottoMadness.java file, load the file LottoGUI.html into your word processor and make one change—the text LottoGUI.class should be LottoMadness.class. Save it under the new name LottoMadness.html. Compile the LottoMadness applet with the javac compiler tool and then try out the applet by loading its Web page into the appletviewer.

Summary

You can create a professional-looking program with a reasonably modest amount of programming by using Swing and Java's event handling features. Although the LottoMadness applet is longer than many of the examples you have worked in during the last 20 hours, half of the program was comprised of statements to build the interface.

If you spend some time running the LottoMadness applet, you will become even more bitter and envious about the good fortune of the people who win these six-number lottery drawings. My most recent run of the program indicates that I could blow $27 grand and the best 266 years of my life buying tickets, only to win a handful of 4-of-6 and 3-of-6 prizes. In comparison to those odds, the chance to make Java programming skills pay off almost seems like a sure thing.

Q&A

Q Is there a way to use different colors in an interface?

A You can use Color objects to change the appearance of each component in several ways. The setBackground() method designates the background elements, and setForeground() sets foreground elements. You must use these methods with the components themselves. The setBackground() method of the applet will not change the color of containers and components within the applet.

Q Do you need to do anything with paint() method or repaint() to indicate that a text field has been changed?

A After the setText() method of a text component is used to change its value, nothing else needs to be done. The Abstract Windowing Toolkit handles the updating necessary to show the new value.

Quiz

After the LottoMadness program has soured you on games of chance, play a game of skill by answering the following questions.

Questions

1. Why are action events called by that name?

    (a) They occur in reaction to something else.

    (b) They indicate that some kind of action should be taken in response.

    (c) They honor cinematic adventurer Action Jackson.

2. What does this signify as the argument to an addActionListener() method?

    (a) "This" listener should be used when an event occurs.

    (b) "This" event takes precedence over others.

    (c) "This" class of objects will handle the events.

3. Which component stores user input as integers?

   (a) JButton

   (b) JTextField

   (c) Neither does

Answers

1. b.

2. c. If the name of another class were used as an argument instead of the this statement, that class would receive the events and be expected to handle them.

3. c. JTextField and JTextArea components store their values as text, so their values must be converted before they can be used as integers, floating-point numbers, or other non-text values.

Activities

If the main event of this hour didn't provide enough action for your tastes, interface with the following activities:

- Add a text field to the LottoMadness applet that works in conjunction with a Thread.sleep() statement to slow down the rate that drawings are conducted.

- Use the TextListener interface and related methods to make sure that users of LottoMadness enter valid numbers from 1 to 50 for the drawings.

To see Java programs that implement these activities, visit the book's Web site at http://www.prefect.com/java24.

PART VI

Putting Your Programming Skills to Work

Hour

HOUR 21

Playing Games with Java

At this point, you have more than enough Java programming skills to be a danger to yourself and others. You can write programs for the World Wide Web and programs to run locally on your computer. The next several hours will test your skills as you apply them to some practical examples of programming.

The program you'll be writing during this hour and the next hour will serve two purposes. First, it will give you a chance to create an object and use it in another program. Secondly, you'll be building gambling skills that will hold you in good stead at the next illicit gambling den you visit. During this hour, you'll create a Die object and test it out with a simple Java program. Once it works, you'll be using the Die object in a Craps applet during Hour 22, "Writing a Game for the Web."

The following topics will be covered during this hour:

- How to play craps
- Creating an object to handle a task
- Generating random numbers for dice rolls
- Drawing dice using polygons

- Determining what to display using `if...then` blocks
- Using methods of the `Math` class
- Storing values in the variables of a class
- Using arguments with methods
- Setting up variables in a constructor method

Craps

Everyone has different recollections of childhood, but who doesn't have memories of skipping school, staying out all night, and blowing all your lunch money at the craps table with some of the neighborhood drug dealers? Most of us don't have these memories, unfortunately, because of restrictive parents and their crazy notions that a good education and sleep were important for their kids.

Luckily, you can simulate a little of that gambling den experience by playing a craps game on your computer. Craps, in case you're particularly sheltered, is a game involving two six-sided dice. The goal is to roll a winning number with the dice before you roll a losing number. Craps has some complicated rules for gambling, but the program you'll write during this hour will focus on dice rolling, winning numbers, and losing numbers. The number of winning rolls and losing rolls will be totaled up as you play, giving you an idea of how often a craps player rolls a winning pair of dice.

When a player rolls the dice for the first time, any combination of the two dice that adds up to 7 or 11 is a winner. Any dice total that equals 2, 3, or 12 is an immediate loser and is called *craps*, as in "Oh, crap, I just lost the money I needed for liposuction surgery!" If the first roll is not an immediate winner or a loser, the total of the dice becomes known as the point. For all successive rolls, the player will win a game if the point is rolled again. However, if a 7 is rolled before the point is rolled, the player craps out.

The following is a sample game rolled by motion picture star Pia Zadora:

1. Pia rolls a 5 and a 6, adding up to 11. She wins the game instantly.

That example wasn't long enough for illustrative purposes, so here's another game from Ms. Zadora:

1. Pia rolls a 6 and a 2. This roll makes 8 the point. On all successive rolls, an 8 will win, and a 7 will lose.
2. Pia rolls a 4 and a 2, adding up to 6. She must roll again.
3. Pia rolls snake eyes—2. She didn't roll the point (8), so she has to roll again.
4. Pia rolls a 3 and 4 (for a total of 7), crapping out.

Now that you know how craps works, it's time to teach the game to your computer. When you're done, you'll be writing a `Craps` applet that you can put on a World Wide Web page.

Organizing the Program

Before you tackle any programming project, spend some time thinking about how it should be implemented. Planning ahead can prevent you from doing work in the program that has to be redone later because it wasn't done correctly. It also can make the finished program easier to understand and easier to maintain later.

If you're particularly organized, you might want to create a flowchart that illustrates the way the program will function. Flowcharts are an effective way to demonstrate the logic a computer should follow as it handles a program. Even if you don't create flowcharts, you should make a list of the things your program must do. Think about each task that must be handled for the program to work, and don't worry about putting them in any order.

For example, the `Craps` applet includes the following list of tasks:

- Roll two dice and add them up
- Figure out if the dice total is a winner or a loser
- Draw the dice on the screen
- Keep track of the point value if the first roll doesn't win or lose
- Count the number of wins and losses
- Create a way for the player to roll the dice

As you can see, almost all aspects of the `Craps` applet will involve the dice. During Hour 10, "Creating Your First Object," you saw how a computer program can be thought of as a group of objects that work together to accomplish a task. One way to conceptualize the `Craps` program is to create an object that represents a six-sided die. If you can create a `Die` class of objects that can roll itself, draw itself, and keep track of its own value, most of the work of a `Craps` applet will be done. An advantage to creating a separate `Die` class of objects is that you can use this class in any program you write that involves dice. The only things left for the applet to do are creating two `Die` objects, asking them to roll themselves, taking user input, and keeping score.

21

Creating a Die Class

The Die class of objects you will create must handle the following tasks:

- Set up an initial value for itself when it is created
- Roll itself
- Keep track of its own value
- Draw itself

Using your word processor, create a new file named Die.java. Each section of the Die class will be described as you enter the text. Begin with the following lines:

```
import java.awt.*;
import java.awt.geom.*;
```

These lines make two packages available to the Die class: Java's main Abstract Windowing Toolkit classes and the java.awt.geom package, which is used for 2D graphics.

> Throughout this section, Die is described as a class of objects rather than as a program. *Class*, *object*, and *program* are largely synonymous in Java, but it's helpful to think of them in the following way: A *program* is a set of computer instructions that handle a task. *Objects* are used by a program to accomplish its work. A *class* is the template that determines how an object is created and what it can do.

After adding a blank line, enter the following statements:

```
public class Die {
    public int value;
```

The first line begins the Die class and indicates that the name of the source file should be Die.java. Die does not use the extends statement along with public class, so it does not inherit any capabilities from other objects. It's a unique class of objects.

The second line creates an integer variable called value. This variable will be used to store the value of the die after it is rolled. Because the object is a six-sided die, the variable will store a value ranging from 1 to 6.

Setting Up Initial Values

The first task the Die object must handle is to set up any variables that are needed when the object is created. Insert a blank line after public int value; and then enter the following:

```
public Die() {
    value = 0;
}
```

This method is called a constructor because it is called automatically whenever another program creates a Die object. The method does only one thing: It sets the value variable equal to 0.

Rolling the Die

The next step is to write a method that handles the rolling of the die. Insert a blank line at the bottom of your file and then enter the following:

```
public void rollValue(int maxValue) {
    double tempValue = Math.random() * maxValue;
    value = (int) Math.floor(tempValue) + 1;
}
```

This method takes one argument, an integer called maxValue. This value will be used to indicate the number of sides on the die. The program you're writing, a Craps applet, always uses six-sided dice. However, by using an argument to enable other types of dice to be used, you make the Die class of objects more useful with other projects you might undertake.

Two methods of the Math class are used in the rollValue() method: Math.floor() and Math.random(). The Math class is one of the standard class libraries that are part of the Java language, and it has several functions to handle mathematic operations. Math.random() generates a random number ranging from 0.0 to 1.0. These numbers are long floating-point numbers such as the following:

```
0.7359693177023363
0.5431408045289557
0.03239819056314541
```

When you multiply Math.random() by a value, you create a random number ranging from 0 to within .001 of that value. For instance, multiplying Math.random() by 6 generates a number ranging from 0.0 to almost 6.0. Adding 1 to this, as the rollValue() method does, generates a random number from 1.0 to almost 7.0.

But just try rolling a six-sided die until you come up with a 2.71570402264! To create a dice-like effect, the number must be rounded down to an integer. The Math.floor()method does exactly this. By using both floor() and random(), the rollValue() method generates a random number from 1 to maxValue and stores the number in the value variable.

Drawing the Die

The last thing the Die class of objects needs to do is draw the die. Instead of displaying the value of the die as text, you can make your program more appealing by showing the die onscreen. Java has several different polygon-drawing methods you can use to depict a die. The final look of a die depends on its value. Figure 21.1 shows six dice with values that range from 1 to 6.

FIGURE 21.1

The possible values on a six-sided die.

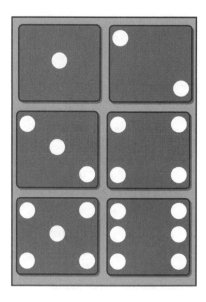

You can show dice in a computer program by drawing a rectangle with rounded corners and circles for each number on a side. One way to handle this procedure in a Java program would be to use a switch...case block with six different sets of drawing statements. One dot could be drawn for a 1, two dots could depict a 2, and so on. However, this solution involves a lot of redundant statements because many of the faces on a six-sided die contain the same dots. As you can see in Figure 21.1, values 2 through 6 all have dots in the upper-left corner and lower-right corner. Using switch and case would require the same statements to be repeated five times for these dots.

Instead of repeating the same statements in several places, you can take a different approach. Figure 21.2 shows each dot that might be seen on a die and the values associated with the dot. You can use this information to draw a die more simply.

Listing 21.1 shows the full source code of the file Die.java. All of the statements you have entered up to this point should look like lines 1–13. Go to the bottom of your file and insert lines 14–37 of Listing 21.1. Save the file when you're done.

FIGURE 21.2

Matching the dots to the values associated with them.

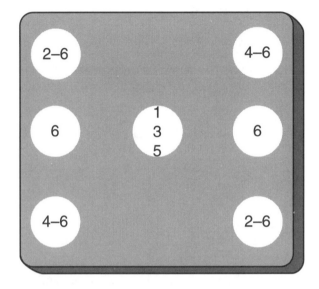

LISTING 21.1   THE SOURCE CODE OF Die.java

```
 1: import java.awt.*;
 2: import java.awt.geom.*;
 3:
 4: public class Die {
 5:     public int value;
 6:
 7:     public Die() {
 8:         value = 0;
 9:     }
10:
11:     public void rollValue(int maxValue) {
12:         double tempValue = Math.random() * maxValue;
13:         value = (int) Math.floor( tempValue ) + 1;
14:     }
15:
16:     public void drawDie(Graphics2D screen2D, float x, float y) {
17:         screen2D.setColor(Color.red);
18:         RoundRectangle2D.Float d1 = new RoundRectangle2D.Float(x, y,
19:             100F, 100F, 20F, 20F);
20:         screen2D.fill(d1);
21:         screen2D.setColor(Color.black);
22:         RoundRectangle2D.Float o1 = new RoundRectangle2D.Float(x, y,
23:             100F, 100F, 20F, 20F);
24:         screen2D.draw(o1);
25:         screen2D.setColor(Color.white);
26:         if (value > 1) {
27:             Ellipse2D.Float s1 = new Ellipse2D.Float(x+5, y+5,
```

continues

LISTING 21.1   CONTINUED

```
28:                    20F, 20F);
29:                screen2D.fill(s1);
30:                Ellipse2D.Float s2 = new Ellipse2D.Float(x+75, y+75,
31:                    20F, 20F);
32:                screen2D.fill(s2);
33:            }
34:            if (value > 3) {
35:                Ellipse2D.Float s1 = new Ellipse2D.Float(x+75, y+5,
36:                    20F, 20F);
37:                screen2D.fill(s1);
38:                Ellipse2D.Float s2 = new Ellipse2D.Float(x+5, y+75,
39:                    20F, 20F);
40:                screen2D.fill(s2);
41:            }
42:            if (value == 6) {
43:                Ellipse2D.Float s1 = new Ellipse2D.Float(x+5, y+40,
44:                    20F, 20F);
45:                screen2D.fill(s1);
46:                Ellipse2D.Float s2 = new Ellipse2D.Float(x+75, y+40,
47:                    20F, 20F);
48:                screen2D.fill(s2);
49:            }
50:            if (value % 2 == 1) {
51:                Ellipse2D.Float s1 = new Ellipse2D.Float(x+40, y+40,
52:                    20F, 20F);
53:                screen2D.fill(s1);
54:            }
55:        }
56: }
```

The drawDie() method takes three arguments:

- A Graphics2D object indicates where all graphics operations should be displayed. All drawing will take place on the applet's main window in the Craps program you'll be writing.
- Two floating-point numbers (x and y) that determine the x and y coordinates where the die should be drawn.

The following things are taking place in the drawDie() method:

- Line 17 sets the current color to red using the red variable of the Color class. All drawing methods that are used after this statement will appear in red until the current color is changed again.
- Lines 18–20 draw a filled rectangle with rounded corners, so a red box appears onscreen that looks like a die without any numbers on it. The first two arguments

to the RoundRectangle2D.Float constructor are the x and y coordinates of the rectangle. These arguments use the same x and y values that were sent to the drawDie() method in line 16. The next two arguments, 100, 100, designate the height and width of the rectangle in pixels. The final two arguments, 20, 20, determine how rounded the rectangle's corners should appear. The higher the number, the more rounded the corners appear to be.

- Line 21 sets the current color to black.

- Lines 22–24 draw an unfilled rectangle with rounded corners using the same arguments as the red rectangle that already has been drawn. These lines create a black outline around the red die.

- Line 25 sets the current color to white.

- Lines 26–54 draw white circles on the die using Ellipse2D.Float objects. Which circles are drawn depend on the value variable, which keeps track of the die's value. The Ellipse2D.Float constructor has four arguments. The first two represent the x and y coordinates of the oval, and the last two represent the height and width of the oval. Because the height and width are equal in these statements (20, 20), the ovals are all circular.

- Lines 27–31 are handled only if the value variable is greater than one. They draw circles in the upper-left and lower-right corners of the die. On a six-sided die, all numbers from 2 upward have circles in these corners.

- Lines 35–40 are handled only if the value variable is greater than 3. They draw circles in the upper-right and lower-left corners of the die.

- Lines 43–48 are handled only if value equals 6. They draw circles in the middle of the left side and the middle of the right side of the die.

- Lines 50–54 take care of the last circle that might be found on a die—the one in the center. This circle is present in the numbers 1, 3, and 5. All of these are odd numbers. Because the modulus operator % produces the remainder of a division operation, you can take advantage of the fact that odd numbers divided by 2 have a remainder of 1, and even numbers have no remainder. The expression value % 2 only equals 1 when value is an odd number. Lines 49–53 draw a circle in the center of the die for odd-numbered die values.

- Line 55 marks the end of the drawDie() method, and line 56 marks the end of the Die class.

Save the file using the name Die.java and compile it. Once it compiles successfully, you will have a Die class of objects that can be used in any program where you want to use six-sided dice.

21

Testing the Die Class

The Die class of objects you have created isn't intended to function as a stand-alone program. If you tried to run it with the java tool, it would result in an error because there is no main() statement in the Die class. To try out your new class, you need to use it inside another Java program. You can do this in the same way you used classes such as Math, Graphics, and Color in your Die class. Create a new file with your word processor and call it TestDie.java. Enter the text of Listing 21.2 and save the file.

LISTING 21.2   THE FULL SOURCE CODE OF TestDie.java

```
 1: class TestDie {
 2:     public static void main(String[] arguments) {
 3:         Die firstDie = new Die();
 4:         Die secondDie = new Die();
 5:         firstDie.rollValue(6);
 6:         secondDie.rollValue(6);
 7:         System.out.println("The first die rolled a "
 8:             + firstDie.value);
 9:         System.out.println("The second die rolled a "
10:             + secondDie.value);
11:     }
12: }
```

This program creates two dice called firstDie and secondDie, rolls each of them using the rollValue() method, and displays the value stored in the value variable of each Die object. The argument of 6 is used with the rollValue() method in lines 5 and 6. This argument causes a dice roll ranging from 1 to 6 to occur, and the result is stored in value.

Compile TestDie.java and run it from the command line with the java tool. The output should resemble the following:

 OUTPUT
The first die rolled a 2
The second die rolled a 5

Run it several times to see that the rolls of the dice are random.

As with most programming languages, Java does not generate completely random numbers. However, the results are random enough for most uses. One use that the Random class would not be sufficient for is encryption. A subclass of Random called SecureRandom can be used in Java programs that encrypt information so it cannot be viewed without being decrypted first.

Summary

This hour provided some practical experience with the object-oriented approach of the Java language. The Die class of objects you created simulates the behavior of a type of real-world object: a six-sided die. Object-oriented programming requires more initial effort than some other approaches, but it has several advantages:

- The structure of the program is more familiar because objects share features such as constructor methods and class variables.
- The program is self-contained, so you can understand what it does without looking at any other programs.
- The program can be instantly reused with other programs.

You now have the Die class of objects to use whenever a die needs to be used in a program. You'll be using it in a Craps applet in the coming hour.

Q&A

Q Does the Craps applet require the use of a class of objects to represent the dice?

A It's not a requirement—you could combine all the dice-related tasks and the score-keeping tasks into the same Java program. If you look at the source code of applets available on the World Wide Web, you'll see many that handle all of their functionality within a single program. However, this type of structure doesn't take advantage of the benefits of object-oriented programming, and the program is harder to understand, harder to reuse elsewhere, and more prone to bugs.

Q Does the public statement in front of a variable declaration mean that the variable can be modified from other Java programs?

A Yes. As you'll see in the Craps applet in the next hour, you can change the value of public variables in other objects. If you create a Die object with the name firstDie, you can set its value variable with a statement such as the following:

```
firstDie.value = 0;
```

Q Can you have more than one constructor method in a class of objects?

A You can have more than one constructor method if they have different argument lists within their parentheses. One constructor could have no arguments, as in public Die(), and another permitted constructor could be public Die (int maxValue). One would be used when Die() is used in a program without any arguments, and the other would be used when Die() is used with a single integer as an argument.

Q Where can I find out the full list of classes that I can use in my Java programs and the `public` methods that can be used with these classes?

A The Java Developer's Kit includes a large number of Web pages that document all classes that are standard parts of the Java programming language. These can be downloaded and you also can view these pages at Sun's Java site with any Web browser. Visit `http://java.sun.com/products/JDK/1.2/docs/`.

Q What colors can be used in conjunction with the `setColor()` method?

A In addition to `red`, `black`, and `white`, you can use the following variables as an argument to `setColor()`: `blue`, `cyan`, `darkGray`, `gray`, `green`, `lightGray`, `magenta`, `orange`, `pink`, and `yellow`. There also are methods of the `Color` class that can be used to create a color based on RGB values, a popular system for specifying a wide range of possible colors. RGB values are used on Web pages with the `BGCOLOR` attribute of the `<BODY>` tag.

Quiz

Roll the dice and put your knowledge of object creation on the line by answering the following questions.

Questions

1. What's the name for a method that is automatically called when an object is created?

    (a) An automat

    (b) A constructor

    (c) An `init()` method

2. In Java, which of the following isn't a synonym for program?

    (a) A class

    (b) A method

    (c) An object

3. What's the name of the method in the `Math` class that rounds a number down to the next lowest integer?

    (a) `floor()`

    (b) `round()`

    (c) `below()`

Answers

1. b. An object's constructor method is called when it is created. The `init()` method might sound familiar because it's handled automatically when an applet is first loaded.

2. b. A program also can be considered as a class of objects or an object itself.

3. a. The `round()` method adds 0.5 to a number before finding the next lowest integer, rounding it off to the closest integer.

Activities

Before you continue to the `Craps` applet, you can expand your knowledge of this hour's topics with the following activities:

- To see whether the `random()` method really generates random numbers, create a short application that rolls 10,000 dice, using an array of integers to keep track of how many times each value from 1 to 6 is rolled. When the dice have finished rolling, display the contents of the array.

- Add an argument to the `drawDie()` method that determines the color of the die. Use a `Color` object for the argument so you can send values such as `Color.blue` and `Color.yellow` to the method.

To see Java programs that implement these activities, visit the book's Web site at `http://www.prefect.com/java24`.

Hour **22**

Writing a Game for the Web

With the Die class you created during the last hour, you can add dice to any of your Java programs. The Craps program you will be writing during this hour uses two dice. Most of the tasks you have to handle in your game are taken care of by the Die class. What's left for your Craps applet is to display information to users, take input from users, and keep score.

The following topics will be covered during this hour:

- Creating an applet
- Using the init() method in an applet
- Using the paint() method to display things
- Using constants in a program
- Putting a button on an applet
- Responding to button clicks
- Creating Die objects
- Using fonts and color

Creating an Applet

All applets you create will have some methods in common. The init() method is called when an applet loads on a page for the first time; you can use this method to set up variables and handle other startup tasks. The paint() method is called whenever something should be updated on the display. It also can be called within a program with the repaint(); statement. The init() and paint() methods will be used in your Craps applet. You also will use the actionPerformed() method, which is called whenever a user does something to a graphical item such as clicking a button or pressing Enter in a text field.

Create a skeletal version of Craps that can be filled in during the hour as each section of the program is discussed. Create a new file in your word processor and enter Listing 22.1. Save it under the name Craps.java, making sure that it is saved in the same folder as Die.java and Die.class.

LISTING 22.1 THE STARTING SOURCE CODE OF Craps.java

```
 1: import java.awt.*;
 2: import javax.swing.*;
 3: import java.awt.event.*;
 4:
 5: public class Craps extends JApplet
 6:     implements ActionListener {
 7:
 8:     // create variables here
 9:
10:     public void init() {
11:         // initialize program
12:     }
13:
14:     public void paint(Graphics screen) {
15:         // display stuff
16:     }
17:
18:     public void actionPerformed(ActionEvent event) {
19:         // receive user input
20:     }
21:
22:      public void checkResult(Die d1, Die d2) {
23:         // check roll and keep score
24:     }
25: }
```

In addition to the init(), paint(), and actionPerformed() methods, this skeletal version of the Craps applet includes a checkResult() method with two Die objects as parameters. As you will see, this method is used to check the results of a dice roll and keep score.

Create Variables to Use

The first task in the Craps applet is to set up all variables that are going to be used in the program. In your word processor, delete the comment line // create variables here and enter Listing 22.2 in its place.

LISTING 22.2 SETTING UP VARIABLES IN Craps.java

```
1: Die die1 = new Die();
2: Die die2 = new Die();
3: int wins = 0;
4: int losses = 0;
5: int point = 0;
6: final String WINNER = "WINNER";
7: final String LOSER = "CRAPS!";
8: String resultText = "";
9: JButton rollButton = new JButton("Roll Dice");
```

Lines 1 and 2 create new Die variables called die1 and die2. These variables are set up in the same way other variables such as strings are created by using the class name, variable name, and the new statement. When this statement is handled in your program, a constructor method of the Die class is called. Because there's nothing in between the parentheses in new Die(), the matching constructor with no arguments is called in the Die class.

In lines 3 and 4, two integer variables are used to keep track of a user's win/loss record: wins and losses. The point integer variable in line 5 stores the point, which is the dice total that must be rolled to win in a craps game after the first roll.

Lines 6 and 7 create strings named WINNER and LOSER. The final statement is used to declare that these variables are constants. A *constant* is a variable that will never change in value as a program runs. To provide another hint that the variables are constants, the names WINNER and LOSER are capitalized.

Because constants never change in value, you might wonder why one should ever be used. You could just use the value of the constant throughout the program. The advantage of using constants is that they can make a program easier to understand. For example, the variables Font.BOLD and Font.ITALIC are constants that hold integer values representing the style of the current font. The statement Font("Helvetica", Font.BOLD, 12) provides more information than Font("Helvetica", 1, 12) does, and both statements make 12 point Helvetica Bold the current font for text display.

Line 8 sets up a string called resultText and sets it up with an initial value of ""—an empty string. The last line, 9, creates a JButton object called rollButton. As this object is created, the string "Roll Dice" is sent to the constructor method of the object. JButton is a class of objects that handle the display and function of clickable user buttons. The rollButton object is given the label Roll Dice. This button is shown in the applet window, and it gives the user a chance to request a dice roll.

Set Up Variables and the Initial Display

A few things need to be done when the Craps applet first runs on a Web page. You need to choose a background color for the window and add the JButton object rollButton to the window. To do these things, replace the comment line // initialize program with Listing 22.3.

LISTING 22.3   THE STATEMENTS INSIDE THE init() METHOD OF Craps.java

```
1: Container pane = getContentPane();
2: FlowLayout flo = new FlowLayout();
3: setBackground(Color.green);
4: rollButton.addActionListener(this);
5: pane.setLayout(flo);
6: pane.add(rollButton);
7: setContentPane(pane);
```

In line 3 of Listing 22.3, the constant Color.green is used with the setBackground() method to choose green as the background color of the applet window. When the paint() method is called automatically to display the applet onscreen, it uses the color defined in setBackground(). If there is no setBackground() statement in a Java program, the default is gray.

Line 4 makesthe `rollButton` object to generate action events when it is clicked. This is done by using the `addActionListener()` method, which is part of the `ActionListener` interface. Line 6 adds the `rollButton` object to the applet window's content pane. The rest of the `init()` method is used to set up the content pane and add it to the applet window.

Display Text and Graphics

The `paint()` method is called any time the text and graphics onscreen should be updated. This situation occurs when the program is run to draw something onto a blank window. The `paint()` method also can be called any time the following takes place:

- The window of the Web browser displaying the applet is resized

- A window or dialog box displayed in front of the applet is moved

- A window is restored to full size after being minimized

- The `repaint()` method is called in a program to force a screen update to occur

In your growing `Craps.java` file, delete the comment line `// display stuff` inside the `paint()` method. Replace it with Listing 22.4.

LISTING 22.4   THE STATEMENTS INSIDE THE `paint()` METHOD OF `Craps.java`

```
 1: super.paint(screen);
 2: Graphics2D screen2D = (Graphics2D) screen;
 3: die1.drawDie(screen2D, 5F, 50F);
 4: die2.drawDie(screen2D, 175F, 50F);
 5: screen2D.setColor(Color.black);
 6: Font f = new Font("Helvetica", Font.BOLD, 15);
 7: screen2D.setFont(f);
 8: if (point != 0)
 9:     screen2D.drawString(point + " wins and 7 craps out.", 5, 200);
10: else
11:     screen2D.drawString("7 or 11 win; 2, 3, or 12 crap out.", 5, 200);
12: screen2D.drawString("Number of wins: " + wins, 5, 220);
13: screen2D.drawString("Number of losses: " + losses, 5, 240);
14: if (resultText != "") {
15:     f = new Font("Helvetica", Font.BOLD, 30);
16:     screen2D.setFont(f);
17:     screen2D.drawString(resultText, 85, 110);
18:     resultText = "";
19: }
```

The following things are taking place in this method:

- Line 2: A Graphics2D object called screen2D is created by casting it from a Graphics object called screen.
- Lines 3 and 4: The drawDie() method of the Die class is called to display two dice. The first argument, screen2D, is the Graphics2D object that tells the Die class to draw something onscreen. The second and third arguments are the x and y coordinates where the dice should be drawn.
- Lines 5–7: The current color is set to black with the Color.black constant, and the current font is set to 15 point Helvetica Bold.
- Lines 8 and 9: If the point value does not equal 0, a string is displayed onscreen using the drawString() method. The string that is displayed is the value of point followed by the text wins and 7 craps out. For example, if point equals 5, the string is 5 wins and 7 craps out. The last two parameters to the drawString() method are the x and y coordinates where the string should be displayed.
- Lines 10 and 11: Using the else statement, if the point value does equal 0, the text 7 or 11 win; 2, 3, or 12 crap out. is shown.
- Lines 12 and 13: The user's win-loss record is displayed along with explanatory text.
- Lines 14–19: This if block statement is handled if the value of the resultText is not empty (the null value ""). If resultText has any text in it, this text is displayed onscreen after the current font is set to 30 point Helvetica Bold. After resultText is displayed, it is set to equal "" again so it will not be displayed twice.

The text displayed in the paint() method depends on several things that are going on in other parts of the program. Because the rolls needed to win or lose change at different points in a game, paint() uses the value of point to determine what should be displayed. The variable point equals 0 at the beginning of a new game of craps because there is no point until the first roll is over. The resultText variable is displayed only when a game is over. It is set initially in another part of the program, the checkResult() method.

Handle User Input

Go to the spot in your Craps program with the comment line // receive user input and replace it with Listing 22.5.

LISTING 22.5   THE STATEMENTS INSIDE THE `actionPerformed()` METHOD OF `Craps.java`

```
1:     die1.rollValue(6);
2:     die2.rollValue(6);
3:     checkResult(die1, die2);
4:     repaint();
```

As you learned during Hour 20, "Responding to User Events with Swing," the `actionPerformed()` method is called whenever an action event occurs on a component that can send out those events. The `Craps` applet has only one user interface component, a `Button` object called `rollButton`, which has been set up with an `ActionListener` object so it can generate action events.

The `rollButton` object in this program is labeled with the text `Roll Dice`. When the button is clicked, lines 1 and 2 call the `rollValue()` method of each `Die` object. The argument, 6, indicates that a number from 1 to 6 should be rolled on each die. When a `Die` is rolled, the `value` variable is updated with the die's new value.

After the dice roll, you should see whether the new total of the dice is a winner or loser. You do this by calling the `checkResult()` method of the applet with two arguments: `die1` and `die2`, the two `Die` objects. The `checkResult()` method is detailed in the next section.

Line 4 calls the `repaint()` method to force the screen to be updated. This method is needed because the dice and other information change with each roll, and those changes should be reflected onscreen.

Check Roll Results and Keep Score

The last thing to handle in the `Craps` applet is scorekeeping. The `checkResult()` method of your program takes two `Die` objects as arguments. Delete the comment line `// check roll and keep score` and replace it with Listing 22.6.

LISTING 22.6   THE STATEMENTS INSIDE THE `checkResult()` METHOD OF `Craps.java`

```
1: if (point == 0) {
2:     point = d1.value + d2.value;
3:     if ( (point == 7) | (point == 11) )
4:         resultText = WINNER;
5:     if ( (point < 4) | (point == 12) )
6:         resultText = LOSER;
7: } else {
8:     if (d1.value + d2.value == point)
```

continues

LISTING 22.6 CONTINUED

```
 9:            resultText = WINNER;
10:        if (d1.value + d2.value == 7)
11:            resultText = LOSER;
12: }
13: if (resultText == WINNER) {
14:     wins++;
15:     point = 0;
16: }
17: if (resultText == LOSER) {
18:     losses++;
19:     point = 0;
20: }
```

Lines 2–6 of this method are handled only if the point variable is equal to 0. The point variable is used throughout this program as an indicator of the current stage of the craps game. When point equals 0, it shows that the current craps game has just finished its first roll, because the point has not been established yet. If point does not equal 0, the current game must be in its second or successive rolls. When point equals 0, line 2 sets point to the sum of the value variables of both Die objects. The value variable keeps track of each die's current value in the game.

Lines 3–6 determine whether a winning roll or a losing roll has happened in the first roll of a craps game. The dice total of 7 and 11 are winners, and the total of 2, 3, or 12 are losers. The OR operator ¦ is used in lines 3 and 5, so if either one equality test or the other is true, the following statement is handled. If point is equal to 7 or point is equal to 11, the resultText variable is set to the value of the WINNER variable, which is the text WINNER. If point is less than 4 or point is equal to 12, resultText is set to the value of the LOSER variable, which is CRAPS!.

Lines 8–11 of this method are handled only if point did not equal 0 in line 1. Line 8 tests whether the current total of the dice is equal to point. If it is, the resultText variable is set to the value of the WINNER variable, which is WINNER. Line 10 tests whether the current dice total equals 7. If it does, resultText is set to equal the LOSER variable, which is CRAPS!

Lines 13–16 are handled if resultText is equal to the WINNER variable, which indicates that the current dice roll was a winner. The wins variable is increased by 1 in line 14 by the increment operator ++. Also, the point variable is set to 0 in line 15 so that a new game can begin.

Lines 17–20 are handled if resultText is equal to the LOSER variable. These lines cause the losses variable to increase by 1 and point to be set to 0 in line 19.

When you're done adding these statements inside the checkResult() method, your program should resemble Listing 22.7. The only differences should be if you indented the program differently, but all statements should be identical. Save your Craps.java file.

LISTING 22.7   THE COMPLETE SOURCE CODE OF Craps.java

```
 1: import java.awt.*;
 2: import javax.swing.*;
 3: import java.awt.event.*;
 4:
 5: public class Craps extends JApplet
 6:     implements ActionListener {
 7:
 8:     Die die1 = new Die();
 9:     Die die2 = new Die();
10:     int wins = 0;
11:     int losses = 0;
12:     int point = 0;
13:     final String WINNER = "WINNER";
14:     final String LOSER = "CRAPS!";
15:     String resultText = "";
16:     JButton rollButton = new JButton("Roll Dice");
17:
18:     public void init() {
19:         Container pane = getContentPane();
20:         FlowLayout flo = new FlowLayout();
21:         setBackground(Color.green);
22:         rollButton.addActionListener(this);
23:         pane.setLayout(flo);
24:         pane.add(rollButton);
25:         setContentPane(pane);
26:     }
27:
28:     public void paint(Graphics screen) {
29:         super.paint(screen);
30:         Graphics2D screen2D = (Graphics2D) screen;
31:         die1.drawDie(screen2D, 5F, 50F);
32:         die2.drawDie(screen2D, 175F, 50F);
33:         screen2D.setColor(Color.black);
34:         Font f = new Font("Helvetica", Font.BOLD, 15);
35:         screen2D.setFont(f);
36:         if (point != 0) {
37:             screen2D.drawString(point + " wins and 7 craps out.",
38:                 5, 200);
39:         } else {
40:             screen2D.drawString("7 or 11 win; 2, 3, or 12 crap out.",
41:                 5, 200);
42:         }
43:         screen2D.drawString("Number of wins: " + wins, 5, 220);
```

continues

LISTING 22.7 CONTINUED

```
44:              screen2D.drawString("Number of losses: " + losses, 5, 240);
45:              if (resultText != "") {
46:                  f = new Font("Helvetica", Font.BOLD, 30);
47:                  screen2D.setFont(f);
48:                  screen2D.drawString(resultText, 85, 110);
49:                  resultText = "";
50:              }
51:          }
52:
53:      public void actionPerformed(ActionEvent event) {
54:          die1.rollValue(6);
55:          die2.rollValue(6);
56:          checkResult(die1, die2);
57:          repaint();
58:      }
59:
60:      public void checkResult(Die d1, Die d2) {
61:          if (point == 0) {
62:              point = d1.value + d2.value;
63:              if ( (point == 7) ¦ (point == 11) )
64:                  resultText = WINNER;
65:              if ( (point < 4) ¦ (point == 12) )
66:                  resultText = LOSER;
67:          } else {
68:              if (d1.value + d2.value == point)
69:                  resultText = WINNER;
70:              if (d1.value + d2.value == 7)
71:                  resultText = LOSER;
72:          }
73:          if (resultText == WINNER) {
74:              wins++;
75:              point = 0;
76:          }
77:          if (resultText == LOSER) {
78:              losses++;
79:              point = 0;
80:          }
81:      }
82: }
```

Compile the Craps.java file using the following command:

```
javac Craps.java
```

After fixing any errors that are caused by typos, you're almost ready to test the program.

Putting the Program on a Page

22

Because the Craps program is an applet, it was designed to run only as part of a World Wide Web page. To place the applet on a Web page, create a new file called Craps.html. Enter Listing 22.8 and save the file in the same folder as Craps.java and Craps.class.

LISTING 22.8   THE SOURCE CODE OF Craps.html

```
1: <html>
2: <head>
3: <title>Craps applet</title>
4: </head>
5: <body>
6: <applet code="Craps.class" width=285 height=250>
7: </applet>
8: </body>
9: </html>
```

Most of the HTML tags on the page are just standard tags that are included on any Web page. The width and height attributes of the <applet> tag determine how big the applet will appear on a page. You can use any dimensions and the applet will still run because Java creates programs that are flexible when it comes to how they are displayed. For optimal appearance, however, use a width of 285 and a height of 250.

In order to see the applet, you need to use a Web browser that can handle Java programs. At the time of this writing, the current versions of Netscape Navigator and Microsoft Internet Explorer cannot handle new features introduced in version 2 of the Java language, although you may be able to use the Java Plug-in with either browser for version 2 support.

You can use the appletviewer tool that comes with the Java Development Kit to test the Craps applet. If you're in the same folder as the Craps.html file, the following command will cause appletviewer to load the applet:

```
appletviewer Craps.html
```

Figure 22.1 shows the output of the Craps applet using appletviewer.

Run the program several times to see the different ways that text and each of the dice can be displayed. Because the dice are drawn with polygons instead of by loading a picture of a die, the applet updates the graphics quickly as you play.

FIGURE 22.1

The Craps *applet on a Web page viewed with the* appletviewer *tool.*

Summary

The Craps applet you have written shows how you can use Java to offer games on a Web site. The step-by-step process of creating a program was detailed, including some of the planning that occurs before you sit down at the computer. Because many of the program's tasks involved rolling or displaying dice, you created a special Die object to handle all of this functionality. Creating this object enables you to use some of the work you did for the Craps applet in other programs later.

You can use this applet on a Web page in its completed form, and all that is required are the files Die.class, Craps.class, and a Web page with HTML tags to load the applet. Thanks to the global reach of the World Wide Web and Java, you can bring the seedy charm of craps games to everyone from Afghanistan to Zambia, including Pia Zadora.

Q&A

Q Do I need to use an import statement to use the Die class or another class of objects that I create in a program?

A If the class you want to use is in the same folder as your program, an import statement is not required. The import statement makes Java's standard classes available in a program. Place special classes you create and other classes you find on the Web or in books in the same folder as the programs that use them.

Q Isn't constant variable an oxymoron?

A Constants never change and variables can change at any time, but it's convenient to call both variables because they serve the same function. Each stores a value for use as a program runs. The final statement is not needed to make a variable a constant in a program—WINNER and LOSER would work the same in the Craps applet without final. However, it's much safer in your programs to ensure that a constant remains constant.

Q **When x and y coordinates are specified in a `drawString()` statement, where are the x and y coordinates in relation to the text that is displayed?**

A Imagine there is an invisible box around the text that is exactly big enough to hold all of the characters. The upper-left corner of this box is the x and y coordinates specified as arguments to `drawString()`.

Quiz

If you've become a gambler thanks to this hour's lesson, feel free to make wagers on your knowledge of programming before you answer the following questions.

Questions

1. What can you do to make the name of a constant stand out in a program?

   (a) Use a foreign language

   (b) Capitalize the first letter

   (c) Capitalize the whole name

2. What method sets the color of the window in an applet?

   (a) `setBackground()`

   (b) `setColor()`

   (c) `setWindow()`

3. If the first dice roll in a craps game isn't a winner or a loser, what do you call the total of the roll?

   (a) The punt

   (b) The point

   (c) The pint

Answers

1. c. If you only capitalize the first letter, the constant name will look just like the names of classes in your programs.

2. a. `setColor()` sets the current color for all successive graphical methods.

3. b.

Activities

Now that you have completed your most sophisticated Java project thus far, you can build your skills with the following activities:

- Add a second button to the `Craps` applet that causes the dice to be constantly rolled until the button is pressed again. The applet will play craps by itself swiftly, and you can see how often winners and losers are rolled.
- Add the capability to make wagers on each game of craps in the `Craps` applet. This capability could be implemented with a choice menu component that lets the user choose bets of $1, $5, or $10 and a text field that displays the player's current winnings.

To see Java programs that implement these activities, visit the book's Web site at `http://www.prefect.com/java24`.

Hour 23

Spicing Up a Web Page

When Java was released to the public in late 1995, its creators had some lofty intentions for the programming language. It was going to revolutionize the way software was produced and distributed, remove the need to write versions of a program for different operating systems, and take full advantage of the Internet as a place to run programs. (They probably wanted to make some money, too.) Although some notable projects created with Java since then advance those goals, many Java programmers worked under somewhat less noble motivation: Show and tell.

For every human who gets a kick out of advancing the causes of human-kind, bettering society, and being the wind beneath someone's wings, there's a human who did something because it looked cool. Animated Java applets are a case in point. There are dozens of different special-effects applets on the Web that do interesting things with text and graphics. During this hour you'll set aside the greater good of Javakind and create one of your own.

The following topics will be covered:

- Controlling an applet with parameters
- Loading images from parameters

- Using offscreen areas for drawing
- Using transparent .GIF files
- Drawing images off the screen's edges

The Pan Applet

One of the common uses for Java applets has been to animate text or images on a World Wide Web page. This kind of animation can be done as an attention-getting move; an online catalog might use moving text to inform visitors of sale items, for example. It also can be done to provide information in a more dynamic way. Several media organizations such as CNN and ESPN have used Java applets as a way to provide constant news and sports updates.

A lot of these applets move graphics or text over a static background to produce an interesting effect. You're going to take the opposite tack with the Pan applet. It will keep something still in the foreground while the background moves. The effect could be useful to draw attention to text or create an interesting logo for a company.

The Pan applet uses the same threaded applet structure you have used in several of the past hours. A thread called runner is created in the applet's start() method and destroyed in the stop() method. The runner object calls the run() method of the program, which loops continuously while the runner object does not equal null.

Three Image objects are used in the program: back, fore, and workspace. The first two objects hold the background image and foreground image that will be displayed. The third is used as an offscreen work area to make the animation appear more smoothly, a trick called double-buffering that you learned during Hour 18, "Creating Animation."

In addition to displaying the background and foreground images, the applet can display a line of text. This text and both images are specified in parameters on the Web page that runs the applet. You can use the following parameters:

- background   This parameter is the filename of the background image that will pan across the applet window from right to left. This image file must be in .GIF or .JPG format and must be located in the same place as the .class file of the applet.
- foreground   This parameter is the filename of the foreground image that will be displayed as the background image moves behind it. This file should be in .GIF format and must have a transparent color. Otherwise, nothing will be visible behind the image. This parameter is optional, so you can choose not to display a foreground image at all.

- text   This parameter is the line of text to display in front of all images that are being displayed. If this parameter is omitted, no text will be shown.
- fontname   This parameter is the name of the font in which the text should be displayed. Arial is the default.
- fontsize   This parameter is the size of the text's font, which defaults to 24.

Displaying the Images

23

All text and images are displayed in the paint() method of the Pan applet. An offscreen Graphics object is used for all drawing methods, and, when everything has been drawn, the offscreen area is copied to the applet window. Using double-buffering produces much better results than displaying each image and string in the window individually.

If a line of text is specified as a parameter, the applet will center it horizontally and vertically onscreen. This is done using a class called FontMetrics, which reports on how large a line of text will be if displayed in a specific font, size, and style. The following statements create a Font object and set up a FontMetrics object that is linked to it:

```
Font f = new Font(fontName, Font.BOLD, fontSize);
FontMetrics fm = getFontMetrics(f);
```

The Font object is used as an argument to the getFontMetrics() method. Once you create the FontMetrics object, you can use two of its methods to help determine how to use the font and center a line of text. These methods are stringWidth(), which indicates how wide the text will be, and getHeight(), which reveals how tall anything in the font will be. In the Pan applet you're going to create, the following statements use these methods:

```
int xStart = (getSize().width - fm.stringWidth(text)) / 2;
int yStart = getSize().height/2 + fm.getHeight()/4;
offscreen.drawString(text, xStart, yStart);
```

The getSize().width and getSize().height statements are the dimensions of the applet window itself. By using these statements with the FontMetrics methods, the program can determine the right location for the text.

Figure 23.1 shows the Pan applet with a line of text centered in the applet window. It's a little harder to distinguish in black and white, but the text is drawn twice—once in black and again in white. The text is drawn at a slightly different place the second time, as shown in the following statement:

```
offscreen.drawString(text, xStart-2, yStart-2);
```

This statement creates a shadow effect that makes the text easier to see over the background.

FIGURE 23.1

A scrolling image running underneath text in an applet.

Workshop: Drawing Images over a Screen's Edges

To create the effect of an image panning from right to left, the Pan applet takes advantage of the way images are displayed with Java. Before taking a look at this applet, you should get Pan running. Create a new file in your word processor called Pan.java, and enter Listing 23.1 into the file. Save it when you're done.

LISTING 23.1   THE FULL TEXT OF Pan.java

```
 1: import java.awt.*;
 2:
 3: public class Pan extends javax.swing.JApplet
 4:     implements Runnable {
 5:
 6:     Thread runner;
 7:     Image back, fore, workspace;
 8:     Graphics offscreen;
 9:     String text;
10:     String fontName;
11:     int fontSize = 24;
12:     int x1 = 0;
13:     int x2;
14:
15:     public void init() {
16:         workspace = createImage(getSize().width, getSize().height);
17:         offscreen = workspace.getGraphics();
18:         // get parameters
19:         String imageBack = getParameter("background");
20:         if (imageBack != null)
21:             back = getImage(getDocumentBase(), imageBack);
22:         String imageFore = getParameter("foreground");
23:         if (imageFore != null)
24:             fore = getImage(getDocumentBase(), imageFore);
25:         x2 = getSize().width;
26:         text = getParameter("text");
27:         fontName = getParameter("font");
28:         if (fontName == null)
29:             fontName = "Arial";
30:         String param = getParameter("fontsize");
31:         if (param != null)
```

```
32:                     fontSize = Integer.parseInt("0" + param);
33:         }
34:
35:     public void start() {
36:         if (runner == null) {
37:             runner = new Thread(this);
38:             runner.start();
39:         }
40:     }
41:
42:     public void stop() {
43:         if (runner != null) {
44:             runner = null;
45:         }
46:     }
47:
48:     public void run() {
49:         Thread thisThread = Thread.currentThread();
50:         while (runner == thisThread) {
51:             repaint();
52:             try { Thread.sleep(200); }
53:             catch (InterruptedException e) {}
54:             x1 = x1 - 1;
55:             x2 = x2 - 1;
56:             if (x1 <= (getSize().width * -1))
57:                 x1 = getSize().width;
58:             if (x2 <= (getSize().width * -1))
59:                 x2 = getSize().width;
60:         }
61:     }
62:
63:     public void paint(Graphics screen) {
64:         Graphics2D screen2D = (Graphics2D) screen;
65:         offscreen.drawImage(back, x1, 0, null);
66:         offscreen.drawImage(back, x2, 0, null);
67:         if (fore != null)
68:             offscreen.drawImage(fore, 0, 0, null);
69:         if (text != null) {
70:             offscreen.setColor(Color.black);
71:             Font f = new Font(fontName, Font.BOLD, fontSize);
72:             FontMetrics fm = getFontMetrics(f);
73:             offscreen.setFont(f);
74:             int xStart = (getSize().width - fm.stringWidth(text)) / 2;
75:             int yStart = getSize().height/2 + fm.getHeight()/4;
76:             offscreen.drawString(text, xStart, yStart);
77:             offscreen.setColor(Color.white);
78:             offscreen.drawString(text, xStart-2, yStart-2);
79:         }
80:         screen2D.drawImage(workspace, 0, 0, this);
81:     }
```

23

continues

LISTING 23.1   CONTINUED

```
82:
83:     public void update(Graphics screen) {
84:          paint(screen);
85:     }
86: }
```

Compile this file with the `javac` compiler tool, and then return to the word processor to create a Web page that contains the `Pan` applet. Enter Listing 23.2 and save it as `Pan.html`. Note that the `width` and `height` attributes of the `<APPLET>` tag should be the same dimensions as the background image to achieve the best results.

LISTING 23.2   THE FULL TEXT OF `Pan.html`

```
1: <applet code="Pan.class" width=460 height=43>
2: <param name="background" value="patch.gif">
3: <param name="font" value="Helvetica">
4: <param name="fontsize" value="25">
5: <param name="text" value="FRED'S APPETITE SUPPRESSANTS">
6: </applet>
```

Before you can see this applet running on a page, you need to put a copy of the image file `patch.gif` in the same folder as `Pan.html`. You can find this file on the book's official Web site at `http://www.prefect.com/java24`. Take the link from the site's front page labeled `Hour 23's Moving Images`, and you'll be able to download `patch.gif`. Get a copy of two other image files called `samsback.gif` and `samslogo.gif` also to save time later.

When you use `appletviewer` to load this Web page, you will see the `Fred's Appetite Suppressants` banner shown in Figure 23.1. No foreground element is specified on the page, so the text appears over a moving background.

The `Pan` applet is able to vary its performance greatly by using parameters to load all images and text. You can create a new Web page by using different images and different parameters. Return to your word processor and create a new file called `Sams.html`. Enter the text of Listing 23.3 and save the file.

LISTING 23.3   THE FULL TEXT OF `Sams.html`

```
1: <applet code="Pan.class" width=229 height=166>
2: <param name="background" value="samsback.gif">
3: <param name="foreground" value="samslogo.gif">
4: </applet>
```

As with the previous example, you need to copy some image files before loading this Web page into `appletviewer`. The files are `samsback.gif` and `samslogo.gif`. As shown in Figure 23.2, this applet shows a moving background underneath a static logo of Sams.net Publishing. The logo makes use of transparency so that the background image can be seen.

FIGURE 23.2

A scrolling image underneath a partially transparent image in an applet.

The panning effect used by this applet is possible because of the way the `drawImage()` method can be drawn to offscreen coordinates. Normally, when you draw an image to an applet window or a workspace, the (x,y) coordinates that you specify are within the display area of the program. Otherwise, the graphics can't be seen. However, there's no prohibition against drawing to coordinates that make most of an image appear offscreen. The `drawImage()` method will display the portion of the image that does appear onscreen and disregard the rest.

By drawing the background image twice at different positions, the `Pan` program makes the image seem to move. The exact positions of the images vary as the program runs, which creates the animation effect, but they always are shown right next to each other. Figure 23.3 shows how this happens with the `Sams.html` page. Black borders have been drawn around the background image so that you can see that it is being drawn twice. The thick black border indicates the visible display area of the applet—everything outside of it would not be seen.

FIGURE 23.3

Two copies of the background image partially displayed in the applet window.

The `Pan` applet uses the integer variables `x1` and `x2` to determine the two x coordinates where the background should be drawn. The images do not move up and down, so no y coordinates are needed. The `x1` variable begins with the value of 0, and `x2` starts out at the width of the applet: 229. The first time that the images are displayed, one copy will be shown at (0,0), filling the entire window, and the other will begin at (229,0), one pixel off the right edge.

In lines 54–55 of the program, both x1 and x2 are reduced by 1. When the repaint() method is called next, each image is displayed one pixel to the left of its last position. Lines 56–59 make sure that neither of the images goes so far to the left that none of it is displayed. If the image moves too far to the left, the x coordinate is set to the width of the applet.

Summary

The Pan applet is an example of producing an interesting visual effect with a few lines of programming. Most of the statements in the program are used to load parameters, store images, and handle the display of non-moving graphics and text. Less than a dozen lines control the values of x1 and x2, and these are all that's needed to move the two copies of the background image and produce the animation.

As you create your own programs and start looking at the programs that others make available on the World Wide Web, you'll pick up more of these tricks. Many of them will probably be used more for the grown-up version of Show and tell—the home page—than any higher purpose.

However, you might find some practical uses for these programs in unexpected places. By using some of the same logic that was needed for the Pan applet, you could write an applet that displays a small section of a large map and enables users to interactively pan to other places on the map.

It isn't an achievement on par with the polio vaccine or inter-league play in Major League Baseball, but a map applet of that kind could be useful to many people browsing the World Wide Web. Because it works fully in conjunction with Web pages, Java makes some types of information more accessible than they would be otherwise. And that's something to get animated about.

Q&A

Q What is the update() method accomplishing in the Pan applet?

A This method is included in the applet to override its existing behavior. The update() method automatically is called each time the screen needs to be redisplayed, either due to a repaint() statement or some other cause. Normally, update() clears the screen by filling it with the background color, and then calls the `paint()` method. This screen-clearing causes a large amount of flickering in an animation program, so `update()` is overridden to prevent it from occurring.

Q **None of the graphics programs that I use has a feature for transparency in `.GIF` files. How is this established for an image such as `samslogo.gif`?**

A Transparency was introduced with a version of the `.GIF` file format called `89a`. In order to use it, you must find a graphics program that can load, edit, and save `.GIF89a` files. If you don't have one of these programs and you save a `.GIF` file, you will wipe out its transparency information.

23

Quiz

Don't pan past this section of the book without testing your know-how by answering the following questions.

Questions

1. Why are threads helpful in controlling an animated program in Java?

    (a) They give other programs that are running more time to operate.

    (b) You can use the `Thread.sleep` method to pause between screen updates.

    (c) Loop statements don't work with animation.

2. Why is a `Graphics` object sent to the `paint()` method of an applet?

    (a) This object contains the necessary information to display something on-screen or on a component.

    (b) The method was set up to take an argument.

    (c) The object signifies that graphics will be used in the method.

3. What method of the `Integer` class is used to convert a string into an integer value?

    (a) `getInt()`

    (b) `load()`

    (c) `parseInt()`

Answers

1. b. Threads have the built-in ability to start, stop, and pause, abilities that correspond well with what an animation program needs to do as it runs.

2. a. The `Graphics` object is used to create a `Graphics2D` object, which is then used to display text, polygons, and image files onscreen.

3. c.

Activities

Unless you're ready to pan this hour's subject matter, do the following activities:

- Add a parameter to the Pan applet that causes the background image to move from left to right instead of right to left.
- Using event-handling and listener classes, make it possible to switch the direction of the Pan animation by clicking the mouse on the applet window.

To see Java programs that implement these activities, visit the book's Web site at http://www.prefect.com/java24.

HOUR **24**

Making Your Knowledge Add Up

Most of the programs you created during the first 20 hours of this book were short tutorials intended to demonstrate a specific aspect of Java programming. These programs can be a useful introduction to how a language works, but when you start to write your own programs, it can be a challenge to make the different things you've learned work together.

The last hour of this book tests how well you can make your skills add up. You'll be creating a working Java program from scratch by using the techniques covered during the past 23 hours. Instead of being shown the specific classes, methods, and other statements to use, you'll face the same task a working programmer would face: an empty document in a word processor that needs to be turned into working source code.

You'll draw upon your knowledge of the following topics as you write the Java program during this hour:

- Adding components to a window
- Arranging components with a layout manager

- Adding components to containers
- Responding to action events
- Reading information from a text field
- Sending information to a text field
- Using your own classes in a Java program

Workshop: A Calculator Component

Imagine that you're a professional Java programmer who has just finished a project and is ready to take on a new assignment. While you're at it, imagine yourself a window office with a nice view of the mountains along with job perks that include a six-week vacation and onsite massage sessions.

Your boss enters your office, and you immediately pay attention for reasons that include her startling resemblance to the actress Ashley Judd.

> Sorry—that was me imagining that your boss looks like the popular star of *A Time to Kill* and *Ruby in Paradise*. The appearance of your own imaginary boss may vary.

Your boss gives you an assignment: Use Java 2 to create `MiniCalc`, a calculator program that should be similar to the one included with Windows 95. That calculator program is shown in Figure 24.1.

FIGURE 24.1

The Windows 95 Calculator.

Your calculator program does not have to be as complex as the one shown in Figure 24.1. It should be able to handle four operations: addition, subtraction, multiplication, and division.

The calculator will need the following buttons:

- Numerals ranging from 0 to 9
- Buttons for the four operators: "+" for addition, "-" for subtraction, "*" for multiplication, and "/" for division
- A "+/-" button that changes a positive number to a negative one, and vice versa
- A "." button to use when entering decimal numbers
- An "=" button to use when the operation should be calculated
- A "C" button to clear the number displayed by the calculator

These buttons can be arranged in any style desired, though if you veer too far from what people expect in a calculator, you run the risk of confusing users.

To make it easier for people to use the calculator, buttons should be disabled at certain times to prevent them from be used, according to the following rules:

- When the program begins, the equals button should be disabled.
- Once the addition, subtraction, multiplication, or division button has been clicked, these four buttons should be disabled and the equals button should be enabled.
- When the equals button is clicked, it should be disabled and the addition, subtraction, multiplication, and division buttons should be enabled.

> By restricting button use in this way, you limit the calculator to use on simple two-number calculations such as 4 + 3 = 7, 2 – 1 = 1, 6 * 2.5 = 15, and 5 / 10 = 0.5. (Other calculators such as the Windows 95 program enable you to handle calculations involving more numbers, such as 3 + 2 * 2 - 5 / 6 = 0.833333.)

Your boss, who I insist on calling Ashley, has one last requirement for this calculator project: You should not be able to run the MiniCalc class as either an applet or an application.

Instead, it should be a subclass of JPanel that can be added to the graphical user interface of both applets and applications.

Listing 24.1 contains the source code of a simple applet that includes the MiniCalc calculator on its interface. When this applet is loaded on a Web page, the calculator should display and be ready to be used.

LISTING 24.1 THE FULL TEXT OF CalcApplet.java

```
 1: import java.awt.*;
 2:
 3: public class CalcApplet extends javax.swing.JApplet {
 4:     MiniCalc calc = new MiniCalc();
 5:
 6:     public void init() {
 7:         setBackground(Color.gray);
 8:         Container pane = getContentPane();
 9:         FlowLayout flo = new FlowLayout();
10:         pane.setLayout(flo);
11:         pane.add(calc);
12:         setContentPane(pane);
13:     }
14: }
```

The CalcApplet program assumes that MiniCalc will be created with a MiniCalc() constructor that takes no arguments. You may choose to design it with a different constructor method.

As you can see in the CalcApplet program, MiniCalc is treated like any other part of a user interface such as JButton objects and JTextField objects. It is created, added to a container, and then the container is added to the applet window.

Listing 24.2 contains an example of HTML code that could be used to display CalcApplet.

LISTING 24.2 THE FULL TEXT OF CalcApplet.html

```
1: <applet code="CalcApplet.class" height=200 width=200>
2: </applet>
```

When you test your own MiniCalc class in an applet, you might choose different HEIGHT and WIDTH attributes with the APPLET tag, depending on how you designed the graphical user interface of the calculator.

Once you have the MiniCalc class working the way you want it to and you compile the file, using MiniCalc in a new program will be as easy as using any other object. Test it by loading an applet such as CalcApplet into a Java 2–capable Web browser such as the appletviewer tool.

The solution to this hour's workshop is offered on the book's Web site along with the solution to every activity in the book. Visit `http://www.prefect.com/java24` and head to the Hour 24 section. If you get stuck while you're working on this project, be sure to visit the Web site for suggestions and other assistance.

Summary

The purpose of *Sams Teach Yourself Java 2 in 24 Hours* is to make you comfortable with the concepts of programming and confident in your ability to write your own applets and applications. Java has an approach that is somewhat difficult to master. (Feel free to scratch out the word "somewhat" in the previous sentence if it's a gross misstatement of the truth.)

As you build experience in Java, you're building experience that will be increasingly relevant in the coming years. If you become knowledgeable in object-oriented programming and distributed network computing, the `MiniCalc` class could prove very useful—there's no better way for a millionaire to spend an afternoon than by projecting the rate of return on no-load mutual funds using a Java program you wrote!

If you haven't already, you should read the appendixes to find out about this book's Web site, other Java books from Macmillan Computer Publishing, and other useful information. Even if you don't, there's one last bit of bad news to deliver. Your 24 hours are up.

At the conclusion of this hour, you are contractually obligated to learn no more about Java programming. You cannot use Internet discussion groups such as `comp.lang.java.programmer` to talk to other people who share your skills. You must not look for Java Users Groups in your area. You cannot search employment World Wide Web sites such as `http://www.careerpath.com` for companies that seek Java programmers. Under no circumstances should you send electronic mail to the author of this book by visiting the Web site `http://www.prefect.com/java24` and asking him questions, making comments, or leveling criticisms in regard to the past 24 hours.

The only legally permissible way for you to continue building your skills as a Java programmer is to read *Sams Teach Yourself Java 2 in 21 Days* or one of the other excellent Java-related books from Macmillan Computer Publishing. If you are caught violating these prohibitions and learning more about Java without spending another cent of your money, there's really only one thing left to be said...

I lied. There's no current law in any jurisdiction that forces you to *Teach Yourself Everything* only by reading our books. You are free to learn freely. My apologies...if I sell enough copies of this book, my name is entered into a drawing with other top Macmillan authors to win special prizes.

My heart's set on a banana-yellow Schwinn Sting-Ray bicycle.

—Rogers Cadenhead

Q&A

Q Does a layout manager have to be specified for a program?

A If one is not used, components will be arranged on an applet window or other container in the same way words are typed onto a page—left to right until there's no more room and then down to the next line. This occurs because the default layout manager, `FlowLayout`, is used if no other manager is specified.

Q The `CalcApplet` program looks different on my version of Netscape Navigator than it does on the `appletviewer` tool. The most noticeable differences are the C and = buttons, which are thinner on Navigator. Why is this?

A Because Java is a language that is presented on many different platforms, some graphical elements will vary depending on the software or operating system being used. Your programs should be presentable on any implementation of Java, but if you're creating a complicated program that arranges numerous components and other visual elements, it's worthwhile to test it on several different systems and Web browsers.

Quiz

To calculate your level of knowledge about this hour's subjects, answer the following questions.

Questions

1. What's the benefit of enabling and disabling components on a graphical user interface?

    (a) The interface looks more interesting.

    (b) You can control how a user actually uses the interface.

    (c) It's easier for the user than if all components are always enabled.

2. In an applet, where is the best place to add components to its content pane?

    (a) The init() method

    (b) A constructor method

    (c) A destructor method

3. What type of variable would be best to use when storing calculator results in the MiniCalc project?

    (a) String

    (b) int

    (c) float

Answers

1. b. and c. This often makes it easier to program and easier to use.

2. a. An applet's init() method serves a similar function to a constructor method in other classes. It is called once when the applet begins running for the first time.

3. c. Because there's a decimal key on the calculator, you must use the float variable type instead of some other numeric type such as int.

Activities

If you'd like to teach yourself even more Java programming in hours 24 and beyond, do the following activities:

- Add a square root button to the MiniCalc class that will display the square root of the currently displayed number.

- Visit developer.com's Java directory at http://www.developer.com to see some other calculators that have been written using Java. Look over any available source files and compare them with your version of the MiniCalc source file.

To see Java programs that implement these activities, visit the book's Web site at http://www.prefect.com/java24.

PART VII

Appendixes

Hour

APPENDIX **A**

Where to Go from Here: Java Resources

Now that you have finished this book, you might be wondering where you can go to improve your Java programming skills. This appendix lists some books, World Wide Web sites, Internet discussion groups, and other resources you can use to expand your Java knowledge.

Other Books to Consider

A worthwhile successor to this book is *Sams Teach Yourself Java 2 in 21 Days*, by Laura Lemay and Rogers Cadenhead. This book teaches Java to people who have had an introduction to programming—either with another language, such as Visual Basic, C, or C++, or a beginning Java book such as this one. Although some of the material in *Sams Teach Yourself Java 2 in 21 Days* will review what you have learned in the past 24 hours of tutelage, the majority of the material will be new. As the co-author, I give the *21 Days* book my completely biased seal of approval as a follow-up to what you've learned here. My mother Gail recommends it, too.

Macmillan Computer Publishing, which includes Sams Publishing, is the leader in Java programming books, and there are numerous books from Macmillan you should consider reading as you develop your skills. The following list includes ISBN numbers, which will be needed at bookstores if they don't currently carry the book you're looking for:

- *Special Edition Using Java 2* by Joe Weber. ISBN: 0-7897-2018-3.
- *Java 1.1 Certification Training Guide* by Cary Jardin. ISBN: 0-7897-1390-X.
- *Developing Professional Java Applets* by K.C. Hopson and Stephen E. Ingram. ISBN: 1-57521-083-5.
- *Tricks of the Java Programming Gurus* by Glenn Vanderburg and others. ISBN: 1-57521-102-5.
- *Mitchell Waite Signature Series: Data Structures and Algorithms in Java* by Robert LaFore. ISBN: 1-5716-9095-6.
- *Mitchell Waite Signature Series: Object-Oriented Programming in Java* by Bill McCarty and Steve Gilbert. ISBN: 1-5716-9086-7.

Several of these books, including the previous edition of this book, *Sams Teach Yourself Java 1.1 Programming in 24 Hours*, have been made available for free on the World Wide Web at the Macmillan Computer Publishing Personal Bookshelf (`http://www.mcp.com/personal/`).

The Personal Bookshelf includes an Online Catalog, links to author Web sites, high-tech job searches, and Web programming utilities. It's a good place to see what's coming up from Sams Publishing and other parts of Macmillan Computer Publishing. The books that are available on the site vary, and you must register before you can start reading them online.

Sun's Official Java Site

As you learned during Hour 3, "Vacationing in Java," the Java software division of Sun Microsystems maintains an active Web site at `http://java.sun.com`.

This site is the first place to go when looking for Java-related information. New versions of the Java Development Kit and other programming resources are available for download, along with documentation for the entire Java class library.

The site is broken down into the following areas:

- **What's New?** This area contains announcements related to upcoming product releases and Java-related events such as JavaOne, the yearly conference for Java programmers. This area also contains press releases from Sun's Java software division.

- **Read About Java:** This area is a good place for information that you're having trouble finding elsewhere. This heading includes a link to the list of Frequently Asked Questions (FAQs) about Java. If you're unfamiliar with FAQ lists, they provide concise answers to as many commonly requested topics as possible. If you encounter a stumbling block as you attempt to accomplish something with the language, visit http://www.developer.com/directories/pages/dir.java.html to see all the topics that have their own FAQ listings.

- **Products and APIs:** This area is a directory of all the development tools and application programming interfaces that can be downloaded from the Java division, including the Development Kit, language documentation, and more than 30 other products and APIs.

- **Applets:** This area is a showcase for Java programs running on the Web, including several dozen by Sun developers that can be readily adapted for use on your own Web pages. There also are links to several applet directories, including developer.com's Java Directory at http://www.developer.com/directories/pages/dir.java.html and the Java Applet Rating Service (JARS) at http://www.jars.com. Be sure to check out the disturbing Bouncing Heads applet, the first Java program I ever saw running on a World Wide Web page.

- **For Developers:** This area is a consolidated resource for all technical information of interest to Java programmers, including complete documentation for the Java language in HTML format. You can find information on language conferences, the for-a-fee programming support programs offered by the Sun Developer Connection, official Java books, and other resources.

- **Java in the Real World:** The area provides a description of what Sun calls its "success stories," which are some of the examples of Java being used at companies, on the World Wide Web, and in stand-alone programs.

- **Business and Licensing:** This area provides licensing and trademark guidelines for using Java products.

- **Support and Services:** This area contains technical support, customer service, and sales assistance for purchasers of Java products and users of Java development tools.

- **Marketing:** This area details the latest marketing and support programs offered by the Java division and other divisions of Sun Microsystems. Programs include the 100% Pure Java Program, which offers guidance for programmers creating Java applications, and the Java Solutions Guide, an online directory of Java-related developers, companies, and products.

- **Employment:** This area lists current job postings for Sun's Java division. Let me know if a high-paying job is posted for a technical writer who can write time-based Java programming guides and doesn't like to leave his house.

- **Java Store:** This area links to Java Gifts, a catalog of official Java merchandise that can be ordered over the Web, including denim shirts, coffee mugs, T-shirts, and caps. Nothing says "I love you" at Christmas like a plush toy depicting Duke, the bicuspid-shaped Java mascot, with fully bendable arms. You also can go straight to the catalog at `http://www.corpstore.com/javagifts/`.

This site is continually updated with free resources of use to Java programmers.

Other Java Web Sites

Because so much of the Java phenomenon has been inspired by its use on Web pages, a large number of Web sites focus on Java and Java programming.

This Book's Official Site

The author of this book offers an official Web site at `http://www.prefect.com/java24`. This site is described fully in Appendix B, aptly named "This Book's Web Site."

The Java Books Page

Those of us who write Java books like to think that you're forsaking all others by choosing our work. However, anecdotal studies (and the number of Java books on *our* shelves) indicate that you might benefit from other books devoted to the language.

JavaWorld, an online magazine that covers the programming language and related technology, maintains the most complete list of Java books that have been published or will be published. You can find it at `http://www.javaworld.com/javaworld/books/jw-books-index.html`.

Elliotte Rusty Harold, himself an author of several Java programming books, maintains a list of current and upcoming Java- and JavaScript-related books at `http://sunsite.unc.edu/javafaq/books.html`.

developer.com's Java Directory

Because Java is an object-oriented language that offers JavaBeans as a means to create self-contained programming components, it is easy to use resources created by other developers in your own programs. Before you start a Java project of any significance, you should scan the World Wide Web for resources you might be able to use in your program.

The place to start is developer.com's Java directory, the Web site that was known previously as Gamelan. This site catalogs Java programs, programming resources, and other information at `http://www.developer.com/directories/pages/dir.java.html`.

developer.com's Java directory is the most comprehensive Web resource of its kind, surpassing even Sun's official site in the depth of its coverage related to applets, JavaBeans, and useful Web sites. It has become the first place that a Java programmer registers information about a program when it is completed. developer.com highlights the best submissions related to Java and other subjects on its What's Cool section, available at `http://www.developer.com/directories/pages/cool.html`.

Java Applet Rating Service

To access another directory that rates Java applets, direct your Web browser to `http://www.jars.com`.

The apple logo of the Java Applet Rating Service (JARS) can be seen on numerous Java applets offered on Web pages. The JARS site also includes news about the language, a job bank, reviews of Java development tools, and other useful information.

JavaWorld Magazine

One of the best magazines that has sprung up to serve the Java programming community is also the cheapest. *JavaWorld* is available for free on the World Wide Web at `http://www.javaworld.com`.

JavaWorld publishes frequent tutorial articles along with Java development news and other features that are updated monthly. The Web-only format provides an advantage over some of its print competitors such as *Java Report* in the area of how-to articles. Because an article is teaching a particular concept or type of programming, *JavaWorld* can offer a Java applet that demonstrates the lesson.

Java Frequently Asked Questions

As a complement to the Java frequently asked question (FAQ) lists that are available on Sun's official Web site, Java programmers using Internet discussion groups have collaborated on their own list of questions and answers.

Elliotte Rusty Harold, one of the keepers of the Java books Web pages, also offers the current Java FAQ list at `http://sunsite.unc.edu/javafaq/javafaq.html`.

Intelligence.Com Java News

Natural Intelligence, a Java consulting company, offers a frequently updated rundown of Java-related headlines called Java News. Each headline is linked to a story about the language that's available on the Web, and the sources include News.com, Sun's Java Developer Connection, companies developing Java-related products, and other sites.

Java News is available at `http://www.intelligence.com/java/`.

Java Newsgroups

One of the best resources for both novice and experienced Java programmers is Usenet, the international network of discussion groups that is available to most Internet users either through an Internet service provider or a news service such as Deja News (`http://www.dejanews.com`) or NewsGuy (`http://www.newsguy.com`). The following are descriptions of some of the several Java discussion groups available on Usenet:

- `comp.lang.java.programmer`   Because this group is devoted to questions and answers related to Java programming, it basically is the place for all subjects that don't belong in one of the other groups. Any Java-related topic is suitable for discussion here.

- `comp.lang.java.advocacy`   This group is devoted to any Java discussions that are likely to inspire heated or comparative debate. If you want to argue the merits of Java against another language, this is the place for it. This group can be a good place to consult if you want to see whether Java is the right choice for a project on which you're working.

- `comp.lang.java.announce`   This group posts announcements, advertisements, and press releases of interest to the Java development community. It is moderated, so all postings must be submitted for approval before they are posted to the group.

- `comp.lang.java.beans`   This group is devoted to discussions related to JavaBeans programming, announcements of Beans that have been made available, and similar topics concerning component software development.

- `comp.lang.java.corba`   This advanced discussion group is devoted to Java-language implementations of CORBA, the Common Object Request Broker Architecture.

- `comp.lang.java.databases`   This group is used for talk related to JDBC, the Java Database Connectivity Libraries, and other solutions for connecting Java programs to databases.

- `comp.lang.java.gui`   This group is devoted to the Abstract Windowing Toolkit, Swing, and other graphical user interface class libraries and development tools.

- `comp.lang.java.help`   This group provides a place to discuss installation problems related to Java programming tools and similar issues that bedevil beginners.

- `comp.lang.java.machine`   The most advanced of the Java discussion groups, this group is devoted to discussing the implementation of the language, issues with porting it to new machines, the specifics of the Java Virtual Machine, and similar subjects.

- `comp.lang.java.programmer`   This group contains questions and answers related to Java programming, which makes it another good place for new programmers to frequent.

- `comp.lang.java.security`   This discussion group is devoted to security issues related to Java, especially in regard to running Java programs and other executable content on the World Wide Web.

Job Opportunities

If you're one of those folks who is learning Java as part of your plan to become a captain of industry, you should check out some of the Java-related job openings that become available. Several of the resources listed in this appendix have a section devoted to job opportunities.

If you might be interested in joining Sun's Java division itself, visit `http://java.sun.com/jobs/index.html`.

JavaWorld offers a Career Opportunities page that often has several openings for Java developers at `http://www.javaworld.com/javaworld/common/jw-jobop.html`.

One tactic that can make Java employers aware of your skills is to register yourself as a resource at developer.com's Java directory. You will be added to the site, and this listing might result in email about Java-related job assignments. To find out about registering yourself, head to `http://www.developer.com/directories/submit_entry.html` in the Add a Resource section of developer.com.

Although this Web page isn't specifically a Java employment resource, the World Wide Web site Career Path enables you to search the job classifieds of more than two dozen U.S. newspapers. You have to register to use the site, but it's free, and there are more than 100,000 classifieds you can search using keywords such as *Java* or *Internet* or *snake charmer*. Go to `http://www.careerpath.com`.

APPENDIX B

This Book's Web Site

One of the advantages of a 24-hour course of study is that it gets you quickly up to speed on a subject. However, because programming is a technical, jargon-packed field, there might be things you're still unclear about. There also might be things I was unclear about—errors and other confusing information that could benefit from a clarification.

If you have questions about any of the subjects covered in this book or suggestions on ways this and other books could be improved, please visit the official Web site for *Sams Teach Yourself Java 2 in 24 Hours* at `http://www.prefect.com/java24`.

This Web site features several different types of information, updated by the author:

- Error corrections and clarifications: When errors are brought to my attention, they will be described on the site with the corrected text and any other material that will help.

- Answers to reader questions: If readers have questions that aren't covered in this book's Q&A sections, many will be presented on the site.

- The source code, class files, and working applets for all programs you create during the 24 hours of this book.

- The full source code for programs that demonstrate all of the user interface components introduced during Hour 19, "Building a Simple User Interface with Swing," including working applets.

- Sample Java programs: Working versions of some programs that were featured in this book will be available on the site.

- Solutions, including source code, for some of the activities suggested at the end of each hour.

- Working applets featured during Hour 4, "Understanding How Java Programs Work."

- Updated links to the sites mentioned in this book: Since the Web changes faster than Roseanne changes surnames, you might try some of the URLs mentioned in this book and discover that they no longer work. If the site has moved elsewhere and I know about the new URL, I'll offer it on my Web site.

- At least one link related to the Dallas Stars: This link is offered for no other reason than the author's unconditional love of professional hockey.

As you might know, the *24 Hours* line of books from Sams Publishing is just over one year old. Your suggestions, comments, and questions on this popular toddler are welcome at any time. You can send email to author Rogers Cadenhead by visiting the book's site. Click the author's name and you'll be taken to a page where you can send email directly from the Web, or find out my current email address for comments related to the book.

This doesn't have to be said, as I learned from the previous edition of this book, but it's offered anyway: Feel free to voice all opinions, positive, negative, indifferent, or undecided. The author has been a user of the Internet and online services long enough to have his parentage questioned in seven spoken languages and one particularly memorable non-verbal one. Any criticism you send will be interpreted as "tough love," and nothing you say could be rougher than what my music teacher said after my audition for the lead in the Yale Elementary School production of *Jesus Christ Superstar.*

                                                                    Rogers Cadenhead

APPENDIX C

Configuring the Java Development Kit

The Java Development Kit is a set of command-line tools that are used to create, compile, and run Java programs. Details on how to acquire and install the current edition of the Kit are available in Hour 1, "Becoming a Programmer."

For many readers, the Kit should work immediately upon being installed if you follow Sun's instructions (and Sun's instructions are on the money). For everyone else, this appendix will show you how to set up the Kit correctly on your system.

If you have downloaded the Kit from Sun Microsystems and have installed it on your system, you're ready to proceed.

Windows 95 and Windows NT Configuration

Using the Java Development Kit requires a command line. Windows 95 and Windows NT users can get to a command line by using the MS-DOS Prompt feature, available as Start, Programs, MS-DOS Prompt from the taskbar.

When you use the MS-DOS Prompt command, a window opens in which you can type commands and use MS-DOS commands to navigate through the folders on your system. The starting folder will be the main Windows system folder on your primary hard drive (usually `C:\WINDOWS`).

The following statement is an example of a command you can use once the Kit has been installed:

```
java -version
```

This command runs `java.exe`, the Java interpreter that is part of the Kit. The text after the name of the program is called an *argument*, and arguments are used to control how a program runs. The argument `-version` causes the Java interpreter to display its version number. It's a good way to test whether the interpreter was installed correctly.

Try this command yourself. If you're using JDK version 1.2—the version for Java 2—the following message should be displayed in response:

```
java version "1.2"
```

Later versions will respond with a slightly different version number. If you're still working with a beta version of the Kit, you will see a message with the text `beta` incorporated into the version number, as in the following:

```
java version "1.2beta4"
```

If you get an error such as the wrong version number or a `File not found` message, your system is having trouble finding the Java interpreter. You need to make some changes to your system's configuration to correct this.

The first thing to do when tackling a Kit configuration problem in Windows is find out where `java.exe` is located on your system. Use the Find Files command (Start, Find, Files or Folders from the taskbar) to search for `java.exe` on the hard drive where you installed the Kit.

If you don't find `java.exe`, you need to reinstall the Kit.

If you find `java.exe`, you might find more than one version of the file if you have past versions of the Kit on your system. Look at the Find window's In Folder column to determine the name of the folders that contain versions of `java.exe`. One of these should include a reference to the folder where you installed version 1.2 of the Kit.

In Figure C.1, there are two versions of java.exe listed in the Find window. The one referring to the current version of the Kit in this figure is C:\jdk1.2\bin.

FIGURE C.1

Result of a Find Files search for java.exe.

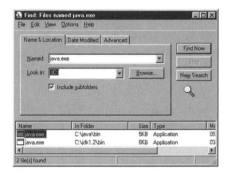

Make a note of the correct folder for the Kit exactly as it is listed under the In Folder heading. This is the Kit's Path folder, and you'll be using it soon.

Checking the PATH Statement

To make sure that your system is looking in the right place for the Kit, you need to look at the PATH setting for your system. PATH indicates where to find a program when you try to run it at an MS-DOS command line.

To display the current setting for PATH, enter the following at a command prompt:

```
path
```

You will see a listing of all folders where Windows looks to find MS-DOS programs; they're separated by semicolons. Here's an example:

```
PATH=C:\WINDOWS;C:\WINDOWS\COMMAND;C:\JDK1.2\BIN
```

In this PATH listing, the text C:\JDK1.2\BIN refers to the Kit's Path folder, which is where the system will look for the file java.exe. There are also two other folders listed in the PATH—C:\WINDOWS and C:\WINDOWS\COMMAND.

Your PATH setting should include a reference to the Kit's Path folder. (Capitalization is not important in this instance—C:\JDK1.2\BIN would be the same as C:\jdk1.2\bin.)

If PATH doesn't include the Kit's Path folder, you need to edit your PATH setting and add it.

Changing Your PATH Setting

When using Windows 95, the PATH setting must be changed by editing autoexec.bat, a text file in the root folder of your system's primary hard drive (usually the (C:) drive).

C

To change the PATH setting on a Windows NT system, you don't have to load a text file for editing. Instead, NT stores all of its Environmental Variables in the System Control Panel. Here you can modify the PATH and any other environmental settings. To change PATH on a Windows 95 system, you must edit the text file autoexec.bat. Right-click the file and select the Edit command to load autoexec.bat into Notepad.

The file autoexec.bat will contain a lot of technical-looking stuff that will be incomprehensible to the MS-DOS novice. Some of it is pretty incomprehensible to everyone else, too.

Thankfully, you can ignore most of the stuff in this file. Look for a line that begins with the text PATH=, SET PATH=, or PATH followed by a blank space. This line, if you find it, is your PATH statement.

Problem: No PATH Statement

If you don't find a PATH statement, you should add one to the autoexec.bat file. Scroll down to the bottom of the text file and add a blank line. On this line, enter the text PATH= followed by the Kit's Path folder. If your Path folder is C:\jdk1.2\bin, the following line would be used when adding a PATH statement:

```
PATH=C:\jdk1.2\bin
```

After making this change, save the file. You must reboot your system before the change takes effect. If the java.exe file is in the folder you've indicated on the PATH statement, you should be able to run java -version successfully.

Problem: No Kit Path Folder in PATH Statement

If you find a PATH statement in the autoexec.bat file that doesn't contain any reference to the Kit's Path folder, look for the text %JAVA_HOME% on that line, followed by text such as \bin.

If you find %JAVA_HOME%, delete it and the text that follows it, up to but not including the next semicolon. Replace this text with the Kit's Path folder. Make sure not to delete any semicolons that are used to separate folder names.

If you do not find %JAVA_HOME% on the PATH statement, place your cursor at the end of the line containing the PATH statement. At that spot, add the text ; followed by the Kit's Path folder. If your Kit's Path folder is C:\jdk1.2\bin, the end of the PATH statement should look like the last part of the following:

```
PATH=C:\WINDOWS;C:\WINDOWS\COMMAND;C:\jdk1.2\bin
```

No other version of the Kit should be referred to on the PATH statement. If you see a folder that refers to a previous version of the Kit on the PATH line, delete the reference to this folder. If this results in a PATH line that contains two semicolon characters in a row (;;), delete one of them.

Save the file after making these changes. You must reboot your system before the new PATH statement takes effect. If the java.exe file is in the folder you've indicated on the PATH statement, you should be able to run java -version successfully.

Fixing Class Not Found Errors

Java programs are compiled with the Kit by running the Java compiler javac with the name of the source file as an argument. For example, if you were in the same folder as the source file BigDebt.java, you could compile it with the following command:

```
javac BigDebt.java
```

> If you have not attempted to compile a Java program yet to test the Kit, you can use the BigDebt.java file from the book's Web site at http://www.prefect.com/java24.

If you get a Class not found error when using the Java compiler on a source file, the first thing to check is whether you have spelled and capitalized the name correctly.

Make sure you're in the folder that contains the source file you're trying to compile, and double-check the filename.

Windows users can use the dir command at an MS-DOS command line to list all of the files in a folder. Each file's full name is displayed along the right-most column of the folder listing. The abbreviated filenames along the left side of the listing should be ignored—they are used internally by Windows to manage the files. In Figure C.2, the full filenames are BigDebt.java and BigDebt.class, not BIGDEB~1 JAV and BIGDEB~1 CLA.

If the name of the source file is correct and there are no errors in the Java source code itself, the Java compiler is having trouble finding tools.jar, a file that contains all of the Java class files needed to successfully compile and run Java 2 programs.

Kit programs such as the Java compiler look for tools.jar in two ways. First, they use the CLASSPATH setting for your system (if one has been set up). Second, they look for java.exe and use that file's location to determine where tools.jar can be found.

Most Class not found errors can be fixed by using the CLASSPATH setting to indicate the location of tools.jar.

FIGURE C.2

FIGURE C.2

A listing of files in an MS-DOS window.

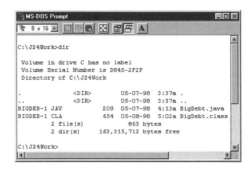

One way to find tools.jar is to open the folder where you installed the Kit (such as \jdk1.2). There should be a subfolder called lib that contains tools.jar.

In Windows 95 or Windows NT, use the Find Files command (Start, Find Files or Folders, Find Files from the taskbar) to search for tools.jar on the same drive where you installed the Kit (as shown in Figure C.3).

FIGURE C.3

Result of a Find Files search for tools.jar.

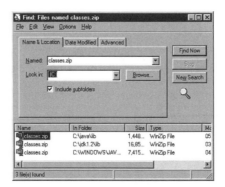

Sometimes there will be more than one file named tools.jar on your system. Some of these might be from past versions of the Kits and other Java development tools, and others could be used by Web browsers that support Java.

Look in the In Folder column to see the full folder name (including hard-drive letter) of each folder that contains a file named tools.jar. Find the one that includes a reference to the folder where you installed version 1.2 of the Kit. (In Figure C.3, it's C:\jdk1.2\lib.)

Make a note of this folder. This folder name followed by the text \tools.jar should be your Kit's CLASSPATH setting.

Checking the CLASSPATH Statement

To make sure your system is looking in the right place for the JDK 1.2 version of tools.jar, you need to look at your system's CLASSPATH setting.

Windows users can display the current setting for CLASSPATH by entering the following at an MS-DOS prompt:

```
echo %CLASSPATH%
```

Make sure to include the percentage marks (%) before and after the term CLASSPATH. If your system has CLASSPATH set up, you will see a listing of all folders and files in which Kit tools will look for Java classes. Each folder and filename is separated by semicolons. Here's an example:

```
.;C:\jdk1.2\lib\tools.jar
```

In this CLASSPATH listing, the text C:\jdk1.2\lib\tools.jar is one place from which Java classes will be loaded. There also is a period (.) listed as the first item—this reference ensures that Kit utilities will also look in the current folder for any classes that cannot be found.

If CLASSPATH doesn't include the reference to the copy of JDK 1.2's tools.jar, you need to edit your CLASSPATH setting and add it.

Changing Your CLASSPATH Setting

The CLASSPATH setting must be changed by editing autoexec.bat, a text file in the root folder of your system's primary hard drive (usually the (C:) drive).

To change the CLASSPATH setting on a Windows NT system, you don't have to load a text file for editing. Instead, choose Settings, Control Panel from the taskbar.

To change CLASSPATH on a Windows 95 system, you must edit the text file autoexec.bat. Right-click the file and select the Edit command to load autoexec.bat into Notepad.

As you might have discovered when adjusting the PATH setting, the autoexec.bat file contains a lot of technical-looking stuff that might make you want to rue the day that the Java language came into your life.

There's no cause for alarm. You only have to worry about one line in this file. Look for a line that begins with the text CLASSPATH=, SET CLASSPATH=, or CLASSPATH followed by a blank space.

Problem: No CLASSPATH Statement

If you don't find a CLASSPATH statement, you should add one to the autoexec.bat file. Scroll down to the bottom of the text file and add a blank line. On this line, enter the text CLASSPATH=.; followed by the Kit's CLASSPATH setting. In the following statement, the Kit's CLASSPATH setting is C:\jdk1.2\lib\tools.jar:

CLASSPATH=.;C:\jdk1.2\lib\tools.jar

Save the file after making this change. You must reboot your system before the change takes effect. If the tools.jar file is in the folder you've indicated on the CLASSPATH statement, you should be able to compile programs successfully.

Problem: No JDK 1.2 Folder in CLASSPATH Statement

If you find a CLASSPATH statement in the autoexec.bat file that doesn't contain any reference to the correct location of tools.jar, look for the text %JAVA_HOME% on that line.

You may find %JAVA_HOME% followed by the text \lib\tools.jar, as in CLASSPATH=%JAVA_HOME%\lib\tools.jar or CLASSPATH=%JAVA_HOME%\..\lib\tools.jar.

If you find %JAVA_HOME%, delete it and any text that follows it, all the way to the next semicolon. Replace it with the correct location of tools.jar. Make sure not to delete any semicolons that are used to separate folder names.

If you do not find %JAVA_HOME% on the CLASSPATH statement, place your cursor at the end of the line containing the CLASSPATH statement. At that spot, add the text ; followed by the correct location of tools.jar. If it's C:\jdk1.2\lib\tools.jar, the end of the CLASSPATH statement should look like the last part of the following line:

CLASSPATH=.;C:\DEV\CHATSERVER\;C:\jdk1.2\lib\tools.jar

No other version of the Kit should be referred to on the CLASSPATH statement. If you see a folder that refers to a previous version of the Kit on the CLASSPATH line, delete the reference to this folder. If this results in a CLASSPATH line that contains two semicolon characters in a row(;;), delete one. Save the file after making these changes. You must reboot your system before the new CLASSPATH statement takes effect. If the correct tools.jar file is in the folder you've indicated on the PATH statement, you should be able to compile and run sample programs such as BigDebt successfully.

UNIX Configuration

To configure the Kit on a Solaris system, add the java/bin or jdk/bin directory to your execution path. This usually can be done by adding a line like the following to your login configuration file (often your .profile, or .login file):

```
set path= (~/java/bin/ $path)
```

This line assumes that you've installed the Kit into the directory java of your home directory. An installation elsewhere will require a change to the directory added to your execution path.

These changes will not take effect until you log out and back in again, or use the source command with the name of the file you changed. If you altered the .login file, the source command would be as follows:

```
source ~/.login
```

Fixing Class Not Found Errors on Other Platforms

To correct any Class not found errors on Solaris systems, the best thing to do is make sure that the CLASSPATH environment variable is not being set automatically at login.

To see if CLASSPATH is being set, enter the following at a command prompt:

```
echo $CLASSPATH
```

If a CLASSPATH value has been set, you can unset it by entering the following command:

```
unsetenv CLASSPATH
```

To make this change permanent, you should remove the command that sets up CLASSPATH from your .profile, .cshrc, or .login file.

These changes will not take effect until you log out and back in again, or use the source command with the name of the file you changed. If you altered the .login file, the source command would be as follows:

```
source ~/.login
```

C

GLOSSARY

Abstract Windowing Toolkit   The basic set of Java classes that can be used to display and control a graphical user interface, which has been extended by the Swing windowing classes. Also called the AWT.

ActiveX   A way to run programs on World Wide Web pages that was developed by Microsoft. ActiveX is an extension of the Component Object Model, and it is a rival of sorts to Java.

applet   A Java program that runs as part of a World Wide Web page.

appletviewer   The Java Development Kit tool that can display applets included on a World Wide Web page.

application   A Java program that does not run as part of a World Wide Web page. Most applications run locally on your computer like other programs you use.

argument   Extra information that is sent to a program when it is run, or information that is sent to a method in a program when it begins.

array   A group of variables that share the same name and store the same kind of information. Each variable in the group is called an element, and elements are numbered so they can be distinguished from each other.

ASCII text file   A text file that does not contain any special character or formatting commands such as centering, boldfaced text, and different point sizes.

attribute   Part of an HTML tag that affects what the tag does. Also, in object-oriented programming, it is a thing that describes an object and distinguishes it from other objects. These attributes are stored in variables.

autodialer   Software that uses a modem to dial a series of phone numbers in sequence.

BASIC   A language designed for use by beginning programmers. Dozens of different versions of BASIC are available.

behavior   The things that an object does, as conducted by the methods of the object.

bit   An integer that can equal 0 or 1. Each byte is made up of 8 bits.

block   A group of statements in a Java program. Blocks begin with a { mark and end with a } mark.

block statement   Another term for a block.

Boolean   A value that can be either `true` or `false`.

browser   Software that can be used to view World Wide Web pages on the Internet.

bug   An error in a program that must be fixed for the program to operate correctly.

byte   A number that can store one of 256 integer values, either 0 to 255 or, in the case of Java, -127 to 128. A byte consists of 8 bits.

byte stream   An input or output stream that is handled as a series of byte values ranging from 0 to 255.

bytecode   The compiled form of a Java source file that is run by a Java interpreter.

C++   An extension of the C programming language developed by Bjarne Stroustrop that includes features such as object-oriented programming, multiple inheritance, and the use of pointers.

character   A single letter, number, punctuation mark, or other symbol.

character stream   An input or output stream that is handled as a series of characters.

check box   A user interface component that presents a box next to a line of text. The box can be checked or unchecked by the user.

choice list   A user interface component that presents a pop-up list of choices from which a single choice can be made. Only one of the selections is visible unless the pop-up list is being displayed.

class   A master copy of an object that determines what behavior and attributes an object should have. Because every Java program is also a class, programs also are called classes.

class method   A method that is associated with a class of objects instead of a specific object.

class variable   A variable that is associated with a class of objects instead of an object and has a value specific to the class.

color space   A system for representing all of the possible colors that can be represented in data, on a display device such as a computer monitor, or both.

command line   A way to operate a computer entirely with the keyboard by typing commands at a prompt. MS-DOS is the most popular operating system that uses a command line.

comments   Lines in a source file that are provided strictly for the benefit of humans trying to understand the program.

compiler   A program that turns a source file into a computer program by interpreting the whole file beforehand and creating a compiled file that can be run. This program is more efficient than an interpreter but is slower to debug.

component   An item such as a clickable button or scrollbar that can be manipulated by a user in a program.

concatenate   To link two things together. This term is often used to describe the process of attaching two strings to each other so they can be displayed together.

conditional   A statement that causes something to happen only if a specific condition is met.

conditional operator   Another term for ternary operator.

constant   A variable that cannot change in value throughout a program.

constructor   A special method that only is handled when an object is being created.

container   A component that can contain other components in a graphical user interface.

decrement   To subtract one from something.

debug   The process of fixing bugs in a computer program.

double-buffering   Drawing graphics to an off-screen work area first in order to improve the quality of animation.

element   A specific variable of an array.

event-handling   Responding to a user's mouse and keyboard use in a program's graphical user interface.

expressions   Statements that involve a mathematical equation or that change the value of something.

floating-point numbers   Numbers that might include a decimal point.

GIF file   An image file format that was developed by CompuServe.

GIF 89a file   A version of the GIF format that includes support for transparent colors.

graphical user interface   The buttons, text fields, and other components of a program that enable a user to interact with the program using a mouse and keyboard. Also called a GUI.

hierarchy   A pyramid-shaped grouping of classes in which the topmost class is the superclass of all classes below it.

HSB values   A color space in which colors are defined by determining the percentage of hue, saturation, and brightness that exist in the color.

hypertext markup language   HTML, the simple programming language used to present information on World Wide Web pages.

icon   A small graphic with limited colors that is associated with a program, user interface component, or other element of a computer system.

increment   To add one to something.

inheritance   The capability of a class of objects to automatically have the attributes and behavior of another object. The extent of this capability is determined by the class's position in the class hierarchy.

inner class   A class that is defined inside of another class as if it were a method. The inner class is used to support the class that contains it.

input stream   An object that's capable of pulling data into a Java program from a source such as a text file or Internet server.

integer   A whole number.

interface   A special type of class that enables a class to inherit methods it would not be able to use through inheritance alone.

Internet Explorer   Web browser software from Microsoft that runs Java programs by using either its own platform-dependent variation of the Java language or Sun's Java Plug-in.

interpreter   A program that turns a source file into a computer program by interpreting each line one at a time. An interpreted language runs programs more slowly than a compiled language does, but it is easier to debug.

initialization   The process of setting something up for the first time in a program. This term is used often in reference to variables.

Java   An object-oriented programming language developed by Sun Microsystems that was first released to the public in 1995. Java programs are compiled into class files that can run on any computer platform that has a Java interpreter.

java   The interpreter that is part of the Java Development Kit.

JavaBeans   Java programs that are created in such a way that they can be used easily as part of other programs.

Java Development Kit   A free set of tools from Sun Microsystems that makes it possible to write and test Java programs in a command-line environment.

Java Foundation Classes   A set of classes that provide sophisticated functionality such as advanced user interfaces, 2D imaging, support for users with disabilities, and other features.

Java WorkShop   Software from Sun Microsystems that enables Java programs to be written in a graphical, point-and-click environment that resembles a Web browser's interface.

javac   The compiler that is included with the Java Development Kit.

JavaScript   An interpreted programming language unrelated to Java that offers limited programming capabilities on a Web page. The source code of JavaScript programs can be included as text on Web pages.

JPG file   An image file format developed by the Joint Photographic Expert Groups, also called a JPEG file. This format is considered the best for presenting photographic images without taking up a lot of disk space.

layout manager   An object that controls how components will be arranged in a graphical user interface.

logic error   A bug that causes a program to do something it isn't supposed to do but doesn't prevent the program from running. These errors must be found during testing, but they can be hard to find.

long integers   Integers that are larger than 2.14 billion or smaller than -2.14 billion.

look and feel   The way that a program looks and how its interface functions when it is used. These can be changed in a Java program to emulate the look and feel of Microsoft Windows, Motif, and a Java-specific look and feel called Metal.

loop   A statement or set of statements that will be repeated in a program.

Metal   Java's own look and feel, which can be used as an alternative to the Windows and Motif look and feel options. This feature is part of Swing.

method   A way to accomplish a task in a Java program. Methods begin with a { and end with a }.

multiple inheritance   The capability of a class of objects to inherit attributes and behavior from more than one superclass.

multithreading   The capability of a program or operating system to run more than one program at the same time. Also known as multitasking.

Navigator   Web browser software from Netscape that includes the capability to run Java programs either with a built-in Java Virtual Machine or Sun's Java Plug-in.

newline   A special character represented by '\N' that causes the display of text to continue at the left-most column of the next line.

object variable   A variable that is associated with an object and has a value that is specific to that object.

object-oriented programming (OOP)   A way of thinking of computer programs as a group of objects that work together, each object containing everything it needs to handle a specific task.

operator   The part of an expression that causes a mathematical operation to occur, such as addition or multiplication, or tests a condition such as equality.

output stream   An object that's capable of sending data from a Java program to a source such as a text file or Internet server.

overriding   Creating a method or variable in a subclass that replaces something it inherited from its superclass.

parameters   Extra information sent to a Java applet when it runs that is included using an HTML tag on a World Wide Web page.

platform   A computer operating system and central processing unit.

platform-independence   The ability of software to run without modification on several different platforms.

point and click   The ability to control a program by using a mouse device and clicking its buttons.

pointer   A variable in a program that points to where another value is stored. Java does not include pointers.

program   A set of instructions that tell a computer what to do. Also called software.

pull-down menus   Menus in a program that you use by clicking a menu title, holding down the mouse, and releasing it over the item you want.

scope   The area of a program in which a variable exists, defined by the nearest { and } marks that surround the variable. A variable's scope is the block in which it was created, and it cannot be used outside of that scope.

short integers   Integers that can range from -32,768 to 32,767.

software   A computer program or group of computer programs designed to work together.

source file   The text file created by a programmer that will be turned into a computer program by an interpreter or a compiler. Also called source code.

sRGB values   Standard RGB, a color space in which a color is described by specifying the percentage of red, green, and blue that exist in the color.

statement   One of the instructions that is handled by the computer when it runs a program.

stream   An object that can send or receive data in a Java program.

string   A group of characters that represent one or more lines of text.

subclass   A class that is below another class in a hierarchy, inheriting attributes and behavior from the classes that are above it.

superclass   A class that is above another class in a hierarchy, giving its attributes and behavior to any classes that are below it.

Swing   Java classes that can expand on the Abstract Windowing Toolkit's ability to display and control a graphical user interface.

syntax error   A bug in a program that is caused by using a statement or other part of the language incorrectly. Syntax errors are easier to find than other errors because they cause error messages.

tab A special character represented by '\t' that causes text to continue at the next column, based on how wide columns have been defined. This character is used to format text for display.

tag An HTML command used on a World Wide Web page to format text, present images, run Java applets, or accomplish similar things. Tags are enclosed within < and > marks.

ternary operator An operator represented by ? that uses a conditional test to set a value. If the test is true, the first value is used, and if it is false, the second value is used. Also called the conditional operator.

text area A user interface component that presents a text field where a user can enter more than one line of text.

text editor Another term for word processor.

text field A user interface component that presents an area where a user can enter a single line of text.

thread A single program that can run as part of a multithreaded system.

ToolTip A line of text that appears when a mouse hovers over a user interface component. This text typically describes the function of the component.

variables Special storage places where a computer program can store information.

VBScript An interpreted programming language from Microsoft that offers limited programming capabilities on a Web page. VBScript is based on Visual Basic, and its source code is included as text on Web pages.

Visual Basic A programming language from Microsoft that speeds up the process of developing windowing software for Microsoft systems.

Visual C++ An object-oriented programming language from Microsoft with extensive support for windowing and many other Windows-specific technologies.

word processor A computer program used for the editing and presentation of text documents.

INDEX